D0547425

LEARNING VACATIONS

Fifth Edition

Gerson G. Eisenberg

Peterson's Guides
Princeton, New Jersey

Copyright ©1986 by Gerson G. Eisenberg and
Peterson's Guides, Inc.
Previous edition copyright 1982

All rights reserved. No part of this book may be
reproduced, stored in a retrieval system, or
transmitted, in any form or by any means—
electronic, mechanical, photocopying, recording, or
otherwise—except for citations of data for scholarly
or reference purposes with full acknowledgment of
title, edition, and publisher and written notification
to Peterson's Guides prior to such use.

Library of Congress Cataloging in Publication Data

    Eisenberg, Gerson G.
      Learning vacations.

      Includes indexes.
      1. Vacation schools—United States—
Directories. 2. Leisure—United States—Directories.
I. Title.
L901.E48   1986   370'.25'73   85-25444
ISBN 0-87866-535-8

Composition and design by Peterson's Guides

Printed in the United States of America

10 9 8 7 6 5 4 3 2 1

For information about other Peterson's publications,
please see the listing at the back of this book.

LEARNING VACATIONS

CONTENTS

FOREWORD

As we approach the twenty-first century, our styles of living, working, and relaxing are undergoing significant changes. In many cases, we are engaged in more than one career, and, through the knowledge explosion and communications revolution, we are exposed to more information than ever before. We are also enjoying better health, and we are living longer. It is likely that our species' life expectancy will increase even more by the year 2000.

Finally, we live in a society where leisure is a part of virtually everyone's life. Leisure, which as little as a century ago was the privilege of only the aristocracy, has been democratized in the more technologically developed societies of the twentieth century. Almost every adult now has time that can be considered prime time or discretionary time for education, entertainment, and travel.

Learning Vacations is a marvelous resource for all of us who want to combine our leisure time with the opportunity for stimulation and enrichment. The fifth edition of this useful work provides detailed information about an extraordinary array of programs throughout the United States and abroad and serves as a valuable guide to satisfying and fulfilling use of leisure.

The author, Gerson Eisenberg, is a thoughtful and energetic individual who has always taken advantage of leisure to grow and learn. Happily for us, a lifelong attraction to learning and a creative spirit have led him to compile and share information about the opportunities for us to follow his splendid example. All of us at the Johns Hopkins University have been privileged to know Mr. Eisenberg as an alumnus, friend, and author; it is a special pleasure for me to recommend to you this fifth edition of *Learning Vacations.*

Steven Muller
President
The Johns Hopkins University

INTRODUCTION

The year was 1874 when Methodist minister John A. Vincent and Ohio businessman Lewis Miller hit upon a unique idea. Why not combine educational, recreational, and social activities with a program of religious instruction and thus create a "learning vacation"?

Since that first, very successful undertaking at Lake Chautauqua in New York State, opportunities for formal and informal learning vacations have grown enormously in number and in popularity. The trend has been greatly influenced by Alumni College Seminar Programs begun at Dartmouth in the 1960s and the Elderhostel movement, a development of the 1970s for those age 60 and over. In addition to such campus-based programs, academic and cultural institutions of all types as well as many commercial organizations now offer vacations with an educational emphasis.

Taking part in so many of these vacations has made me into what I jokingly call a "professional seminarian." At any rate, since no central source of information concerning such programs formerly existed, I was motivated to undertake such a compendium, which was originally published in 1977 and concentrated on the learning vacation programs of academic institutions.

Since that edition, I have added categories on travel; archaeology, science, and history; arts and crafts, etc., as shown in the current Table of Contents.

It is interesting to note that a century after the original learning vacation, ever-increasing numbers of people favor vacations that are more than an escape from their regular routine. They are looking for the mental stimulation, personal challenge, and social opportunities that only a learning vacation can give.

Gerson G. Eisenberg

ON USING THIS BOOK

Material in the fifth edition of *Learning Vacations* is arranged by categories denoted by chapter headings with listings alphabetized by the state—and then foreign country—in which the sponsoring institution is located. In the case of foreign sponsors, the address of their U.S. headquarters or representative is given, as is the foreign address of such sponsor.

As aids, two indexes are provided, namely (1) Sponsor and (2) Geographic (indicating where the program takes place). Trips going to several locations are designated in this index under headings such as "U.S. Regional" or "Worldwide," as appropriate.

All listings of programs are based on recent information and, even though subject matter or particular trip destinations may change from year to year, can be considered indicative of current and future programs and trips. Where the sponsor's offerings are numerous, the examples given were considered most representative.

Costs are accurate as of the time programs took place and are offered as a guide. In the case of travel programs, a price range is often given to cover variations in trip lengths, destinations, mode of travel, etc. *All current costs should be confirmed directly with the program sponsors.*

Readers are encouraged to contact program sponsors directly for up-to-date descriptions of their trips and programs. Although phone numbers are listed with many entries, *it is generally preferable to make such requests for information by mail,* if time allows.

This fifth edition of *Learning Vacations* contains a greater variety of courses that may be taken for college credit than previous editions. It should, therefore, be of interest to serious students and teachers looking for these kinds of courses, as well as to those seeking learning vacations of this type.

As there are programs in *Learning Vacations* for all age groups, directories of those for children and families as well as those for high school youth have been included for the reader's convenience.

—G.G.E.

ACKNOWLEDGMENTS

Learning Vacations could not have been produced without the assistance of others whom I wish to thank.

First and foremost my wife, Sandy, who gave devoted and untiring assistance in numerous areas. Among these, she tracked down program material, helped with editing, acted in a general supervisory capacity, and as always continues to be my most valued PR person.

I also wish to give credit to the following:

John Curtis, a graduate student of the Johns Hopkins University and Ph.D. candidate, for his research and other skills.

Gerald Z. Levin, my former research director, for his additional assistance.

Anne Stiller and Sandy Adams of Baltimore, for their editing, and Carol Meyers, for her typing and special expertise in other areas.

Tracie Cornish-Seth, also of Baltimore, for her computer skills.

In addition, I wish to acknowledge the contributions of my friend Pam Mendelsohn of Arcata, California, and author of her own work *Happier by Degrees,* for her fine reviews and for publicizing the concept of learning vacations, as well as for her many helpful suggestions for this edition.

Finally, I want to thank Richard Bohlander of *Peterson's Guides* for his excellent work in editing and for suggestions for this manuscript as it took final form.

—G.G.E.

1 *SEMINARS AND WORKSHOPS ON AND OFF CAMPUS*

Dartmouth Alumni College

Covering a wide range of topics, this chapter includes study programs for individuals and families on campuses and elsewhere in the United States and Canada. The experience of sharing one's knowledge, in and out of the classroom, with others of diverse backgrounds is always rewarding.

Recreational facilities, if on campus, are generally available and free to learning vacation participants.

> *Men and methods make universities, not halls, nor books, nor instruments.*
> *Daniel Coit Gilman*

CALIFORNIA

Stanford University
Stanford Summer College
Bowman Alumni House
Stanford, California 94305

Program
Annual Alumni College centered on a specific topic; 6 days, August. Recent topics have included Soviet Union: Rut, Reform or Revolt; Technology and You; and The New Families.

Accommodations
Modern dormitories.

Children
There is no program for children; parents must make their own arrangements for child care and stay in a different dormitory.

Cost
Day students: $500 per person, $950 per couple (includes lunch and academic program). Resident students: $700 per person, $1350 per couple (includes room, meals, and academic program).

Recreation
Organized recreation plus free use of campus swimming pools, tennis and volleyball courts, and golf course.

Comment
Stanford's alumni college programs date back to 1966, attracting 175 to 250 participants. The faculty includes Stanford professors, guest lecturers, and performers. Programs encompass lectures, group discussions, and field trips.

Further Information
Jenee Zenger, Director
(415) 497-2028

> *Thought makes man wise—*
> *Wisdom makes life durable.*
> *Sakini*

CONNECTICUT

Connecticut College
Vacation College
Office of Continuing Education
102 Fanning Hall
New London, Connecticut 06320

Program
Program of noncredit courses for singles, couples, and families; 1 week; summer.

Accommodations
College dormitories.

Children
Special children's program of planned activities.

Cost
$250 per person, complete.

Recreation
Tennis, swimming, ocean beaches, and golf nearby.

Cultural Opportunities
Mystic Seaport Museum, historic Stonington, museums nearby.

Comment
Vacation College was first offered in 1979. Its courses are taught by Connecticut College faculty members; participants may attend as many courses as they like. Usually forty adults and children attend annually.

Further Information
(203) 447-7566

University of Connecticut
Division of Extended and
*   Continuing Education*
U-56, Room 128
One Bishop Circle
Storrs, Connecticut 06268

Program
Young People's Institute; 1–2 weeks, June–July. A residential program for gifted youth, with a focus on computers, studio arts, and theater; grades 5–11.

Accommodations
Dormitory, double occupancy.

Cost
$400 per week, including room and board, instruction, and recreational activities.

Recreation
University field house, track, swimming, tennis, horseback riding.

Cultural Opportunities
Library, art museum, Nutmeg Summer Playhouse, Merlin D. Bishop Center.

Comment
A nationally recognized institute, in operation since 1982.

Further Information
Deborah C. Huntsman, Program
   Manager
(203) 486-3231

Education makes the man.
James Cawthom

DISTRICT OF COLUMBIA

American University
Washington Summer Seminar
Massachusetts and Nebraska
*   Avenues, N.W.*
Washington, D.C. 20016

Program
The Washington Summer Seminar for college-bound high school students offers a pair of 2-week sessions on the theme Government in Action. Participants learn about political parties, pressure groups and lobbying, foreign policy, the three branches of the federal government, and more.

Accommodations
Dormitories on campus.

Cost
$850 per session, complete.

Recreation
Swimming, tennis, track and field.

Cultural Opportunities
Resources of Washington, D.C. Scheduled field trips to museums and other sites, including a theater performance.

Comment
The Washington Summer Seminar for high school students was established in 1974. It grew out of American University's Washington Semester program for college students first held in 1947. For each summer session, two

faculty members are assigned to the group of approximately thirty participants. In addition, students meet party officials, congressmen, members of the press, White House staff members, and others. College credit granted.

Further Information
Director
Washington Summer Seminar
(800) 424-2600

FLORIDA

Museum of Science, Inc.
3280 South Miami Avenue
Miami, Florida 33129

Programs
(1) Summer Science Camp for children, four 2-week seminars, June–August. Courses for preschoolers to high school students. Subjects include marine biology, art, rocketry, chemistry, sailing, computer science; field trips and instruction by certified teachers. Also Saturday computer programs for children.
(2) Adult schedule of classes, excursions, and lectures; year-round. Recent offerings included astronomy and microcomputers.
(3) Holiday Science Programs at Christmas and Easter.

Accommodations
Participants arrange their own.

Cost
(1) Classes $30–$100, most in the $65–$85 range; lower rates for members (family dues: $35 annually).
(2) and (3) Write for information.

Comment
(1) Summer Science Camp was first offered in 1967 and attracts participants from throughout the United States. Several courses involve field trips; all are taught by certified faculty. The 2-week sessions make family vacation planning easier.

Further Information
Mr. Chris Migliaccio, Education
    Director
(305) 854-4245

University of West Florida
Office of Conferences and
Workshops
Pensacola, Florida 32504

Program
Conferences, workshops, and seminars designed to meet the needs of special or professional groups and individuals. Past topics have included Audit and Accounting Review, Supervisory Management, Productivity, Nursing Supervision, and Stress Management.
Accommodations
A limited number of dormitory efficiency apartments available on campus; hotels in Pensacola and Pensacola Beach. Write for details.

Cost
Write for details.

Comment
Programs of professional development in most fields, allowing participants to update and improve skills and offering them intellectual and cultural opportunities. The faculty is drawn from the university, from the community, and from out of state. Participants include professionals and others interested in career

development. Continuing education credits are available.

Further Information
George M. Faulk, Director
(904) 474-2156

ILLINOIS

Northwestern University
Alumni College
2003 Sheridan Road
Evanston, Illinois 60201

Program
Annual Alumni College, 5 days, July or August. Selected topics revolve around a broad theme like The Persistence of Myth, with lectures, discussions, and field trips.

Accommodations
Air-conditioned dormitory; each participant has a private sleeping room in a suite with shared living room and bathroom.

Cost
$500 includes academic program, housing, meals, and excursions.

Recreation
Tennis courts, beach swimming, social hours.

Comment
Social activities and mealtime breaks allow opportunities for interchange with faculty and enrich the intellectual experience. There are also receptions and field trips to performing arts events, such as the Ravinia Festival. A reading list is sent to enrollees for background apropos of the selected topic. NOTE: Program eligibility limited to adults.

Further Information
Jane Essley, Coordinator of Special
  Programs
(312) 491-8550

> *The quality of a person's life is in direct proportion to their commitment to excellence, regardless of their chosen field of endeavor.*
> **Vincent Lombardi**

INDIANA

Indiana University
Mini-University
Bloomington, Indiana 47405

Program
Mini-University, 5-day program, third week in June. A variety of courses are offered in areas such as the arts, business, domestic issues, health, international affairs, human growth and development.

Accommodations
Indiana Memorial Union or residence halls.

Children
Professionally supervised recreational activities for ages 7–16; nursery school for ages 2–7. Babysitters available in the evening for a nominal fee.

Cost
Tuition: adult, $55; child, $40. Single and double rooms in residence halls: $115–$200 (meals included); in Indiana Memorial Union: $165–$275 (room only).

Recreation
Swimming, tennis, golf, group picnics, racquetball, basketball, hot-air balloon rides. Lessons in riding and horsemanship at nearby stables for additional fee.

Cultural Opportunities
Fine arts library, Brown County Playhouse, faculty reception, School of Music performances, various campus tours and exhibits.

Comment
The Mini-University was first offered in 1972. It is an educational vacation for the entire family, with activities ranging from a picnic to courses on politics and music. The courses, designed by professors of Indiana University, combine relevancy, controversy, and facts. Discussion is a classroom staple.

Further Information
Director
Indiana Memorial Union, M-17
(812) 335-7352

IOWA

Iowa State University
Office of Continuing Education
102 Scheman Building
Ames, Iowa 50011

Program
College Week, annually in June. Nearly one hundred short sessions on a wide variety of topics, including computers, golf, wellness, floral design, photography.

Accommodations
Double rooms and dining facilities in air-conditioned university residence halls. Convenient shared bathrooms, linen service, washers and dryers available.

Children
Teens may attend courses. Child care is available locally for younger children, who may stay with parents in residence halls.

Cost
Enrollment fee, including tuition: $50; materials fees may be added. Room and board: $45 per person (double occupancy), $60 per person (single).

Recreation
Swimming, golf, canoeing, tennis, and use of university facilities.

Cultural Opportunities
Musical performances, seminars on other cultures, dinners, and receptions.

Comment
Classes are designed to be of interest to men and women of any age. Many are taught by ISU faculty. Participants can explore new ideas and improve skills.

Further Information
Kathy Beery, College Week Coordinator
B3 Curtiss Hall
Iowa State University
Ames, Iowa 50011
(515) 294-6616

It's not the least of functions of a true university to maintain a climate favorable to the growth of new ideas and novel practices and then sit back and see what happens.
Romeyn Berry

> *Self-education is fine when the pupil is a born educator.*
> *John Shell*

KENTUCKY

Pine Mountain Settlement School
Bledsoe, Kentucky 40810

Programs
(1) Appalachian Family Week; July. Music, dance, outdoor education, cultural heritage of the region.
(2) Weekend programs on various topics; April–October. Subjects include wildflowers, medicinal plants, spinning and weaving.
(3) Additional programs for children and adults; write for details.

Accommodations
Dormitories.

Cost
Low-cost daily tuition and lodging; write for details.

Recreation
Softball, tennis, swimming, hiking, picnicking.

Cultural Opportunities
Founders Museum with 11,000 volume library; chapel.

Comment
Since its founding in 1913, the Pine Mountain Settlement School has continually adapted its program to the changing needs of the Appalachian region. Its programs, attended by some 6500 people annually, provide insight into the local culture and environment.

Alcoholic beverages not allowed on campus.

Further Information
James Urquhart, Director
(606) 558-4361

> *No problem can stand the assault of sustained thinking.*
> *Voltaire*

LOUISIANA

Tulane University
Latin American Summer Center for Latin American Studies
New Orleans, Louisiana 70118

Program
Summer session program in Mexico, 6 weeks. Courses available in Latin American cultures, history, political science, language, art history; held at Ibero-American University, Mexico City. Participants must take two courses.

Accommodations
Host families.

Cost
Tuition and fees: $700 for two courses; room and board: $470.

Comment
Based in Mexico City, the forty participants in the program take frequent excursions within and outside the city. Focus is on Mexican history, art, and culture, as well as on all aspects of the Spanish language.

Further Information
Dr. Gene Yeager, Associate Director
(504) 865-5164

> *Education has really only one basic factor . . . one must want it.*
>
> G. E. Woodberry

MAINE

University of Maine at Presque Isle
Conferences and Special Programs
Presque Isle, Maine 04769

Programs
(1) Academic courses, 3–5 weeks, May–August. Subjects include writing, psychology, economics, history, art, education.
(2) Youth camps, July–August. Gymnastics, computers, basketball.
(3) Colorado and European study tours available; write for information.
(4) Elderhostels program, July.

Accommodations
Residence halls available.

Cost
(1) Courses per credit hour: $47 (undergraduate); $52 (graduate).
(2) $95–$300, depending on length.
(3) and (4) Write for information.

Recreation
Golf, tennis, hiking, fishing, camping in scenic Aroostook County.

Cultural Opportunities
Visiting nearby New Brunswick, Canada, provides a cross-cultural experience.

Comment
Courses are open to high school students, undergraduates, teachers, and other adults. Enrollment averages about 115 people each summer session, ten to twenty per class.

Further Information
Robert M. Whitcomb, Director
(207) 764-0311, ext. 204

> *I have yet to see any problem (however complicated) which, when you looked at it in the right way, did not become still more complicated.*
>
> Paul Anderson

MARYLAND

The Aspen Institute for Humanistic Studies at Wye Plantation
Box 222
Queenstown, Maryland 21658

Program
Weekend seminars year-round, for executives and others, that carry the concern for traditional values into the examination of contemporary institutions and attitudes and the changes required to cope with the problems and challenges of the late twentieth century. Subjects have included Energy and Resources; The American Constitution; Human Rights and Social Justice; and Food, Water, and Climate.

Accommodations
Wye Plantation House and adjacent buildings at Cheston-on-Wye.

Cost
$350, single; $550, couple.

Comment
The Institute was founded in 1949 at Aspen, Colorado, and has since established branches nationwide and abroad with the center at Wye as its largest base and, because of its proximity to Washington, the logical center for activities in the areas of governance.

It has brought together leading citizens from the public and private sectors of the United States and abroad to consider interrelated issues of the human mind and spirit in contemporary society.

Mortimer Adler, the eminent philosopher, lectures at the Institute several times each year.

Further Information
(301) 827-7168

Recreation
Afternoon schedule allows opportunities for sailing, tennis, boating, and deep-sea fishing.

Cultural Opportunities
Historic tours, visits to museums, libraries.

Comment
The Johns Hopkins Alumni College has been held annually since 1975 at St. Mary's College. Its family-oriented program usually attracts around one hundred participants per session. All programs involve faculty members from Hopkins and visiting scholars.

Further Information
William J. Evitts, Director, Alumni
   Relations
(301) 338-7963

*Johns Hopkins University
   Alumni College
3211 North Charles Street
Baltimore, Maryland 21218*

Program
One-week session, summer, centered around a particular topic. Recent examples: Archaeology and the Bible; American Music—From Colonies to Copland; Getting Out the Word—Language as a Commodity; Geology—Chasms in Earth, Time, and Perspective.

Accommodations
College dormitories.

Children
Programs scheduled for children and teenagers.

Cost
$440 adult tuition per session includes room, board, and books; lower rates for children.

*St. Mary's College of Maryland
Office of Summer Programs
St. Mary's City, Maryland 20686*

Program
Adult learning vacation, 1 week, annually in June. Topics generally cover aspects of American and Maryland history. Lectures, field trips, and social activities provide a full program. Recent themes: Colonial Barony to Free State, The Southern Maryland Legacy, and New Perspectives on Maryland's Past.

Accommodations
Air-conditioned residence hall; catered meals.

Cost
$340 (full program, room and board); $120 (nonresident, including lunch).

Recreation
College facilities; sailboats, tennis courts, gym, and pool.

Cultural Opportunities
Concert, theater, trips to historic
homes and museums.

Comment
Courses are taught by St. Mary's
College faculty and visiting lecturers.
St. Mary's City offers numerous
experiences in four centuries of living
history. There are no prerequisites for
the programs.

Further Information
(301) 863-7100, ext. 330

> *The ideas which civil
> servants and politicians and
> even agitators apply to
> current events are not likely
> to be the newest.*
>   **J. M. Keynes**

MASSACHUSETTS

Brandeis University
Waltham, Massachusetts 02254

Program
Alumni College Seminars on varied
topics (e.g., science, literature, and
music), 3-day weekend, June.

Accommodations
Campus housing.

Cost
$200 (including housing).

Recreational/Cultural
Opportunities
University facilities, including art
collection, renowned library, theater.

Comment
Of recent origin, these seminars
combine with many social and cultural
activities to round out the weekend.

Further Information
Office of Alumni Relations
Gryzmish 113
(617) 647-2307

Exploration Summer Program
124 High Rock Lane
Westwood, Massachusetts 02090

Program
Exploration Summer Program on
campus of Wellesley College, with
workshops for high school and junior
high school students in most areas of
academic study; two 3-week sessions,
July and August.

Accommodations
Dormitories.

Cost
Day students: $475 for 3-week session;
$900 for two 3-week sessions. Resident
students: $1100 for one session, $2100
for both; includes tuition, room, and
board.

Recreation
Swimming, tennis, golf, sailing.

Cultural Opportunities
Mini-courses, guest speakers, trips to
Boston, university visits, concerts,
museums.

Comment
The Exploration Summer Program
began in 1977. It has two separate
divisions, one for students entering
grades 7–9, the other for students
entering grades 10–12. Students select
two from more than sixty workshops in
the humanities, social sciences,

science, and technology. The program helps students explore future career fields, deepen academic interests, and form new friendships. Instructors are graduate and undergraduate students from Wellesley, Harvard, MIT, Yale, and other leading institutions. Average number of participants is fifteen per workshop. Minimum age is 12 years.

Further Information
Arnold H. Singal, Executive Director
(617) 329-4488

Hampshire College
Amherst, Massachusetts 01002

Programs
A variety of programs for high school students and teenagers: Summer Studies in Mathematics, a residential program for students of high ability, 6 weeks; Summer Institute for Film, Photography, and Video for high school students; dance and athletic programs for ages 10–18; academic enrichment for ages 10–16.

Accommodations
Campus residences.

Cost
Write for information.

Recreation
Swimming, sauna, tennis, hiking, bike paths.

Cultural Opportunities
Harold F. Johnson Library, historic sites nearby, theatrical and musical productions.

Further Information
Rosemary Morgan
Director, Summer Programs
(413) 549-4600, ext. 524

MICHIGAN

Michigan State University
Summer Youth Programs
27 Kellogg Center
East Lansing, Michigan 48824

Programs
A variety of summer youth camps in specific subjects; 4 days to 8 weeks. Examples: Ballet Conference (age 12 +); Computer Camp (ages 11–15); High School Science and Engineering Camps; High School Band, Journalism, and Music Workshops.

Accommodations
University residence halls.

Cost
Varies with program. Some offer scholarships. Write for information.

Recreation
Swimming, tennis, racquetball.

Cultural Opportunities
Concerts, theater.

Comment
Courses are taught by MSU faculty and are divided into classroom and outdoor instruction with time allotted for relaxation. Attendance generally varies between twenty and fifty per camp.

Further Information
Clayton Wells
Director, Summer Conferences
(517) 355-4540

Our universities have become the research and training centers on which American professions depend.
            John F. Kennedy

MISSOURI

Saint Louis University and
   Copper Mountain Institute
Metropolitan College
221 North Grand Boulevard
St. Louis, Missouri 63103

Programs
(1) Management Seminars, topics such
as Stress Management and Situational
Leadership; 1 to 3 days, July–August.
(2) Other summer programs ranging
from Continuing Legal Education to
Advanced Jewelry Making.

Accommodations
Hotel or condominium.

Children
Children's program available.

Cost
$315–$495 includes class materials,
luncheons, and refreshments.
Example: Stress Management (2 days),
$495. Housing: $30 per person per day
(double occupancy).

Recreation
Tennis, golf, hiking, rafting, biking,
horseback riding.

Cultural Opportunities
Colorado Philharmonic at Copper
Mountain, June–July; Repertory
Theatre of Saint Louis University;
restored village nearby; annual
Festival of Arts and Crafts.

Comment
Copper Mountain is a year-round
resort sixty miles west of Denver that
has been in operation since 1978.
Programs are structured to encourage
families to accompany participants.
Management Seminars enable those in
executive and managerial positions to
deal effectively with relevant problems
and decision making. Seminar leaders
are university professors and
professionals well qualified in their
fields. Credit is available.

Further Information
(314) 658-2330

*That's what education
means—to be able to do what
you've never done before.*
   George Herbert Palmer

MONTANA

University of Montana
Center for Continuing
   Education and Summer
   Programs
Main Hall #125
Missoula, Montana 59812

Programs
Wide variety of short summer
programs, for ages 5 years and older;
generally for credit, e.g.:
(1) Computer camp, for youth and
young adults, 10 days.
(2) "Step Ahead" programs for high
school students to explore professions
(radio/TV, health, business, theater,
forestry), 4 days.
(3) Courses for adults (health and
fitness, home economics, journalism,
sports, history), 3 weeks.

Accommodations
University dormitories.

Cost
Tuition: Varies with number of credit
hours and whether in-state or out-of-
state enrollee. Write for information.

Room: $42 per week per person (double occupancy).

Recreation
Wide variety of campus facilities, including swimming pool and tennis courts; located near wilderness areas.

Cultural Opportunities
Library, summer theater, concerts, lectures, films, tours; ghost towns and mining sites nearby.

Comment
Summer programs provide education in a spectacular setting. In addition to courses already mentioned, an aerospace education workshop is offered, and the University conducts institutes on glaciers at Glacier and Yellowstone national parks.

Further Information
(406) 243-0211

NEBRASKA

Chadron State College
Family "Vacation" College
Chadron, Nebraska 69337

Program
Several 1-week sessions covering the topic Western Heritage Review. Features discussion, with visits to Fort Robinson, Museum of the Fur Trade, and Mount Rushmore; also, the American Indian Perspective, with a visit to the Mission School Museum and the National American Indian Art Show on the Pine Ridge Reservation. Academic credit may be available.

Accommodations
College dormitories and cafeteria.

Children
Babysitting services provided when needed.

Cost
$225 per week, ages 12 and up (includes room, board, and tuition). Off-campus package, $130 per week. Lower rates for children.

Recreation
Boating, fishing, horseback riding, camping; location near Chadron State Park allows for use of its facilities.

Cultural Opportunities
Fort Robinson and museums, Post Playhouse, library.

Comment
Most time is spent actually experiencing the rich heritage of the Pine Ridge region. Instruction in a living-room-style classroom is combined with the experience of actually being at the historic sites where the events took place.

Further Information
Michael K. Coffee, Director of
    Conferences and Community
    Education
(308) 432-6374/6376
In Nebraska:
(800) 682-5100, ext. 6374

Concordia Teachers College
800 North Columbia Avenue
Seward, Nebraska 68434

Programs
(1) Writing for the Church, August.
(2) Perspective in Rural Life Crises, 4 days, July; mainly for clergy.
(3) Teaching Gifted Children, 4 days, July.

Accommodations
Some air-conditioned units with private baths; facilities depend on full-time-student housing demands.

Cost
Tuition: $117; room and board: $15 per day.

Recreation
Golf, swimming, tennis (at city facilities).

Comment
Concordia Teachers College was established in 1894. It is a Lutheran institution with religiously oriented courses but allows participation by those of all denominations. Courses provide opportunity for individual and professional growth.

Further Information
Dr. Richard Zuick
(402) 643-3651

NEVADA

The Joy Lake Community
P.O. Box 1328
Reno, Nevada 89504

Programs
Various workshops and seminars in holistic health and personal growth. Examples:
(1) Ayurveda—the science of self-healing.
(2) Leonard Energy Training—a way of health and renewal.
(3) The therapeutic use and application of crystals and crystal devices.

Accommodations
Cabins or camping.

Cost
Tuition ranges from $100 to $400 for 3- to 6-day courses. Room and board are extra.

Recreation
Hiking (old logging roads nearby), swimming, horseback riding, etc.

Cultural Opportunities
Aviaries, Whittell Audubon Society.

Comments
Joy Lake is located on a forested 80-acre site in the eastern Sierras. Established in 1983, the site was once an "Old West" attraction called "Sundown Town" with which Buster Keaton was associated. All courses are led by trained practitioners in the holistic healing arts. Certain courses are approved for continuing education credit in nursing by the state of California. Community is a member of the American Heart Association.

Further Information
Registrar
(702) 323-0378

> *He who binds his soul to knowledge steals the key to heaven.*
>
> *N. P. Willis*

NEW HAMPSHIRE

Dartmouth Alumni College
Hanover, New Hampshire 03577

Program
Annual, generally of 12 days, summer. A central theme is chosen and explored in many aspects. Recent examples:

Keep the Wheels Turning and The Challenge of Change.

Accommodations
College dormitory; also deluxe accommodations available at Hanover Inn, located on campus.

Children
The Dartmouth Alumni College is family oriented; there is a Junior Program for young people ages 7–17.

Cost
$1295 per couple for tuition, room, and board; lower prices for younger couples and children.

Recreation
Campus facilities for swimming, tennis, golf, fishing, and camping.

Cultural Opportunities
Library, films, theater, art exhibitions, concerts, etc.

Comment
Dartmouth's Alumni College, founded in 1964, is the oldest of its kind in the country. It offers a cohesive and intensive academic program with small group discussions supplementing faculty lectures. Topics are explored from many perspectives, including historical, social, and literary. The enthusiasm of participants and their high rate of return attest to the Alumni College's excellence.

Further Information
Steven L. Calvert, Director
(603) 646-2454/3309

But, soon or late, it is ideas, not vested interests, which are dangerous for good or evil.
J. M. Keynes

NEW YORK

Albert Einstein College of Medicine
Montefiore Medical Center
Department of Psychiatry, 1312 ECHS
Bronx, New York 10461

Program
Cape Cod Institute, June–August. A series of weeklong courses on topics of current interest to mental health professionals. Morning classes leave afternoons free for leisure and study.

Accommodations
Participants arrange their own. Write for recommendations.

Cost
Tuition: $325 for one program, $250 for each additional program.

Comment
The Institute has been held annually since 1980 and has offered more than seventy-five courses to a growing audience from North America and overseas. It offers in-depth exposure to the ideas and methods of leading clinicians, researchers, theorists, and mental health and medical experts. Continuing education credit approved by the American Psychological Association for psychologists; 15 credit hours of category one of the Physician's Recognition Award of the AMA; the college has applied for CEUs from Massachusetts chapter of NASW. Courses are held in the Provincetown and Eastham areas of Cape Cod, Massachusetts.

Further Information
Gilbert Levin, Ph.D., Professor and Institute Director
(212) 430-2311

The American Jewish Committee
Academy for Jewish Studies
165 East 56th Street
New York, New York 10022

Program
Seminars in Jewish Studies (culture, history, problems, etc.):
(1) 5 days, July—Skidmore College, Saratoga Springs, New York.
(2) 5 days, August—Williams College, Williamstown, Massachusetts.
(3) Special Family Program, 5 days— Williams College, Williamstown, Massachusetts.
All programs are from Monday through Friday, with orientation Sunday evening; weekend stayovers may be arranged at additional cost.

Accommodations
(1) Skidmore College residence facilities (air conditioned).
(2) and (3) Dodd House on Williams College campus, private or semiprivate baths.

Cost
(1) and (2) $340 per person (tuition, room, and board).
(3) $150 additional per child, ages 9– 12.

Recreation
Campus facilities.

Cultural Opportunities
(1) Saratoga Performing Arts Center nearby.
(2) and (3) Tanglewood nearby.

Comment
The Academy for Jewish Studies was founded in 1974 by the American Jewish Committee; in addition to the summer seminars mentioned above, correspondence courses on all aspects of the Jewish experience, as well as short courses for group study and videotapes suitable for individual or group viewing, are available. The Williams College Family Seminar was designed with preteen and teenage children in mind.

Further Information
The Academy for Jewish Studies
(212) 751-4000, ext. 434

> *Persistence and determination alone are omnipotent.*
> *Calvin Coolidge*

Chautauqua Institution
Schools Office
P.O. Box 1098
Chautauqua, New York 14722

Program
Annual courses in virtually all the fine and applied arts, plus over one hundred Special Studies courses; 2 days to 8 weeks; summer. Special Studies subjects include handicrafts, foreign languages, language arts and literature, basic skills of learning, cultural and behavioral studies, practical daily skills, recreation, exercise, and more. There is also a weeklong Age Fifty-Five Plus residential program.

Accommodations
Residence halls, hotels, private homes, rooming houses, apartments. The Accommodations Referral Service is a telephone answering service that can be used by calling (716) 357-6204.

Children
Programs for children ages 2 and up. Day camps held.

Cost
Varies widely; write for information.

Recreation
Eighteen-hole golf course, beaches, tennis courts, shuffleboard, lawn bowling, boating, swimming.

Cultural Opportunities
Programs in amphitheater, including lectures, symphony orchestra, religious services, and opera in English. There is also a Chautauqua Literary and Scientific Circle.

Comment
Established in 1874, the Chautauqua Institution has become an international center for continuing education. It is, in fact, where the concept of learning vacations began. For art courses, professionally oriented younger students share instruction and facilities with serious amateurs of all ages. The Special Studies courses are designed for the hobbyist or vacationer. Lessons for beginning through advanced students given by teachers from colleges, universities, and other educational institutions throughout the United States and abroad. Over 1900 enrolled in all Chautauqua courses in 1985. College credit is available for most art and some Special Studies courses.

Further Information
Jean Quinette, Coordinator for Schools
(716) 357-4411

*Cornell Adult University
Summer Vacation Study
626B Thurston Avenue
Ithaca, New York 14850*

Programs
(1) Variety of weeklong adult and family programs on Cornell campus throughout the summer. Adults select from among seminar and workshop topics including art, history, politics, photography, writing, and field natural history.
(2) Seminars on various topics by Cornell faculty and guest lecturers in other U.S. locations, 3 to 7 days, May–October.

Accommodations
(1) Donlon Hall or Hurlbutt House dormitories; meals at North Campus Union.
(2) Hotels, lodges, rustic camps.

Children
(1) Summer learning and recreational program for ages 3–17. Daily morning activities include instruction in topics from zoology to video communication; field trips, picnics, games, and sports.

Cost
(1) Adult: $440 per week for tuition, room, and board. Youth: $225 per week for tuition, room, and board.
(2) $225–$500 including housing (double occupancy), meals, and academic program.

Recreation
(1) Golf, tennis, swimming, trails, gardens. Nearby: Cayuga Lake, parks, wineries.

Cultural Opportunities
(1) Lectures, concerts, films, theater, art exhibits; use of libraries and other campus facilities.

Comment
Established in 1968, the Cornell Summer and related programs are among the most comprehensive in the nation. The summer program on campus attracts 1500 participants annually. All courses are taught by Cornell faculty or qualified guest lecturers.

Further Information
Ralph Janis, Director
(607) 256-6260

> *For the more a man knows,*
> *the more worthy he is.*
> *Robert of Gloucester*

Land's End
Presbytery of Northern New York
Star Route Box 5
Saranac Lake, New York 12983

Programs
Seminars in various aspects of faith education and human relations, 3–5 days, year-round. Recent seminars have dealt with marriage enrichment, conflict management, Bible study, ethics, Central America.

Accommodations
Twin-bedded rooms, two to a room. No pets.

Cost
Varies with seminar. Examples: $123 (5 days), $85 (3 days), all inclusive.

Recreation
Swimming, boating, fishing, tennis, volleyball, badminton, croquet; golf and skiing nearby.

Comment
The Presbytery's mission at Land's End is to provide quality programs, outstanding leadership, and private study opportunities to assist pastors, lay persons, churches, and nonprofit organizations in renewing their lives and mission in Christ's name. Average group size is twelve; Continuing Education Units (CEUs) available. Land's End is a well-maintained, attractively furnished rustic lodge, situated in a wooded area on the shore of upper Saranac Lake.

Further Information
Rev. Jean Anne Swope, Executive Director
(518) 891-4034

Long Island University
Southampton Campus
Summer Program
Southampton, New York 11968

Programs
Five-week sessions and 1-week intensive courses, June–August. Course topics include social and natural sciences, arts and humanities; graduate and undergraduate levels. Also noncredit courses for personal enrichment.

Accommodations
Dormitories for those taking classes for credit.

Children
Programs in science for high school students and gifted children in grades 4–6. Day Camp (ages 5–12) and Kinder Camp (ages 3–4).

Cost
Tuition: $171–$182 per credit hour. Housing: $60–$75 per week (lower for LIU students). Meal plans: $45–$60.

Recreation
Swimming, tennis, fitness trail, university facilities.

Cultural Opportunities
Campus library, art galleries, summer theater, museums, botanical gardens.

Comment
The Summer Program has been held annually since 1977. Classes are scheduled at varied times to accommodate differing schedules. Courses include regular departmental offerings, intensive workshops, and

personal and professional enrichment courses.

Further Information
Alice Flynn, Summer Program
(516) 283-4600, ext. 114

Mohonk Mountain House Tower of Babble Language Program
Mohonk Lake
New Paltz, New York 12561

Programs
Foreign language immersion programs; weekend programs held several times yearly, with 15 hours of instruction; weeklong session in January provides 45 hours of instruction. Evening programs focus on international arts and culture. A dozen languages at all levels.

Accommodations
Single or double rooms, with or without bath; meals included.

Cost
$100 tuition, credit additional; single rooms: $69–$137 per day; double rooms: $132–$212 per day. Some additional expenses.

Comment
The language immersion concept was developed by Dr. Henry Urbanski, chairman of the Department of Foreign Languages at State University of New York College at New Paltz. It has proven an efficient, effective method of learning and reinforcing a foreign language. Classes are small, and learning is enhanced by the secluded, relaxing atmosphere of Mohonk Mountain House, a full-service resort and conference center, founded in 1869 on 2000 wooded acres near New Paltz, New York.

Further Information
Faire Hart, Public Relations
(914) 255-1000
(212) 233-2244 (New York City)

> *Only a mediocre person is always at his best.*
> **Somerset Maugham**

The Rensselaerville Institute Asimov Seminars
Rensselaerville, New York 12147

Program
Philosophical seminars led by Isaac Asimov (with assistants), 5 days, July or August. Recent topics: Artificial Intelligence: Are We Being Outsmarted? and Biotechnology: Man-made Evolution? In general, seminars assess the impact of an emerging technology and consider reactions to possible large-scale future emergencies.

Accommodations
Two modern residences, turn-of-the-century estate home; single and double rooms. Meals by master chef in the Weathervane, a full-service restaurant.

Cost
$530 for tuition, room, and board; couples at discount rate.

Recreation
Tennis, swimming, volleyball, hiking; socializing with Dr. Asimov and guest experts.

Comment
Campus situated in one hundred–acre estate in the hamlet of Rensselaerville

(on National Register of Historic Places); twenty-seven miles southwest of Albany. The Rensselaerville Institute is an independent educational center chartered in 1963 as the Institute on Man and Science. The Asimov Seminars (in which Dr. Asimov is joined by experts in various fields) began in 1973. Seminars encourage the interaction of participants.

Further Information
Asimov Seminar Director
(518) 797-3783

---

*Sagamore Lodge and
    Conference Center
Sagamore Institute
Sagamore Road
Raquette Lake, New York 13436*

Programs
Year-round workshops in various subjects: leadership, professional development, human relations, personal growth, recreation; 3 days to 1 week in length.

Accommodations
Dormitory, single and double rooms at Sagamore Conference Center near Raquette Lake, New York, approximately 130 miles northwest of Albany; camping facilities.

Cost
$20–$200 tuition, depending on workshop (example: $140 for Training for Workshop Leaders, 5 days). $125–$190 for room and board.

Recreation
Swimming, boating, fishing, hiking, cross-country skiing, bowling.

Comment
Established in 1971, Sagamore Institute specializes in the fields of

education, professional development, environmental studies, and social change. Workshops are conducted by experts in their respective fields (professors, psychologists, consultants). More than 1000 people participate in the various programs annually; average attendance per workshop is thirty.

Further Information
Howard Kirschenbaum, Executive Director
(315) 354-5311

The price of greatness is responsibility.
        Winston Churchill

---

*Skidmore College
Saratoga Springs, New York
    12866*

Programs
(1) Skidmore Senior Seminar, Northeastern Senior Seminar; 6–7 weeks, beginning late June. Weeklong seminars on a variety of subjects for persons over 55.
(2) Judaic Studies Program; three weeklong seminars, mid-July and early August; cosponsored by the American Jewish Committee and the Academy for Jewish Studies. Lectures, discussions, and other experiences to deepen understanding of Jewish texts and concepts.

Accommodations
Single or double dormitory rooms.

Cost
(1) $235–$255 per week, complete.
(2) $325 per week, complete.

Recreation
Tennis, horseback riding, campus athletic facilities.

Cultural Opportunities
Saratoga Performing Arts Center, Newport Jazz Festival, theater, concerts.

Comment
Northeastern Senior Seminar is sponsored by a network of colleges and universities. Its variety of programs and locations enables people 55 and over to enjoy the intellectual stimulation of college life. Through weekly travel, participants can take advantage of study opportunities at all network institutions, which offer a total of nineteen programs. Write for details.

Further Information
Dean of Special Programs
(518) 584-5000

State University of New York College at Potsdam
Raymond Hall
Potsdam, New York 13676

Program
Annual 1- to 6-week undergraduate and graduate courses in music, education, and liberal arts. Special workshops and seminars; June through early August.

Accommodations
University residence halls.

Cost
Tuition: varies with course. Housing: $50 per week (double); $75 per week (single). Cafeteria meals, $65 per week. Camping nearby. Write for details.

Recreation
Swimming, tennis, golf, boating, hiking.

Cultural Opportunities
Crane School of Music, Music Theatre North; art galleries.

Comment
A campus of the State University of New York, located in the western Adirondack Mountains. A variety of summer courses are available. Children are allowed. The campus is convenient to Ottawa, Montreal, and the Thousand Islands. College credit available.

Further Information
Director, Continuing Education and
    Lifelong Learning
(315) 267-2000

Wainwright House
Center for Development of Human Resources
260 Stuyvesant Avenue
Rye, New York 10580

Program
Courses, seminars, and workshops for people in pursuit of intellectual, psychological, and physical development; throughout the year. Topics include global issues, psychology, health, philosophy, and religion. Skill-oriented sessions focus on the professions. Among the annual core programs arc A Better World, Spiritual Guidance, and Receptive Listening.

Accommodations
Available for weekday and weekend students.

Cost
Tuition: $5–$300, depending on course. Lodging: $20–$30 per night. Meals:

$4.50–$8. Weekend rates, tax-deductible membership option.

Comment
Wainwright House, a Normandy-style château on Long Island Sound, close to I-95 and the Rye train station, is a nonprofit, nonsectarian educational center established in 1941. Programs are meant to help people discover their own spiritual path. Courses emphasize learning, sharing, group support, spiritual growth, and wholeness.

Further Information
Dr. Franklin E. Vilas Jr., Executive
    Director
(914) 967-6080

The world is full of educated derelicts.
                    Calvin Coolidge

NORTH CAROLINA

Charlotte Yiddish Institute at
    Wildacres
Charlotte Jewish Community
    Center
Box 13369
Charlotte, North Carolina
    28211-0080

Program
Charlotte Yiddish Institute at Wildacres, 4 days in spring. Program includes lectures, language workshops, literature, shabbat, services, etc.

Accommodations
Heated rooms with baths in two main lodges at Wildacres, Little Switzerland, North Carolina, a retreat

in the Blue Ridge Mountains of western North Carolina.

Cost
$125 per person (double occupancy), including tuition, board, and gratuities.

Recreation
Tennis, golf, and hiking nearby.

Cultural Opportunities
Many opportunities directly related to program.

Comment
First held in 1979, the Charlotte Yiddish Institute provides an entire program devoted to aspects of that language. Institute leaders have included professors, newspaper editors, and Yiddish Theatre performers. Knowledge of Yiddish is vital for participants. Maximum enrollment is one hundred. The institute is for adults only.

Further Information
Baila Pransky, Coordinator
(704) 366-5564/7846

University of North Carolina at
    Chapel Hill
Vacation College
Program in Humanities and
    Human Values
209 Abernathy Hall–0024
Chapel Hill, North Carolina
    27514

Program
Annual Vacation College seminars on social, cultural, and historical topics; 4–6 days each, late June–early August. Recent topics have included The Middle Ages, The Renaissance, World War I, Russia and America, Heroes.

Accommodations
Choice of university residence halls or more luxurious Carolina Inn (at additional cost).

Children
No programs for children.

Cost
$195 registration fee includes tuition, banquets, picnic, and reception. Room and most meals additional. Write for information.

Recreation
Swimming, golf, tennis.

Cultural Opportunities
Films related to seminar topic, concerts, planetarium, art museum film series, library special collections, National Humanities Center nearby.

Comment
Vacation College was first held in 1979. Enrollment is limited to fifty per seminar. Each seminar has a faculty coordinator plus guest lecturers, many of whom are university faculty members.

Further Information
Warren A. Nord, Director
(919) 962-2211

OHIO

College of Wooster
Alumni House
Wooster, Ohio 44691

Program
Annual 6-day program on social or cultural issues, early to mid-June. Recent subjects: cross-cultural dynamics, medical ethics, the arts and humanities.

Accommodations
Dormitories; College Inn, with private baths and air-conditioning, available at extra cost. No pets.

Children
Youth program for ages 3–15. Recreation, movies, special field trips.

Cost
$245 per adult (tuition and dormitories). Teens and children lower.

Recreation
Tennis, golf, swimming, bowling.

Cultural Opportunities
Concerts, plays, Andrews Library, Frick Art Museum, Ohio Light Opera, Cleveland Art Museum, Seiberling Mansion in area.

Comment
Courses conducted by faculty of the college, distinguished alumni, and guest scholars.

Further Information
Marjorie Kramer
Director, Alumni Relations
(800) 362-7386 (Ohio)
(800) 321-9885 (out-of-state)
(216) 263-2324

Lakeside on Lake Erie
236 Walnut Avenue
Lakeside, Ohio 43440

Programs
(1) Financial Planning, 1 week.
(2) Ten programs of 1-week duration featuring daily educational and cultural events, summer. Included are religious and academic guest speakers, concerts, films, and the like.

Accommodations
Hotels, rental cottages, guest houses.

Cost
Adults: $6.50 per day; youth: $4.50 per day. NOTE: Figures are for entrance or participation fees; there is an extra charge for some events.

Recreation
Tennis, swimming, sailing, shuffleboard, miniature golf, volleyball, archery, roller skating, and more.

Cultural Opportunities
Extra concerts, movies, etc.

Comment
Established in 1873, Lakeside on Lake Erie is a nonprofit resort supported by the United Methodist Church. It serves thousands of visitors in the summer and functions as a conference center throughout the year. No alcoholic beverages or motorbikes are allowed.

Further Information
Tom Edwards, Executive Director
(419) 798-4461

Ohio Wesleyan University
Summerweek
Delaware, Ohio 43015

Program
Annual seminars on a variety of topics explored in depth through lectures, discussions, field trips, etc.; 7 days, May–June.

Accommodations
Air-conditioned residence hall; four persons to a three-room suite.

Cost
$260 per person includes all program activities, room, most meals, local transportation.

Recreation
Golf, tennis, swimming.

Cultural Opportunities
Music and theater performances.

Comment
Established in 1976, the Summerweek program is small, emphasizing a family atmosphere among participants. Speakers include Wesleyan faculty, alumni, and others. Examples of topics are Quest for Balance: Needs, Resources, Values; and The Constitution-Vision and Reality.

Further Information
Laura M. Newman, Director of Alumni
    Relations
(614) 369-4431

Adversity reveals genius, prosperity conceals it.
                    Horace

OREGON

University of Oregon
Grace Graham Vacation
    College
Housing Office
Eugene, Oregon 97403

Program
Grace Graham Vacation College, a 1-week seminar for adults, usually held in August. Topics generally focus on cultural history, contemporary issues, or future perspectives.

Accommodations
Private rooms.

Cost
$550 per person includes tuition, room and board, special events.

Recreation
Golf, tennis, racquetball, bowling, swimming, gym, and more.
Cultural Opportunities
Art museum, pioneer museum, libraries, Maude Kerns Arts Center.

Comment
Organized in 1964, the Grace Graham Vacation College is based on a century-old concept of the Danish Folk School. All seminars are led by university faculty or visiting specialists. Limited enrollment (maximum of eighty per session) encourages free exchange of ideas and close interaction.

Further Information
Housing Office
(503) 686-4277

PENNSYLVANIA

Marywood College
2300 Adams Avenue
Scranton, Pennsylvania 18509

Programs
(1) On-campus programs, 2 weeks: computer programming and data processing; financial management; money and banking; religion; dynamics of speech communication. 3-credit courses, July.
(2) Music Camp for students, 2 weeks, July.
(3) College-for-Kids; 3-week program for children ages 4–16, July.

Accommodations
Campus residences for women (dorms or apartments); men at nearby college or motels. No pets.

Children
College-for-Kids, mentioned above.

Cost
(1) $125 per credit.
(2) $70.
(3) $55.
Accommodations not included.

Recreation
Swimming, racquetball, tennis, alpine and water slide nearby.

Cultural Opportunities
Band concerts, summer-stock theater.

Comment
The college offers credit and noncredit programs for all ages and interests.

Further Information
Sr. Loretta Mulry, Dean
(717) 348-6258

Pennsylvania State University
University Park Campus
Alumni Vacation College
105 Old Main
University Park, Pennsylvania
  16802

Program
Weeklong session annually, July. Program includes lectures and discussions on cultural, political, or scientific issues (Changing American Families, Current Research at the University, The New Decade).

Accommodations
Dormitories, shared baths; nearby motels and hotels available.

Children
Youth programs for all age groups, including pioneer crafts, caving, canoeing, and theatrical makeup.

Cost
$185 tuition (adults); $170 tuition (children). Dormitory room and board $100–$125 (less for children 9 and under).

Recreation
Golf, paddleball, tennis, squash, handball, swimming, hiking, fishing, boating, picnicking.

Cultural Opportunities
Libraries, art museum, summer-stock theater, musical productions.

Comment
Alumni Vacation College provides an open forum where varied viewpoints are expressed through informal interaction, lectures, and group discussions. Non-alumni are welcome.

Further Information
Program:
Heather Ricker Gilbert, Assistant
    Executive Director
Penn State Alumni Association
(814) 865-6516
Registration:
Gretchen A. Leathers, Conference
    Coordinator
410 Keller Conference Center
(814) 863-4563

Slippery Rock University of
    Pennsylvania
Slippery Rock, Pennsylvania
    16057

Program
Vacation College: 1-week courses during summer on varied subjects, e.g., living wills, investments, gardening, antique markets, music.

Accommodations
Dormitories with single and double rooms and shared bath arrangements.

Cost
$195 per week inclusive of room and board.

Recreation
Swimming, tennis, golf, gymnasium.

Cultural Opportunities
Nearby historic sites, evening cultural presentations.

Further Information
Professor Tim Walters
ATTN: English Department
(412) 794-2510/7266

RHODE ISLAND

Brown University
Summer College
Box 1920
Providence, Rhode Island 02912

Program
Annual 1-week educational experience taught by Brown faculty, June. Several topics offered each session, with lectures, discussions, and workshops. A recent example is The Making of Foreign Policy; previous workshops have dealt with business planning, film, physical fitness, and public speaking.

Accommodations
Dormitory rooms.

Cost
Approximately $470 per person (tuition, room, and board); $400 for nonresident participants.

Recreation
Tennis, squash, swimming, golf, historic walking tours.

Cultural Opportunities
Libraries, art galleries, theater, Museum of Rhode Island.

Comment
The Summer College was first offered in 1972 and attracts an average of 125 participants annually. The lecture/

discussion series is led by prominent Brown faculty members. Workshops offer a hands-on experience in specific skills, with maximum interaction between participants and faculty.

Further Information
Sallie K. Riggs
Associate Vice-President, University
   Relations
(401) 863-2785

> *The only sure weapon against bad ideas is better ideas.*
> *W. Griswold*

VERMONT

The Experiment in
   International Living
School for International
   Training
Kipling Road
Brattleboro, Vermont
   05301-0676

Programs
(1) Intensive foreign language courses; 2 weeks, January, July, August. Emphasis on speaking and listening and on cultural awareness. Languages offered are French, Spanish, German, Japanese, Chinese, and Russian. (2) Global Education Summer Institute, consisting of general sessions on key concepts in global education; small-group work sessions. Write for more information.

Accommodations
Double-occupancy dormitories with shared bath. On-campus dining hall. Motels available nearby.

Cost
(1)Tuition: $320; room and board: $95 per week.

Recreation
Swimming, hiking.

Cultural Opportunities
Marlboro Music Festival, theater, folk dancing.

Comment
The school is located on a multicultural, multilingual campus that offers a distinctive opportunity for language practice and cultural exchange outside the classroom. Individual or group tutorials are available.

Further Information
(1) Susan Schuman
Special Language Programs
(802) 257-7751, ext. 292
(2) Global Education Summer Institute
(802) 257-7751, ext. 224

VIRGINIA

Eastern Mennonite College
Harrisonburg, Virginia 22801

Program
Three 3-week terms, May–July. First-term courses: Introduction to Computers, New Testament, Psychology for Teaching Adolescents, Humanities, Horticulture; second term: Faith and Practice, Plant Pest Management, Colonial America, Humanities; third term: Faith and Vocation, Speech Communiction, Principles of Economics.

Accommodations
Dormitory facilities. Smoking and drinking are prohibited.

Children
Children are welcome; no special activities are planned.

Cost
$175 per credit hour, $50 audit; $55 per week, room and board.

Recreation
Basketball, tennis, gym.

Cultural Opportunities
Luray Caverns and Shenandoah Cavern; also Natural Bridge.

Comment
Eastern Mennonite College was founded in 1917; it is located in the Shenandoah Valley, which contains many areas of scenic and historic interest. Average size of class is twelve to fifteen.

Further Information
Marie Hertzler Horst, Director of
   Summer School
(703) 433-2771, ext. 105

> *I have taken all knowledge to be my province.*
> *Francis Bacon*

Ferrum College
Ferrum, Virginia 24088

Program
Summer classes, 3 weeks, May–June. Varied subjects in biology, business, computers, history, mathematics, religion, etc., all offering 3–4 college credits.

Accommodations
Student residential facilities.

Cost
Tuition: $270–$360. Room and board: $230.

Recreation
Horseback riding, hiking, tennis, swimming, track, softball, tubing. Within driving distance are the Blue Ridge Parkway, Philpot Lake, Fairy Stone State Park, and Smith Mountain Lake.

Cultural Opportunities
Stanley Library on campus. Nearby are the Blue Ridge Institute and the Booker T. Washington Museum.

Comment
Ferrum College, founded in 1913, is a relatively small institution whose campus location (about thirty-five miles from Roanoke in the foothills of the Blue Ridge Mountains) offers an attractive setting for summer study.

Further Information
(703) 365-2121

Washington and Lee University
*   Alumni Colleges*
Office of Summer Programs
Lexington, Virginia 24450

Program
Annual seminars, two 1-week sessions, July. Recent topics include Great Writers and 18th-Century France.

Accommodations
Modern air-conditioned furnished apartment with bath; private dining room.

Children
Junior program for ages 6–16.

Cost
$500 (single), $800 (double); includes room, board, and tuition. Junior program: $150 per child.

Comment
Programs with suggested readings on the topic. Optional afternoon program

includes lectures, plays, entertainment, and meals with the faculty. Maximum enrollment is seventy-five adults. (Of a recent group, fifty percent were returning for a second session.)

Further Information
Robert Fure, Ph.D., Director of
    Summer Programs
(703) 463-8723

It is well to live that one may learn.
                Miguel de Cervantes

WASHINGTON

Western Washington University Center for Continuing Education Bellingham, Washington 98225

Program
Adventure in Science and Arts: three 5-day sessions for students in grades 6–12, July. Features more than twenty-five workshops in the following areas: arts and humanities, science and nature, psychology and personality, economics, electronics, technology, and computers.

Accommodations
University residence halls.

Cost
Tuition: $125 per session; room and board: $125 per session.

Comment
Adventures in Science and Arts was first offered in 1982. Workshops schedule intense 5- to 6-hour daily

sessions, usually with grades 6–8 and 9–12 in separate groups. Instructors are University faculty, graduate students, and community resource people. Applicants must submit a one-page essay on their background and interests, plus a nomination letter from a knowledgeable adult. Commuting students are welcome.

Further Information
Lina Sullivan, Publications and
    Promotions Coordinator
Center for Continuing Education
(206) 676-3320

CANADA

*Couchiching Institute on Public Affairs
25 Adelaide Street East, Suite 1711
Toronto, Ontario M5C 1Y6
Canada*

Program
Annual summer seminars, 4 days, late July or August. Lectures and discussion workshops on topics of Canadian or general interest.

Accommodations
Choices abound, from rustic to motel.

Cost (Canadian dollars)
CIPA Members: $270–$335 (double occupancy).
Nonmembers: $320–$385 (double occupancy).
Student rates are lower.

Recreation
Swimming, sailing, tennis, hiking.

Cultural Opportunities
Leacock Festival.

Comment
The Couchiching Institute, established in 1931, is Canada's oldest public affairs forum. It features prominent speakers from around the world. Its proceedings are taped, then broadcast by the Canadian Broadcasting Company.

Further Information
Lee Walsh, Director
(416) 362-4752

Georgian College of Applied Arts and Technologies
School of Continuous Learning
One Georgian Drive
Barrie, Ontario L4M 3X9
Canada

Programs
Short-term courses and workshops (predominantly evening or weekend), spring and summer, in business, computers, health care, language, etc. Various locations in the Georgian Bay area north of Toronto, including Barrie, Orillia, Owen Sound, and Parry Sound.

Accommodations
Contact Huronia Tourist Association, Midhurst, Ontario.

Cost (Canadian dollars)
Varies with course length. Examples:
(A) Introductory and Microcomputer: fourteen or fifteen sessions each (42–45 hours), $45–$48.
(B) Conversational French: ten sessions (30 hours), $48.
(C) Photography: ten sessions (30 hours), $71.

Recreation
Canoeing, sailing, tennis, golf, horsemanship, camping (depending on location).

Cultural Opportunities
Public libraries; Simcoe County Museum, Midhurst.

Comment
The Continuous Education Program was first offered in 1970. The instructors are professionals in their fields. General enrollment is twelve to fifteen students per class.

Further Information
Ted Dunlop
(705) 722-1544

> *For God's sake, stop researching for a while and begin to think.*
>   *Walter Hamilton Moberly*

Mount Allison University
Department of Continuing Education
Centennial Hall
Sackville, New Brunswick E0A 3C0
Canada

Programs
(1) French and English Language Intensive Immersion Programs; 6 weeks. Daily classes, a variety of activities, weekend excursions. Students live and work together; program stresses cultural as well as linguistic experience.
(2) Weeklong current events and United Nations forum for high school students, July.
(3) New England Maritime Connection, a 1-week program of lectures, field trips, and entertainment. Children's programs available.

Accommodations
University dormitories, single and double rooms; meals available from on-campus food service.

Cost (Canadian dollars)
(1) $1500, includes tuition, room, board, books, activities.
(2) $200, includes tuition, room, and board.
(3) Call or write.

Recreation
Outdoor track, swimming, gymnasium, tennis, hiking, boating.

Cultural Opportunities
University library, art gallery, fine arts studios, music conservatory.

Comment
Instructors for courses are university teachers and qualified professionals. Extracurricular activities are designed to supplement classwork.

Further Information
(1) Marilyn McCullough
Director, Department of Continuing Studies
(506) 364-2266/2265
(2) Gordon Watson, Program Director
St. Margaret's Bay, Nova Scotia
BOJ 1R0
Canada
(902) 826-7678
(3) Professor Gwen Davies
Center for Canadian Studies
(506) 364-2543

Apprehending technology in its completeness . . . is what we should expect education . . . to achieve.
Eric Ashby

University of Guelph Summer Campus Continuing Education
Room 160, Johnston Hall
Guelph, Ontario N1G 2W1
Canada

Program
Session of unconventional university courses emphasizing the pleasure of learning, 1 week. Recent subjects include drawing, French, bird-watching, free-lance writing, management techniques, and more.

Accommodations
Modern university residences.

Children
Complete youth program for ages 4 and up.

Cost (Canadian dollars)
Average 1-week course tuition: $95; for youth programs: $75; approximately $400 per week for room and two meals a day for family of four.

Recreation
Swimming, tennis, jogging, hiking, golf, bicycling, squash; social events.

Cultural Opportunities
Art gallery and library on campus. Guelph is near Toronto, Niagara Falls, and the Stratford Shakespeare Festival.

Comment
Summer Campus was first held at Guelph in 1976. The program of academic, cultural, recreational, and social activities appeals equally to families, couples, and individuals. Some courses have limited enrollment.

Further Information
Kathy Freeburn
Program Coordinator, Continuing Education Division
(519) 824-4120, ext. 3956

2 *JOURNEYS FAR AND NEAR*

Foundations for Field Research

*S*ightseeing with a purpose. This chapter includes cultural journeys and trips led by scholars and specialists to all areas of the globe. A wide variety of choices are offered, ranging in length from a few days to several months, during all seasons of the year.

> *The vitality of thought is in adventure, ideas won't keep. Something must be done with them.*
>
> *Alfred North Whitehead*

ALABAMA

University of South Alabama
Continuing Education
2002 Old Bayfront Drive
Mobile, Alabama 36615

Programs
(1) British Studies Program at the University of London, 3–5 weeks, July–August. Course work in a variety of disciplines, research at London archives, field trips, and free travel are all included.
(2) Mexico Tour, 9 days, late November. History, architecture, and sightseeing in Yucatan and along the Caribbean coast.

Accommodations
(1) University dormitories.
(2) First-class hotels.

Children
(1) Not permitted.
(2) Children may accompany parent.

Cost
(1) Approximately $2000, including airfare, tuition, and housing.
(2) Approximately $700, including airfare, local transporation, rooms, and some meals.

Comment
(1) The British Studies Program is a cooperative program of several U.S. and English institutions. Classes are taken for credit, including accelerated courses for professional enrichment. There are usually between thirty and sixty students taught by six or seven faculty members, who are drawn from both English and American schools.
(2) The Mexico Tour combines visits to pyramids and other historical sites with relaxation at resorts. Average group size is twenty to thirty. Guides have an intimate knowledge of local culture and provide special contacts for the group. Local travel by motorcoach.

Further Information
Patricia B. Mullins, Travel
    Coordinator
(205) 431-6409

ARIZONA

Arizona State University
Tempe, Arizona 85287

Programs
Varied summer travel/study.
(1) Mexican Language and Culture Immersion Program in Gungjuato, Mexico, 3 weeks, July–August.
(2) Criminal Justice in England and Scotland, 1 month, late May through late June.
(3) Social Science, Art, Literature, in Florence, Italy, 3 weeks, June–July.

Accommodations
(1) With Mexican family.
(2) and (3) Hotels.

Cost
(1) $360, tuition.
(2) $1770, tuition, airfare, some meals.
(3) $985, tuition (7 credit hours), room, side trips.

Comment
The Mexican and Italian trips afford opportunities to learn the languages of those countries, as well as to study their history and culture. The Mexican trip, in addition, is a total "immersion" experience through contact with Mexican families.

Further Information
(1) Office of Summer Sessions
Academic Services Building, #110
(602) 965-6611

(2) Professor Tom Schede
328 Wilson Hall
(602) 965-7040

(3) Professor Pier Raimondo Baldwin
Department of Foreign Languages,
    Room C434
(602) 965-3362

> *To know one thing well is to have a barbaric mind.*
>   *Robert Graves*

***Southwestern Mission
Research Center
Arizona State Museum
University of Arizona
Tucson, Arizona 85721***

Program
Annual 3-day travel/study program to northern Sonora, Mexico; spring and fall.

Accommodations
Motels (double occupancy) with bath.

Cost
$225, includes round-trip bus transportation from Tucson.

Comment
Program gives participants an introduction to contemporary, colonial,

and ancient Mexico. Featured is a visit to Father Kino's missions. Average group size is thirty-two; tours are conducted by members of the research center.

Further Information
Dr. Charles W. Polzer, S.J., Associate
    Director
(602) 621-6281

CALIFORNIA

***Gordon Frost Indian Folk Art
    Tour
P.O. Box 471-LV
Newhall, California 91321***

Program
One folk art study tour per year to Guatemala, Mexico, and/or Peru, 2 or 3 weeks, July–August. Visits to key centers of Indian art and culture to see craft processes, ceremonial events, spectacular scenery, pre-Columbian ruins, and national museums.

Accommodations
First-class or best available.

Cost
$1375 land arrangements, 2 weeks.
$1995 land arrangements, 3 weeks.

Comment
Each tour is led by Gordon Frost, folk-art collector and photographer, who has 20 years' experience in Mesoamerica and South America. Groups are limited to fifteen people.

Further Information
Gordon Frost
(805) 255-7577

> *Here is the world, sound as a nut, perfect . . . but the theory of the world is a thing of shreds and patches.*
> *Ralph Waldo Emerson*

Los Angeles World Affairs Council
900 Wilshire Boulevard
Los Angeles, California 90017

Programs
(1) Diplomatic Tours: fully escorted trips featuring private briefings by U.S. and foreign officials. Recent examples include People's Republic of China, 25 days; Ecuador and Peru, 14 days; Egypt, Jordan, and Israel, 23 days; and Scandinavia and Leningrad, 18 days.
(2) Forum Abroad Series: 1-week, one-city tours including briefings. Recent destinations include Washington, D.C.; Rome, Italy; and London, England.

Accommodations
First-class.

Cost
Varies with program.
(1) For two examples above: China, $4850 (land), $969 (airfare from Los Angeles); Egypt, Jordan, and Israel, $3377 (land), $1075 (airfare).
(2) For Washington, D.C., example above: $1450 (land), $318 (airfare).

Comment
The Los Angeles World Affairs Council was organized in 1953 and now has over 9000 members. Its travel programs are designed so participants can experience the habits and customs of people in other countries.
Participants are strongly encouraged to attend the scheduled diplomatic briefings while on tour. Membership in the Los Angeles or other World Affairs Council is required. Tours are limited to twenty-four people.

Further Information
Camilla B. Evans
Director, Diplomatic Travel Program
(213) 628-2333

San Diego State University
College of Extended Studies
5630 Hardy Avenue
San Diego, California 92182

Programs
(1) Spanish Language Experience in Mexico, twice yearly. Language and cultural learning through immersion, particularly through the chance to live with a Mexican family in either Mexico City or Cuernavaca.
(2) Other study tours of varying lengths to a number of destinations. Examples: Classical Alliance Tours (Mediterranean, South America, Orient), Shakespeare and Dickens in England, Autumn in the Canyonlands, Baja Whale Watching.

Accommodations
(1) Housing and meals with Mexican families.
(2) Vary with trip. Write for information.

Cost
(1) Tuition and fees: $275 for Mexico City, $450 for Cuernavaca; includes 3 units of credit. Housing, meals, and travel to Mexico are additional.
(2) Examples: Autumn in the Canyonlands, $435 (includes transportation, room, and fees); Baja cruise, $1295 (includes on-board accommodations, meals, and program); Shakespeare and Dickens, $1849 per person (double occupancy; includes

airfare, room, some meals, theater performances).

Comment
The tours feature leaders from the academic and professional worlds, who give lectures and other presentations. Tours show the authentic culture of the destinations visited. Minimum age is 18. College credit is available.

Further Information
Jan Wahl or Faye Rose
(619) 265-5152

> *Man's mind, once stretched by a new idea, never regains its original dimensions.*
> *Oliver Wendell Holmes*

San Jose State University
Travel-Study Programs
Office of Continuing Education
Washington Square
San Jose, California 95192-0135

Program
International travel-study programs, 2–4 weeks, throughout the year. Trips emphasize language, history, culture, health care, law enforcement, and other topics. Recent destinations include Kenya, China, Alaska, France, Mexico.

Accommodations
Usually first-class hotels. Some programs use college residence halls.

Cost
Write for information. Trips may be tax deductible as an educational expense.

Comment
San Jose State has offered travel-study programs since the late 1960s. Trips are developed for special groups (teachers, health-care professionals, journalists) as well as for the average traveler. All programs include contacts and visits not available to most tourists by taking advantage of ties between the university and other educational institutions, agencies, and associations around the world. College credit is available.

Further Information
(408) 277-3781

Stanford University
Bowman Alumni House
Stanford, California 94305

Programs
(1) Seminar in China, including Taiwan and Hong Kong, 23 days, fall.
(2) College on the Mississippi, 11-day cruise, Minneapolis–St. Paul to St. Louis.
(3) Antarctica, 16 days, air and sea, winter.

Accommodations
(1) Vary; primitive in interior China.
(2) Riverboat (*Delta Queen*).
(3) Deluxe and first-class hotels land, plus ship (*Society Explorer*).

Cost
(1) $4676 from San Francisco (including airfare).
(2) $1890–$3200, according to accommodations.
(3) Ship fares vary according to accommodations: $5300–$6800; airfare: $1400.

Comment
Eligibility for these trips is limited to membership in the Stanford Alumni Association as an alumnus, alumna, or friend (dues: $30).
(1) Trip led by Professor Arthur P. Wolf, an anthropologist with many

years of research experience in China and Taiwan and also an expert on Chinese society.

(2) Led by Professor Don Fehrenbacher of history department and an authority on Mark Twain, and by other distinguished faculty members.

(3) Led by Drs. Donald Kennedy, president of Stanford, and Robert A. Helliwell, authority on Stanford's Center for Polar Research.

Further Information
Stanford Alumni: Travel/Study
     Association
Bowman Alumni House
Stanford, CA 94305-1618

> *The world is a book and those who stay at home read only one page.*
> *St. Augustine*

COLORADO

University of Colorado at
*   Boulder*
Koenig Alumni Center
Campus Box 459
Boulder, Colorado 80309-0459

Programs
Eight to ten trips annually, generally 2- or 3-week duration, with different destinations in Europe and Asia. Examples:

(1) Renaissance Waterways Cruise, 2 weeks, July; features stops and/or stays in London, Holland, and Belgium.

(2) The Golden Ring of Russia, air/river-cruise trip, 2 weeks, August; stays in Moscow, Leningrad, and

Copenhagen, combined with Volga River cruise.

(3) Other trips within $2000–$4000 range.

Accommodations
Deluxe or first-class hotels; modern, with comfortable ships for cruise portions.

Cost
(1) $2460, including airfare from Chicago.

(2) $2775, including airfare from Chicago.

Comment
Trips are usually accompanied or led by faculty members knowledgeable in an area appropriate to the destination, e.g., an art historian, the University's president, or a history professor, who lecture during journey.

Further Information
Special Events Coordinator
(303) 492-8484

University of Northern
*   Colorado*
Department of Foreign
*   Languages—Study Abroad*
Greeley, Colorado 80639

Program
Foreign language study for students to complete second or third semester of language study in French or German at UNC. Study Abroad centers in Tours, France, and Bayreuth, Germany. Permits earning 13–16 hours of credit.

Accommodations
With families.

Cost
$4000 (Colorado resident students), including airfare, room, and board.

Cultural Opportunities
Study tours preceding courses to
various areas in France and Germany,
depending on language and course
selected. Also 1- to 3-day side
excursions.

Comment
Small groups (up to fifteen students)
are accompanied by UNC faculty
members who are familiar with
localities of study and who act as both
educators and group leaders.
Accommodations are with non-
English-speaking families, permitting
practice in language of choice.

Further Information
Dr. Kathleen Ensz
Chairperson, Department of Foreign
    Languages
(303) 351-2040

CONNECTICUT

*American Institute for Foreign
    Study
102 Greenwich Avenue
Greenwich, Connecticut 06830*

Programs
Academic Year Abroad; Summer
Programs (2–6 weeks); Mini Programs
(8–10 days; winter, spring, summer);
Learning Holidays Abroad for adults
(9–24 days). A large variety of
educational programs to Europe,
China, Japan, and Australia.

Accommodations
Tourist hotels, student residences, host
families.

Cost
Wide range of prices. Summer
Programs, $1900–$3100; Mini

Programs, $700–$1100; Learning
Holidays, $1200–$3000. Most prices
include two meals, room, fees, and
other expenses.

Comment
Since its founding in 1964, nearly
350,000 teachers and students have
traveled under the auspices of AIFS.
Counselors (usually one per eight
students) accompany participants
throughout and are joined by resident
experts at each stop.

Further Information
(203) 869-9090

*Choate Rosemary Hall
Programs Abroad Office
Box 788
Wallingford, Connecticut 06492*

Program
Study trips abroad for high school
students, age 14 and older. Various
destinations; classes in language and
culture, with field experience. Spring
and summer vacation trips (2–6 weeks)
have been to England, China, Mexico,
Greece, and others; academic-term
programs (2 months) are usually held
in Spain and France. Some programs
have language prerequisites.

Accommodations
Hotels, host families, youth hostels,
camping, as appropriate.

Cost
Ranges from $1390 for England (2
weeks) to $2660 for Spain (6 weeks);
costs include round-trip airfare, local
transportation, tuition, room, and
some meals. Academic-term programs
are charged at the regular school
residence fee, plus airfare. Some
scholarships may be available.

Comment
Choate was founded in 1896 as a preparatory school for boys. It has offered travel programs since the early 1960s. Beginning in 1974, Rosemary Hall joined with Choate to provide coeducational instruction. Trips combine classes with excursions under the direction of school faculty. Most trips are preceded by an orientation period at the school. Academic credit is available.

Further Information
William N. Wingerd
Director, Programs Abroad
(203) 284-5365

Lindblad Travel, Inc.
One Sylvan Road North
P.O. Box 912
Westport, Connecticut 06881

Programs
Tours and cruises worldwide throughout year. Recent examples: (1) Golden Ring of Ancient Russian Cities, 17 days; (2) China by Motorcoach, 17 days; (3) Yangtze River Cruise, 3 weeks; (4) A Thousand Miles Up the Nile, 15 days.

Accommodations
Luxury hotels, large and small cruise ships, safari camps, as appropriate.

Cost
Minimum costs for the above tours are:
(1) $1790.
(2) $2295.
(3) $3795.
(4) $1980.
Prices do not include airfare.

Comment
Lindblad has organized tours worldwide since 1958 and continues to offer unusual itineraries. River cruising is a specialty, with many vessels chartered for its exclusive use.

Lindblad has been a pioneer of travel to China and offers briefings on these trips, presented by sinologists living in Hong Kong. Historical and cultural aspects are featured on other trips.

Further Information
(800) 243-5657
or
(203) 226-8531

> *Nothing in life is to be feared.*
> *It is only to be understood.*
> *Marie Curie*

DELAWARE

University of Delaware
Continuing Education
Clayton Hall
Newark, Delaware 19716

Program
Study trips in the northeastern U.S., 1–6 days, year-round. Recent examples: day-trip to the National Arboretum and Brookside Gardens; day-trip to Treasure Houses of Britain exhibit at the National Gallery of Art; Performing Arts Weekend (3 days) at Saratoga and Tanglewood.

Accommodations
Comfortable hotels and motels on overnight trips.

Cost
Day-trips range from $35 to $90. Others vary, for example, Saratoga and Tanglewood: $275. Trips include

round-trip motorcoach; room and meals may be extra.

Comment
Each study trip focuses on a particular theme (art, architecture, history, music, etc.). There are always opportunities to view performing arts events, tour museums, sightsee, and plan family excursions. The trips are led by university faculty or other experts. Advance study notes are provided; many trips are preceded by special orientation sessions.

Further Information
Sally W. Cohen, Program Specialist
(302) 451-8839

DISTRICT OF COLUMBIA

Academic Travel Abroad, Inc.
1346 Connecticut Avenue, N.W.
Washington, D.C. 20036

Programs
(1) Study Tours Abroad. A variety of educational tours for various groups: colleges and universities, in conjunction with courses and lectures; professional organizations, focusing on practices in another country; secondary- or private-school students, led by a teacher; alumni and continuing education.
(2) Russian Language Seminar. Five 10-week sessions of intensive language classes and cultural activities in Leningrad, Moscow, Krasnodar, or Sochi. Academic credit available.
(3) Museums and cultural programs. Cultural and historical study tours, often with a specific theme or focus. Recent trips: Paris to Beijing by train;

textiles in Turkey; performing arts in the U.S.S.R.

Accommodations
Deluxe or first-class; student rate where appropriate. All levels of accommodation are based on the request of the sponsor.

Cost
Varies according to destination, length of tour, season, accommodations, and size of group. Write for further information.

Comments
Established in 1950 to aid universities in planning foreign-study programs, Academic Travel Abroad specializes in arranging study-abroad experiences for all types of educational, cultural, and professional institutions. All programs have an educational component; most are short-term (2–6 weeks) and are led by professors or others with special expertise.

Further Information
Anne H. Waigand
College and Continuing Education
    Programs
(202) 785-3412
Margot Mininni
Soviet and Eastern European
    Programs
Mara Delli Priscoli
Museum, Cultural, Professional
    Programs

Bishop Wilkins prophesied that the time would come when gentlemen, when they were to go on a journey, would call for their wings as regularly as they call for their boots.

Maria Edgeworth

Canterbury Cathedral Trust in America
2300 Cathedral Avenue, N.W. Washington, D.C. 20008

Program
Motorcoach tour of English and French cathedrals, monasteries, and châteaus of religious significance; 2 weeks; September.

Accommodations
First-class and tourist hotels.

Cost
$2520, not including airfare.

Comment
Trip sponsored jointly by Canterbury Cathedral Trust in America and English Homes and Country Tours of East Sussex, England. It focuses on both Catholic and Protestant religious sites and is limited to twenty-five participants.

Further Information
(202) 328-8788

George Washington University Alumni House
714 21st Street, N.W. Washington, D.C. 20052

Programs
Academic and cultural trips to changing destinations, varying seasons. Examples:
(1) The Best of Eastern Europe and Yugoslavia, 2 weeks, July–August; featuring visits to Prague, Budapest, Dubrovnik, etc.
(2) The Golden Ring of Russia, 2 weeks, August–September; featuring visits to Moscow, Leningrad, Copenhagen, etc.
(3) The Côtes du Rhône Passage, 2 weeks, October; air, rail, and ship to French Riviera, Monte Carlo, etc.

Accommodations
First-class.

Cost
(1) $2199 per person, including airfare from Washington, D.C.
(2) $2725 per person, including airfare from Washington, D.C.
(3) $2950 per person, including airfare from Washington, D.C.

Comment
Trips are part of Alumni Program and usually guided by a faculty member or someone else with expertise on the area being visited. Group size is twenty to fifty.

Further Information
Sandra H. Lear, Director
(202) 676-6435

The John F. Kennedy Center for the Performing Arts
Washington, D.C. 20566

Programs
Varied travel, United States and foreign; recent examples:
(1) Alaskan Summer Adventure (air/sea), 12 days in August.
(2) China Explorers (air/sea), 18 days, late October.

Accommodations
Cruise ships and first-class hotels.

Cost
(1) $2400 to $7800, depending on ship accommodations; price does not include airfare.
(2) $3700 to $9500, depending on ship accommodations; price includes round-trip airfare from Washington, D.C., to ship departure point in Kobe, Japan.

Comment
The Kennedy Center conducts several trips annually for its members, as in

above examples. The Alaskan Summer Adventure is aboard the Royal Viking Line, highlighting Vancouver, British Columbia, and Ketchican, Juneau, and Sitka, Alaska. China trip includes Japan and Hong Kong.

Further Information
Friends of the Kennedy Center Tour
    Information
(202) 254-8700

National Trust for Historic
*   Preservation*
1785 Massachusetts Avenue,
*   N.W.*
Washington, D.C. 20037

Program
Domestic and foreign study tours include train trips, cruises, and air tours; emphasis on preservation of architectural and historic sites. Programs have included: Historic Savannah and Charleston, Hudson River Cruise, Two Weeks at Oxford, Two Weeks in Florence, Great Trains of Europe.

Accommodations
Vary with trip. Single and double cabins on all cruises.

Cost
Range: $1000–$6000 per person for 7- to 17-day tours. Example: Oxford, 2 weeks; $2335, includes airfare, room, board, and all activities.

Comment
The National Trust for Historic Preservation, a private, nonprofit membership organization, was chartered by Congress in 1949 and acts as a clearinghouse for information on state and federal programs relating to preservation. It provides advisory and technical assistance to private organizations, libraries, individuals,

and government units. Its study tour program accepts members, who join for a $15 fee. Travel programs offer participants access to sites or people they would not normally be able to visit on their own, with an opportunity to meet professionals in the field of preservation. Tours feature presentations by scholars and guest lecturers. National Trust representatives accompany each tour.

Further Information
Manager, Special Programs
(202) 673-4138

FLORIDA

Florida State University
Center for Professional
*   Development and Public*
*   Service*
Tallahassee, Florida 32306

Programs
(1) Summer Programs in Florence, Italy; 3- or 8-week sessions, June–August.
(2) Oxford Adult Summer Program; two 3-week sessions, July–August.

Accommodations
(1) First-class or tourist-class hotels.
(2) Private room in 700-year-old Christ Church.

Cost
(1) $1775, 3 weeks, first-class accommodations (double occupancy); $1870, 8 weeks, tourist-class accommodations (triple occupancy). Includes room and some meals; airfare not included.
(2) $1750 for one session; $3250 for both. Includes room and meals; airfare extra.

Comment
Academic credit is offered in both
programs, and a desire for lifelong
learning is encouraged. Both programs
began in 1983; neither is designed to
include children.
(1) Led by FSU faculty, participants
choose 3 or 8 weeks of study and travel
to other cities. Enrollment is limited.
Participants in the 3-week session are
usually adults; in the 8-week session,
students. Up to 10 semester hours may
be earned.
(2) Students participate in small
seminar groups led by Oxford tutors
and gain knowledge of the 700-year-old
culture surrounding the university.
Afternoons are free; visits to other
cities are available. Nine seminars
with world-class scholars are offered
with 3 semester hours of credit in each
session.

Further Information
Valerie Bensen, Travel Program
    Coordinator
(904) 644-3801

> *No man's knowledge here,*
> *can go beyond his*
> *experience.*
>   *John Locke*

Hanns Ebensten Travel, Inc.
513 Fleming Street
Key West, Florida 33040

Program
Tours to unusual destinations
worldwide, 1–3 weeks, throughout
year. Tours emphasize wildlife, culture
(ancient and modern), and
archaeology. Some regular
destinations include Hudson Bay
(Canada), England, Egypt, and Nepal.

Accommodations
Vary with tour: luxurious private
homes, outdoor camping, a yacht, or
small hotels and lodges.

Children
A few programs suitable for children:
Discover Galapagos, Great White
Bears (Hudson Bay). Discounts can be
arranged.

Cost
Some examples: Hudson Bay, 7 days,
$2700 plus airfare; Egypt, 18 days,
$3700–$6700, all inclusive; Himalayas
(Nepal, India), 26 days, $6100–$9000,
all inclusive. Price ranges indicate a
difference in air accommodations.

Comment
Hanns Ebensten tours, which began in
1972, are led by experienced, mature
leaders with detailed knowledge of the
destination. Groups vary in size from
five to twenty-four with many limited
to small groups.

Further Information
(305) 296 9935

IDAHO

International Swedish
    University Programs
c/o Mrs. Joanna Wallin, U.S.
    Representative
645 Lincoln Drive
Idaho Falls, Idaho 83401

Programs
Recent examples:
(1) Swedish language (beginning to
advanced), comparative social studies,
international economic studies; two
sessions of approximately 3 weeks at

University of Lund; July and August.
(2) Swedish language (beginning to advanced); several sessions at the University of Stockholm, July and August.
(3) Swedish language and folklore at Malung, Dalarna, 3 weeks, June–July.

Locations
(1) The City of Lund is approximately 300 miles southwest of Stockholm.
(3) Course held at the Malung Folk High School in the Province of Dalarna.

Accommodations
(1) and (2) Student dormitories.
(3) Students and instructors live in double rooms at the school.

Cost
(1) Approximately $385 for Swedish language, $500 for other courses. Double room with bath, $160; meals extra.
(2) Approximately $220 for language course. Single room with bath, $130; meals extra.
(3) Approximately $560, includes full room and board.

Comment
The International Swedish University was established at Lund in 1975 to coordinate study programs for foreign students. Small classes with close teacher contact allow for concentration on individual interests. Certification is given on course completion and college credit is available.

Further Information
Joanna Wallin
(208) 523-1039

> *If I should not be learning now, when should I be?*
> *Lacydes*

ILLINOIS

The Chicago Council on Foreign Relations
Suite 721
104 South Michigan Avenue
Chicago, Illinois 60603

Programs
Trips worldwide. Examples:
(1) Focus China, 1 month, late August through September.
(2) Focus Egypt, 18 days to 3 weeks.
(3) Focus Canada, late September.

Accommodations
First-class hotels.

Cost
(1) $4300 per person (including airfare from Chicago).
(2) $3565 per person (including airfare from Chicago).
(3) Write for information.

Comment
The Chicago Council on Foreign Relations was founded in 1922. The trip to China emphasizes current life-styles, as well as provides a historical perspective, while the Egyptian trip emphasizes the realities and myths of archaeology and includes briefings on artifacts by curators.

Further Information
Susan Katz, Director of Travel
(312) 726-3615

Fun Safaris, Inc.
P.O. Box 178
Bloomingdale, Illinois 60108

Program
Numerous tours to both eastern and southern Africa with emphasis on special interests such as wildlife,

farming, horticulture, conservation, and ornithology. Recent tours: Southwest Africa/Botswana, 18 days; Zambia/Zimbabwe, 18 days; safari to Kenya/Tanzania; and a special Grand Circle Tour to South Africa.

Accommodations
First-class hotels; permanent and mobile tents in wildlife areas; tree houses and houseboats in Zimbabwe.

Cost
Varies with program and destination. Examples above: $3245–$3440 for Kenya/Tanzania; $4495 for Zambia/Zimbabwe. Some tours require membership in sponsoring organizations. Write for information.

Comment
Fun Safaris has been in operation since 1974. It has arranged tours sponsored by a number of special interest groups: zoological societies, botanical associations, university groups, and professional organizations in medicine, farming, real estate, interior design, and human relations.

Further Information
Bonnie Fogg
(800) 323-8020
    or
(312) 893-2545

New Trier Extension Study/Travel
3013 Illinois Road
Wilmette, Illinois 60091

Programs
Twenty-four year-round study-travel programs in U.S. and abroad for adults and high school students, including:
(1) Michigan bicycling, 3 days.
(2) Vienna, 9 days.
(3) Japanese culture for high school students, 3 weeks.

Accommodations
Tourist-class hotels, host families, dormitories, or other facilities, as appropriate.

Cost
(1) $99.
(2) $999, including airfare.
(3) $2499, including airfare.

Comment
New Trier Extension Study/Travel, begun in 1979, is a unique cooperative program of several Chicago-area high schools. Faculty trip leaders are drawn primarily from these schools; participants come from all over the country. Some adult trips are planned in conjunction with those offered by the University of Pittsburgh in its informal program.

Further Information
William Boyd, Director
(312) 256-7070

Northeastern Illinois University Mini-U
5500 North St. Louis Avenue
Chicago, Illinois 60625

Program
Spanish in Costa Rica, 2 or 4 weeks, February. Participants live with Costa Rican families and receive daily formal instruction.

Accommodations
Costa Rican homes. Pension or hotel accommodations available.

Children
Children and spouses are welcome.

Cost
$485, 2-week session; $695, 4-week session (airfare not included). Also $5 registration fee.

Comment
This is a total immersion program, offering an experience of Latin American culture in a friendly and peaceful environment. Participants receive Spanish instruction in small groups based on their proficiency level. Guest speakers lecture on political and social issues. Costa Rican professors encourage participants to use the language outside the classroom, in interaction with Costa Ricans. Excursions to beaches, national parks, and ecological preserves are available.

Further Information
Dr. Edgardo Pantigoso
Department of Foreign Languages and
    Literatures
(312) 583-4050, ext. 8220

Every change of scene is a delight.

                                    Seneca

*Northern Illinois University
Office of International and
    Special Programs
De Kalb, Illinois 60115*

Program
Numerous programs, usually focused on a particular subject, various locations worldwide, 3–8 weeks, all seasons. Some recent examples: Adult Education in India and Nepal, Gerontology in Japan, International Business Education in Europe, Outdoor Education in Hawaii.

Accommodations and Cost
Write for information.

Comment
The university offers a different schedule of programs each year covering a wide range of topics and geographical areas of the world. All programs combine travel and study, with academic credit available.

Further Information
Orville E. Jones, Assistant Dean
Office of International and Special
    Programs
(815) 753-1988

*Western Illinois University
International Programs
100 Memorial Hall
Macomb, Illinois 61455*

Programs
(1) European Travel for Educators, 3-week tours to European countries with emphasis on various educational fields, June–July. Recent examples: United Kingdom Environmental Education Camping Tour, Science Education in European Schools.
(2) Undergraduate Tour of Northwestern Europe, 3-week tour of seven major countries for the undergraduate university student, May–June.
(3) Mexican Culture, 2-week tour designed for high school students, June–July. Program includes tours of Mexican cities and historic landmarks.
(4) Independent Travel-Study: For qualified applicants at either the undergraduate or graduate level. Participant makes independent travel arrangements and works with a WIU faculty member.

Accommodations
(1) and (2) Bed and breakfast, shared baths.
(3) Double occupancy, private baths.

Cost
(1) $1699, all inclusive for above examples.
(2), (3), and (4) Write for information.

Comment
(1) Tours are planned to combine educational activities with enjoyable travel. They provide elementary and secondary school teachers with an opportunity to meet European counterparts. Leaders are experienced educators and scholars. Credit available.
(2) Tour features visits to five major cities with the opportunity for students to develop their own program. Sightseeing geared to student interests. Undergraduate credit available.
(3) The program provides an opportunity for high school students to earn college credit while visiting cultural sites and major cities in Mexico. Opportunities for relaxation and recreation are included.
(4) Independent Travel-Study is a unique program that requires each participant to meet with a faculty tutor before and after the travel experience (in the U.S. or abroad). Two to 6 semester hours of credit available.

Further Information
Dr. Robert E. Gabler, Director
(309) 298-2426

INDIANA

Purdue University Calumet
Hammond, Indiana 46323

Program
Summer program in Madrid, Spain; 5 weeks; June–August. Courses include Spanish Conversation, Spanish Novel, and independent study projects. Weekend excursions, tour of Andalusia region.

Accommodations
In Madrid, student dormitories; on tours, first-class hotels.

Cost
$1300, includes all expenses except tuition.

Comment
The program is conducted by Dr. Celestino Ruiz, a Purdue professor who is a native of Spain. Dr. Ruiz has led the program since its inception in 1981 and takes participants to unusual places not regularly visited. Program designed for people of diverse ages who are at least high school seniors.

Further Information
Dr. Celestino Ruiz
Department of Foreign Languages and
    Literature
(219) 844-0520, ext. 378

KENTUCKY

Audubon Center for Economic
Education
215 West Seventh Street
Owensboro, Kentucky 42301

Program
Economics and the Humanities, in Washington, D.C., 7 days, late June.

Accommodations
Rooms, double occupancy.

Cost
$500 for transportation, room and board, theater tickets; tuition extra.

Cultural Opportunities
Sightseeing tours of Washington, theater tickets to Kennedy Center, concerts at Wolf Trap, and the like.

Comment
The program, designed for elementary and secondary school teachers and interested lay persons, stresses fundamental economic principles reflected in history, art, architecture, and other areas of the humanities.

Further Information
Robert L. Graham, Director
(502) 686-4329

LOUISIANA

University of New Orleans
International Study Programs
Box 1315
New Orleans, Louisiana 70148

Programs
International summer schools in:
(1) Orleans, France; 6 weeks.
(2) Innsbruck, Austria; 5 weeks.

Accommodations
Dormitories during the academic session, hotels during tours. Some students may live with host families during the program.

Cost
(1) and (2) $2695, including New Orleans–to–Europe airfare.

Recreation
(1) Special tours through the Loire Valley, as well as Normandy, Brittany, and Paris.
(2) University of Innsbruck Program: Special tours into Bavaria and through Austria include hiking in the Alps. Also use of university's recreational facilities.

Cultural Opportunities
Prestudy and poststudy tours, weekend field trips to other European countries.

Castle restoration program in Belgium. Museums, performing arts, and other attractions during the academic program.

Comment
The university offers separate programs for college and high school honors students. The International Summer School began in 1973 and has grown to include several locations and programs. Instructors include UNO faculty, guest professors from other U.S. colleges, and instructors from various institutions in the home country. Most instruction is in English, although foreign-language study is recommended. There are specific prerequisites and course requirements for some programs. College credit available.

Further Information
(504) 264-7116

MARYLAND

Baltimore Hebrew College
Teen Study Group
5800 Park Heights Avenue
Baltimore, Maryland 21215

Program
Annual Teen Study Tour to Eastern Europe and Israel for teenagers 15–18 years old, 7–8 weeks, summer. Itinerary includes Holland, Czechoslovakia, Hungary, Austria, and Israel.

Accommodations
Hotels and dormitories.

Cost
$2600, includes round-trip airfare from Baltimore.

Comment
This study tour was first offered in 1969. The group (maximum size of thirty-five) is accompanied by a faculty member from the Hebrew College High School and two others and is joined by resource people in Israel. Tour emphasizes both general and Jewish points of interest in Europe, including a concentration camp. Informal language and history instruction, activities with Israeli students, and extensive trips throughout Israel. No membership or enrollment requirements.

Further Information
Dr. Samuel Litov
Baltimore Hebrew College, High
    School Division
(301) 578-6933/6934

The path to culture should be through a man's specialism, not bypassing it.
                  Eric Ashby

Catonsville Community College
800 South Rolling Road
Catonsville, Maryland 21228

Programs
Travel study tours to Greece, Italy, and Egypt as detailed below:
(1) Ancient Greece; annual 3- to 4-week tour of Greece, Turkey, and the Aegean Islands; early June.
(2) The Art of Italy, annual or semiannual 3-week tour; summer term.
(3) Egypt, annual art history tour, January.

Accommodations
First-class and tourist.

Cost
(1) $2300, four weeks, including airfare and most meals.
(2) $2000, including airfare and partial board.
(3) $2000, including airfare and meals.

Comment
These travel-study tours were first offered in 1981. They are led by Dr. Dian Fetter, professor of arts and humanities at Catonsville Community College, and emphasize art, culture, history, archaeology, and religion of areas and sites visited. They are preceded by orientation slides and lectures. Group sizes vary from a minimum of twelve (to Italy) to a maximum of twenty-five (to Egypt).

Further Information
Dr. Dian Fetter
(301) 455-4326

Dundalk Community College
Travel Study Tours
7200 Sollers Point Road
Baltimore, Maryland 21222

Programs
(1) Annual Holiday Course in Scandinavian Culture; 2 weeks, late summer. Offered in conjunction with the Danish Institute; features visits to businesses and social institutions.
(2) Other trips: Japan, China, Middle East, U.S.S.R., and more.

Accommodations
(1) Tourist-class hotels.
(2) Write for information.

Cost
(1) $2300, all inclusive.
(2) Examples: Far East, $2800; Middle East, $2100 (both all inclusive).

Comment
Study tours are led by Don Schaffer, associate professor of history and political science. Enrollment for the Scandinavian course, which has been held for the past 11 years, is limited to twenty-five. Trip may be taken for college credit or audited.

Further Information
Professor Don Schaffer
(301) 522-5795

Essex Community College
Travel Study Tours
7201 Rossville Boulevard
Baltimore, Maryland 21237

Programs
(1) Cycle Tours, study-travel programs to different regions of the United States, each focusing on a specific topic, approximately 1 week, throughout the year. Recent examples include: in New England—History of Fishing, Robert Frost; in the South— New Orleans—Its Creole Culture and Cuisine, Faulkner's Mississippi.
(2) Independent thematic tours in the United States and abroad, 2–3 weeks, throughout the year. Recent examples include: Byzantium and the Eastern Mediterranean and the Natural History of Australia and New Zealand.

Accommodations
First-class or deluxe.

Cost
(1) From $350 to $1000 for transportation, room and board; tuition extra.
(2) From $1500 to $3200 for transportation, room and board; tuition extra.

Comment
Essex Community College has been offering these programs since 1975. All tours are led by faculty members or others with expertise in the program theme. The Cycle Tours include a series of lectures prior to departure and a posttrip seminar. For out-of-town participants, there is a trip-only option, and a bibliography will be supplied. Lectures and discussions en route are an important feature of every trip. Between 1 and 6 college credits are available.

Further Information
Vernon Walton
Coordinator, Travel Studies
(301) 522-1617

> *Those with the courage to tread this path to real discovery are actively discouraged and have to set about it in secret.*
> *George Spencer Brown*

Goucher College
Department of Modern
Languages
Towson, Maryland 21204

Program
Annual trips to France or, in alternate years, to the Soviet Union, Germany, Latin America; 3 weeks; winter.

Accommodations
Write for information.

Cost
Approximately $1400, all inclusive.

Comment
These trips stress the language and culture of the country visited, including its history and historic sites, art, cathedrals, castles, handicrafts, and more. Some knowledge of the

language of the country visited is a prerequisite. College credit available.

Further Information
(301) 337-6223

Harford Community College
Office of International
Education
401 Thomas-Run Road
Belair, Maryland 21014

Program
Travel-study tours, arranged independently or with a group, 1 week to 1 semester. Recent trips include: Three Cultures of Mexico, Baroque in Germany and Austria, Mansions of Newport, and the Stratford Shakespeare Festival (Canada).

Accommodations and Cost
Write for information.

Comment
Travel-study tours were first offered in 1976. They are designed primarily for Harford Community College students and area residents but are open to others by arrangement. Group size averages ten to twenty. Pretrip classes are held for briefing purposes.

Further Information
Dr. Claire Eckels
(301) 836-4293

International Council for
Cultural Exchange
1559 Rockville Pike
Rockville, Maryland 20852

Programs
(1) Summer Course Trips to northern Italy, southern French Riviera, and Britain focusing on art, languages,

advanced music, social sciences, etc. College credit obtainable.
(2) Year-round cultural tours and programs for executives, managers, and other adults; subjects include languages, art, cooking, music, opera, skiing, and Mardi Gras.
(3) Year-round high school language programs and advanced music.
(4) Year-round group seminar programs worldwide. All programs are of 2–3 weeks' duration.

Accommodations
As appropriate to program, including host family living, college residences, and deluxe hotels.

Cost
Varies with program; $1781 average for 3-week European trip (including airfare).

Comment
The International Council for Cultural Exchange is a nonprofit organization established in 1982 that manages and administers cultural exchange trips, programs, courses, and seminars. It works in affiliation with some major European educational institutions.

Further Information
Dr. Stanley I. Gochman
(301) 983-9479

The ends are achieved by indirect means . . . a remark made by a teacher in the middle of a discussion, a book picked up in someone's room . . .

Harold Taylor

> *Success is a journey, not a destination.*
>
> *Ben Sweetland*

Johns Hopkins University Alumni Travel Program
Alumni Relations Office
3211 North Charles Street
Baltimore, Maryland 21218

Programs
Trips to foreign countries, year-round.
Recent examples:
(1) Soviet Union, 2 weeks, summer.
(2) Scandinavia, 2 weeks, summer.
(3) Mediterranean cruise, 2 weeks, fall.
(4) South America, 2 weeks, winter.

Accommodations
First-class or superior tourist-class
hotels.

Cost
(1) $2600 (airfare included from
gateway city).
(2) $2400 (airfare included from
gateway city).
(3) $2595–$3975 (airfare included from
gateway city).
(4) $2600 (airfare included from
gateway city).

Comment
The Johns Hopkins University Alumni
Travel Program began in 1972 with a
trip to Italy. Groups are led by either
faculty members or Alumni Office
representatives and have English-
speaking experts in countries visited.
Ample leisure time is allotted for
independent sightseeing or shopping.
Tours generally include meetings with
Hopkins alumni living in countries
visited.

Further Information
William J. Evitts, Director
(301) 338-7963/7966

Loyola College
4501 North Charles Street
Baltimore, Maryland 21210

Programs
Travel Study Tours to Europe and
Mediterranean areas. Recent
examples:
(1) Four Faces of Europe (Amsterdam,
Rome, Florence, and Paris).
(2) Israel, 9 days, late December.

Accommodations
(1) Low-budget hotels.
(2) First-class hotels and kibbutz.

Cost
(1) $1100, includes transportation,
room, and breakfast.
(2) $1185, includes transportation,
lodging, and most meals.

Comment
Travel Study trips have been offered by
Loyola College since 1976. All are
preceded by some orientation.
(1) Led by Dr. Bernard Nachbar of
Philosophy Department, and student
oriented. Focus is on European art and
history; up to thirty-five participants.
(2) Led by Dr. Webster Patterson of
Theology Department, emphasizing
archaeological excavations and
historic sites in Jerusalem's old city
and new city. Tour also includes
Masada, Qumran, Bethlehem, Galilee,
and a short stay at a kibbutz in Acre.
Up to thirty-five participants.

Further Information
(1) Dr. Bernard Nachbar
(301) 323-1010, ext. 2031
(2) Dr. Webster Patterson
(301) 323-1010, ext. 2219

> *For my part, I travel not to go anywhere, but to go. I travel for travel's sake. The great affair is to move.*
>   *Robert Louis Stevenson*

Roland Park Country School
Evening School
5204 Roland Avenue
Baltimore, Maryland 21210

Program
Educational tours emphasizing art, culture, and related topics are offered annually. Recent examples:
(1) A Taste of Italy, a 2-week trip led by noted Baltimore cooking teacher Germaine Sharretts.
(2) A 2-week cultural tour of Belgium and the Netherlands led by art historian Kay Cavanaugh.

Accommodations
First-class.

Cost
(1) $2398.
(2) $2295.
Prices include airfare and $150 contribution to the school.

Comment
Roland Park Country School tours were first offered in 1979. Trip leaders are either faculty members or other specialists in tour themes. An orientation lecture is always given before departure, and a related evening course or special program may also be offered. Average group size is twenty to forty.

Further Information
Peggy Patterson, Evening School
    Director
(301) 323-5500

Towson State University
Towson, Maryland 21204

Programs
(1) Annual art semester in Florence, Italy; fall, spring, summer.
(2) European Cities program, 3 weeks, January.
(3) Annual Modern Language Department 1-month summer programs in Madrid, Spain.

Accommodations
Hotels and motels.

Cost
(1) $1650 for airfare, room, and board; tuition additional.
(2) Approximately $1700 for airfare, room, and board; tuition additional.
(3) $1700 for airfare from New York, room, board, and excursion to Costa del Sol; tuition additional.

Comment
(1) The art semester in Florence was first offered in 1979. Participants may select courses of interest, including studio courses. Emphasis is on the Renaissance and art of northern Italy.
(2) Begun in the mid-1970s, the European Cities program focuses on the history, geography, and cultural aspects of leading Western European cities. College credit available.
(3) Since it began in 1984, the summer program has given participants both a chance to learn about Spanish life and culture and an academic language program in Spain. Credit available.

Further Information
G. Franklin Mullen, Director of
    Academic Affairs
(301) 321-2032
    or
(1) Helen Pullen
Art Department
(301) 321-2801

(2) Dr. James DiLisio
Chairman, Geography Department
(301) 321-2973

(3) Dr. Jorge Giro, Chairman
Modern Language Department
(301) 321-2878
    or
Dr. Armin Mruck, Professor of History
(301) 321-2909

The Ward Foundation
655 South Salisbury Boulevard
Salisbury, Maryland 21801

Program
Annual Waterfowl Art Exhibition and
tour of Chesapeake Bay Islands, 6
days, October.

Accommodations
During the tour: hotels, with meals at
various special locations.

Cost
Tour: $255 per person (double
occupancy); painting competition
exhibition: $25 per person.

Comment
The annual exhibition and tour is a
celebration of waterfowl art and its
traditions that brings together the
most talented carvers and painters
working in this field.

Further Information
(301) 742-4988

William Mueller Associates, Inc.
1108 Bellemore Road
Baltimore, Maryland 21210

Program
Short summer seminars in Cambridge,
England. Some designed for physicians
and health-care workers, others for
lawyers and law students.

Accommodations
College residence halls of Cambridge
University.

Cost
$900–$1100 includes lodging, most
meals, field trips, and activities.
Airfare additional.

Cultural Opportunities
Concerts, theater, art festivals.

Comment
The seminars are offered in
cooperation with the University of
Maryland School of Medicine and
School of Law. Seminar faculties
include both British and American
instructors. Physicians receive CME
credit in Category I; nurses receive
continuing education credit through
the Maryland Nurses Association.

Further Information
Dr. William R. Mueller
(301) 323-4180

MASSACHUSETTS

Anatolia College
Summer Institute in Hellenic
Studies
130 Bowdoin Street
Boston, Massachusetts 02108

Program
Annual 6-week Summer Institute each
July and August in Thessaloniki,
Greece. Courses in Greek art, history,
archaeology, language, and philosophy
taught in English.

Accommodations
School dormitories in Thessaloniki,
located in northern Greece about 200
miles from Athens.

Cost
$1500 (airfare not included).

Recreation
Tennis, playing fields, gymnasium, individual travel.

Cultural Opportunities
Library, archaeological museum, optional dinners and excursions with local host families.

Comment
Anatolia College, founded in 1886, is a Massachusetts-chartered school offering 6 years of secondary education to Greek youth. College credits are earned through rigorous and academically demanding course work, taught in English. Features include an outstanding faculty, course-related field trips, and a small-group environment. The Summer Institute has been endorsed by the Fulbright Foundation in Greece. Mainly for college students or graduates, the Institute is open to adults with proper academic credentials.

Further Information
(617) 742-7992

> *The ends are achieved by*
> *indirect means.*
>   *Harold Taylor*

Boston University Alumni Association
10 Lennox Street
Brookline, Massachusetts 02140

Programs
(1) Tour of Switzerland and Munich, with optional side trips to Bavarian Alps and Black Forest, 8 days.
(2) Project Amazon, 9-night cruise from Manaus, Brazil, exploring native plants, animals, and primitive cultures.
(3) Cruise on *Royal Viking,* from Hong Kong, with ports of call in southern China, Philippines, Indonesia, and Malaysia, 14 days.

Accommodations
(1) Write for specific information.
(2) Cruise ship *Society Explorer.*
(3) Ship mentioned above.

Cost
(1) $759 per person.
(2) $2490 (not including airfare).
(3) $3650 per person (from Boston or New York).

Comment
(1) Designed for cooks, artists, poets, and University friends.
(2) Designed for working scientists; ornithologist and botanist accompany group on land explorations and give evening lectures.
(3) Includes lectures on ship.

Further Information
(617) 353-2228

Esplanade Tours
38 Newbury Street
Boston, Massachusetts 02116

Programs
Tours to England, France, and Italy, ranging from 9 days to 2 weeks.
(1) English Country Gardens; 9 days; spring, summer, fall. Exploring gardens of all sizes and varieties along with special homes in West Sussex, Kent, and Essex counties.
(2) Medieval Southern France, 2 weeks, spring. Focusing on medieval castles, châteaus, and towns.
(3) Southern Italy and Sicily, 2 weeks, spring and late summer. Highlighting archaeological wonders of southern

Italy, along with art and architecture of Sicily.

Accommodations
(1) and (3) First-class hotels.
(2) Cruise ship *Athos*.

Cost
(1) $1795 per person (double occupancy), including airfare from New York.
(2) $2195 per person (double occupancy), including airfare from New York.
(3) $1985 per person (double occupancy), including airfare from New York.

Comment
All trips have educational content and are led by those with special expertise in their fields:
(1) Bob Thomson, garden specialist.
(2) Marie-Reine Bernard, a graduate in art history from the University of Toulouse who has lectured for many years on this subject.
(3) Led by experts in archaeology; a highlight the ruins of Pompeii.

Further Information
(617) 266-7465

The Humanities Institute, Inc.
Box 18
Belmont, Massachusetts 02178

Programs
Three-week summer seminars in Great Britain, Ireland, and Continental Europe. Campuses at Cambridge, Edinburgh, Dublin, and Athens, with others to be added. Seminars focus on the humanities, including literature, history, philosophy, and art.

Accommodations
Vary according to site.

Cost
$900–$1800 depending on site. Airfare and college credit additional.

Cultural Opportunities
Classes are supplemented by tours, tutorials, field trips, and other activities depending upon content. The cities in which the seminars take place provide a variety of concerts, theater, and art.

Comment
The Humanities Institute has been sponsoring summer seminars abroad since 1975. They are designed to attract a wide variety of people wishing to combine academic pursuits with travel and sightseeing. Serious commitment to the academic program is expected of all registrants. Instructors are drawn from host universities and other institutions. University credit available.

Further Information
Dr. Martha B. Mueller, Director
(617) 484-3191

Iberian Art Tour
c/o Cerel's Travel Center
19 Main Street
Natick, Massachusetts 01760

Program
Recent example: Iberian Art Tour, escorted tour of Spain and Portugal exploring Phoenician artifacts, Roman ruins, great mosques, etc.; 17–19 days.

Accommodations
First-class hotels.

Cost
$2500 per person (double occupancy), including airfare from Boston.

Comment
Trip led by Kay Stein, art historian, archaeologist, and veteran tour leader

to these countries, who has also conducted trips to Italy and China. Ample leisure time allowed; size of groups averages twenty to twenty-five.

Further Information
(617) 653-2400

[Classics] are the only oracles which are not decayed.
        Henry David Thoreau

MICHIGAN

Oakland University
Department of Sociology and
    Anthropology
Rochester, Michigan 48063

Program
Recent example: China Highlights Study Tour; 15 days, May. Hong Kong, Beijing, Shanghai, and Canton are among the cities visited.

Accommodations
First-class hotels.

Children
Permitted under special conditions.

Cost
$2900 includes round-trip airfare from Detroit, rooms, some meals, all fees.

Comment
Tour led by an experienced Mandarin-speaking American professor visits historic temples and other sites, as well as the most important cities of modern China. Credit option. Group size averages twenty to twenty-five.

Further Information
Richard or Marsha Stamps
(313) 375-0246/0600

MINNESOTA

Minneapolis Society of Fine
    Arts
2400 Third Avenue, South
Minneapolis, Minnesota 55404

Program
Year-round trips to foreign and domestic locations emphasizing art, architecture, cultural history, etc. Recent examples:
(1) Archaeological Treasures of Mexico, 10 days, winter.
(2) San Francisco, 4 days, spring.
(3) Heart of the Arts, Holland and Belgium, 2 weeks, late spring.
(4) The Best of Japan, 3 weeks, fall.

Accommodations
Comfortable hotels and inns as appropriate to trip.

Cost
(1) $1895, includes airfare.
(2) $1095, includes airfare.
(3) $2645, includes airfare.
(4) $4510, includes airfare and tax-deductible contribution.

Comment
The Minneapolis Society of Fine Arts trips offer unusual travel opportunities combining educational and cultural enrichment with recreational enjoyment. They are led by Peggy Lindborg, membership coordinator, who accompanies participants throughout the trips. Trips are limited in size.

Further Information
Peggy Lindborg, Volunteer Travel
    Coordinator
(612) 935-7265

> *Progress always involves risk; you can't steal second base and keep your foot on first.*
> Frederick Wilcox

University of Minnesota, Duluth Continuing Education and Extension
403 Darland Administration Building
10 University Drive
Duluth, Minnesota 55812

Program
Summer study in England. Courses and travel based at the University of Birmingham, 4 weeks, July–August.

Accommodations
University residence halls.

Cost
$1750 includes program, accommodations, breakfast, and round-trip airfare from Minneapolis.

Comment
Participants may select from four courses on a credit or noncredit basis. Topics include literature, architecture, and contemporary British society; all include visits to relevant sites in southern England. Some instructors are faculty members of the University of Birmingham; others from faculty of University of Minnesota. Participants must be at least 18 years of age; usually about eighty people enroll. Extensive field trips are part of each course; weekends are left free for travel.

Further Information
Greg Fox, Program Director
(218) 726-8113

MISSISSIPPI

University of Southern Mississippi
Box 56
Southern Station
Hattiesburg, Mississippi 39401

Program
Annual domestic trips. Examples:
(1) New York Theater, 4 days, November.
(2) Utah Ski Experience, 5 days, March.
Overseas trips also planned though not scheduled at time of publication.

Accommodations
(1) Hotels.
(2) Condominiums (Breckinbridge).

Cost
(1) $625 per person, including airfare.
(2) $550 per person, including airfare.

Comment
These trips, which are accompanied by University staff, have been given for several years; other general overseas trips to be added.

Further Information
Dr. William Bufkin
(601) 266-4189

NEW HAMPSHIRE

Dartmouth Alumni Colleges Abroad
308 Blunt Alumni Center
Dartmouth College
Hanover, New Hampshire 03755

Program
Travel-study trips to various destinations around the world.

Sponsored by Dartmouth College
(sometimes with a co-sponsor) and led
by Dartmouth faculty. Trips feature
lectures, field trips, and discussions on
topics related to the destination.
Recent destinations include:
(1) Alaska, land and sea cruise, 12
days.
(2) Russia, 2 weeks, August.
(3) Rhone River Cruise, 2 weeks, June.

Accommodations
Hotels, cruise ships, other as
appropriate to tour.

Cost
(1) $3100–$3600, depending on ship
accommodations.
(2) $2975 per person.
(3) $3175 per person.

Comment
Instructors provide an in-depth look at
various aspects of the history, art, and
culture of places visited. Participants
are assigned advance reading to
supplement trip lectures.

Further Information
Steven L. Calvert
Director, Alumni/Continuing
   Education
(603) 646-2454

NEW JERSEY

Fairleigh Dickinson University
223 Montrose Avenue
Rutherford, New Jersey 07070

Programs
(1) M.B.A. for Executives Program.
Summer Session at Wroxton College,
England, 2 weeks, August. The
Summer Session is part of the
Silberman College of Business
Administration.
(2) British Studies Program at

Wroxton College, 4 weeks, summer.
This is a fully accredited program
designed to accommodate graduates,
undergraduates, and those wishing to
audit.
(3) British Studies Program, semester-
long programs at Wroxton College,
spring, summer, fall. Courses open to
graduates and undergraduates.

Accommodations
At Wroxton College, in Wroxton, near
Banbury, Oxfordshire, England.
Housed in a Jacobean mansion that
dates from 1618, the College was
renovated by Fairleigh Dickinson
University in 1965 and subsequently
was declared a national monument.
Single, double, and triple rooms.

Costs
(1) Write for information.
(2) $177–$202 per credit hour; $694 for
room, board, and fees.
(3) $5303 for tuition, room, and board.

Comment
Courses are conducted at Wroxton
College, the Shakespeare Institute at
Stratford, the University of Warwick,
and the North Oxfordshire College of
Art in Banbury. Instructors are drawn
from these institutions and elsewhere,
and courses are taught by the lecture
and tutorial method commonly used in
British universities. For the British
Studies Program, a variety of courses
are offered, and many include field
trips and optional weekend tours to
sites of national historic and cultural
interest.

Further Information
(1) Dr. Paul Lerman
College of Business Administration
(201) 460-5416
(2) and (3) Eileen McDonough Rogers
Executive Director, University
   Continuing Education
(201) 460-5010

Kean College of New Jersey
TRAVELEARN
Union, New Jersey 07083

Program
Annual travel-study programs
throughout the world, 2–4 weeks,
summer and January intersession.
Recent examples: Geology of Hawaii, 4
weeks, summer; Contemporary London
Theatre, 2 weeks, January.

Accommodations
College facilities, tourist or first-class
hotels, depending on program.

Cost
Varies with destination and duration.
Examples above: Hawaii, $1795;
London, $1000. Includes program,
accommodations, round-trip airfare
from New York. Participants must also
pay either tuition or continuing
education fee. Costs might be
deductible as an educational expense.
Write for information.

Comment
The TRAVELEARN program was first
held in 1973. It features annual theme
journeys to locations throughout the
world and continually adds new topics
and destinations. Though designed for
educators, in recent years more than
one third of the participants have been
non-educators, of all ages and
backgrounds. Each program includes
predeparture readings, lectures,
seminars, and field experiences. All
programs are supervised by college
faculty specialists. Average group size
is twenty.

Further Information
Ethel J. Madsen, Coordinator of
    International Studies
(201) 527-2163

> *Knowledge is the great sun of*
> *the firmament.*
> *Daniel Webster*

NEW YORK

American Friends of the
    Hebrew University
Office of Academic Affairs
11 East 69th Street
New York, New York 10021

Programs
(1) Summer courses in English at the
Hebrew University, Jerusalem; two
consecutive 3-week sessions. Courses
in the Hebrew and Arabic languages
are also offered. One year of college
required.
(2) Summer Ulpan (intensive Hebrew
language course), 2–3 months,
depending on student's progress.
Related tours, lectures, and social
events are scheduled.

Accommodations
University dormitories.

Cost
Write for information.

Comment
The Hebrew University of Jerusalem
was founded in 1918. Its summer
programs, as well as its programs for
overseas students, give participants
opportunities to gain insight into
fundamentals of Jewish culture and to
acquire proficiency in Hebrew.

Further Information
In the United States:
Write to the address above.
(212) 472-2288

In Canada:
Canadian Friends of the Hebrew
    University
1 Yorkdale Plaza, Suite 208
1 Yorkdale Road
Toronto, Ontario M6A 3A1
Canada
(416) 789-2633

American University of Cairo
866 United Nations Plaza
New York, New York 10017

Program
Six-week summer session includes
courses in many subjects with an area
focus. Examples include: Islamic Art
and Architecture, Egyptology,
International Business Management,
Arab Society; undergraduate and
graduate levels. Instruction in
English; intensive Arabic language
program also available.

Accommodations
University housing for single students;
assistance given in finding off-campus
housing.

Cost
Tuition: $1250 for two undergraduate
or graduate courses; $1375 for
intensive Arabic language program.
Housing: $170 per month.

Recreation
University sports facilities; others
available in city.

Cultural Opportunities
Cairo is the chief city and cultural
center of Arab society.

Comment
The university was established in 1919
and has a small campus on the central
square of Cairo. Since 1979 it has
accepted students from abroad for its
summer session. It is a multinational
facility: faculty members are drawn

equally from America and Egypt, with
about ten other nations represented;
students come from thirty-five nations.
The university is incorporated in
Washington, D.C.

Further Information
In the United States:
(212) 421-6320

In Egypt:
Ismael Safwat, Registrar
American University in Cairo
P.O. Box 2511
Cairo, Arab Republic of Egypt

American Zionist Youth
*   Foundation*
515 Park Avenue
New York, New York 10022

Programs
(1) Summer programs for high school
and college students (18–22 years of
age) at various locations in Israel; 6
weeks, June–August. Programs
feature work with Israeli youth on a
kibbutz, as well as seminars on
contemporary issues facing Israel. Also
music and art, Yiddish culture, etc.
(2) Short-term programs in Israel,
including winter seminar and spring
project; long-term programs in Israel,
including graduate program and
apprenticeship, 6 months to a year.

Accommodations
Hotels, youth hostels, nature study
centers; double or triple rooms.

Cost
(1) $1400–$2000, depending on
program (includes round-trip airfare
from New York). Registration fee: $40.
(2) Examples: Spring Project in Israel,
6 weeks, $990 (including airfare);
Touring Program, 6 weeks, $2000;
Combined Kibbutz/Touring, 6 weeks,
$1875.

Comment
The American Zionist Youth
Foundation, begun in 1963, sponsors
educational programs and services for
American Jewish youth, with the goal
of bringing them closer to Israel and
Judaism. Program leaders are college
graduates, fluent in Hebrew and
English, with travel experience in
Israel. Group size averages forty.
Academic credit available.

Further Information
Dr. Victor Benel
Director, Israel Program Center
(212) 751-6070

The Asia Society
725 Park Avenue
New York, New York 10021

Programs
(1) Dance and Textile Tour of
Indonesia, exploring religious, social,
and artistic settings; 23 days; summer.
(2) The Buddhist Trail, investigating
history and modern traditions of
Buddhism; 20 days; winter.
(3) National Treasures of Korea,
Japan, and Taiwan, with visits to
historic, religious, and artistic centers;
3 weeks; spring.

Accommodations
First-class or best available hotels.

Cost
(1) $5978, including airfare from New
York.
(2) $5998, including airfare from New
York.
(3) $6598, including airfare from New
York.
All costs include tax-deductible
contribution to Asia Society.

Comment
The Asia Society, founded in 1956, is
an educational organization whose aim

is to increase knowledge of Asian
countries and their importance to the
United States. Also sponsors trips, acts
as a consultant to educators, operates
museum, etc.
(1) and (3) Led by Dr. John S. Major,
director of Asia Society, assisted by Dr.
Valerie Steele, expert on textiles and
fashions.
(2) Led by Dr. Leonard Van der Kuip,
Oriental scholar.

Further Information
Claire Fair
(212) 288-8400

Columbia University
Broadway and 116th Street
New York, New York 10027

Programs
A variety of overseas travel, by both
air and combined air and sea. Recent
examples:
(1) Land of the Mayas, air and sea, 2
weeks, January.
(2) Classical Mediterranean, air and
sea, 3 weeks, June–July.
(3) Morocco, 2 weeks, November.

Accommodations
First-class.

Cost
Write for information.

Comment
The cruise portion of the air and sea
trips is by the four-masted schooner
Sea Cloud, the world's only tall ship for
passengers. All trips are accompanied
by Columbia University faculty.

Further Information
Jessie Mygatt
Alumni Federation
Box 400, Central Mail Room
(212) 280-3237

Cornell Adult University
626B Thurston Avenue
Ithaca, New York 14850

Program
Study tours to various destinations in the United States and abroad. Recent examples: Mediterranean, India, Hawaii, Japan, Soviet Union. Tours include daily lectures and discussions with Cornell faculty and guest lecturers.

Accommodations
Hotels, resorts, cruise ships.

Cost
Domestic trips: $200–$500; overseas: $1500–$4000, some including airfare.

Comment
The Cornell Adult University was established in 1968. Its travel and seminar programs attract about 2000 participants annually, in groups ranging from 25 to 125. Locations and destinations are often designed to provide a field experience in addition to classroom instruction.

Further Information
Ralph Janis, Director
(607) 256-6260

Council on International
Educational Exchange
205 East 42nd Street
New York, New York 10017

Programs
International travel and study programs of varying duration up to full academic year. Examples:
(1) Views of Japan, educational and sociological emphasis; 3½ weeks; July.

(2) Japanese Business and Society, for advanced college undergraduates, graduates, and young professionals; 7 weeks; late June to August.
(3) Film Study Center in Paris, 1 semester or full academic year.

Accommodations
Vary according to trip: private homes, inns, hotels.

Cost
(1) $2700 (West Coast departure) to $3500 (East Coast), all inclusive.
(2) $3600 (West Coast departure), $3900 (East Coast).
(3) $3385, semester; $5075, full academic year.

Comment
Founded in 1947, the Council on International Educational Exchange arranges and administers international travel and study programs for its member institutions, for other exchange organizations, and for individual students, teachers, and other international travelers from the academic community. The Council also organizes conferences and workshops. College credit is available for certain programs.

Further Information
(1) and (2) Margaret Shuba, Program Director
(212) 661-1414
(3) Cynthia Settler

In traveling . . . a man must carry knowledge with him, if he would bring home knowledge.
Samuel Johnson

> *Travel, in the younger sort, is a part of education; in the elder, a part of experience.*
> *Sir Francis Bacon*

Hebrew University of Jerusalem
Rothberg School for Overseas Subjects
11 East 69th Street
New York, New York 10021

Programs
(1) Short courses for credit, on varied subjects (Bible, Jewish history, Jewish music, Hebrew and other Middle East languages and studies, etc.), July and August.
(2) Excavating Jerusalem, archaeological course with fieldwork. (See Chapter 3.)
(3) Summer in Kibbutz, 8 weeks.

Accommodations
Hebrew University dormitories.

Cost
(1) Tuition: generally $235–$295 per credit hour; housing: $140 per session.
(2) Tuition: $295; housing as above.
(3) $2000 (includes airfare with European stopover).

Recreation and Cultural Opportunities
Facilities of University include swimming pool and other sports; also libraries. There is a wide variety of cultural events in Jerusalem.

Comment
Summer programs offer insight into Jewish culture in the unique setting of Jerusalem. Kibbutz program involves 1-month stay combining living with work-study; followed by 1-week tour with last 3 weeks at Hebrew University. All courses (except for special language courses) given in English.

Further Information
(1) and (2) (212) 472-2288
(3) Kibbutz Aliyah Desk
27 West 20th Street
   New York, New York 10011
(212) 255-1338

Institute of International Education
809 United Nations Plaza
New York, New York 10017

Programs
(1) British University Summer Schools held at Oxford, London, Edinburgh, Canterbury, Stratford-upon-Avon; 6-week session, July–August. British history, political science, literature, etc.; designed for graduates and college seniors.
(2) British Archaeology Program, 1 month, July. One-week seminars and tour in Cambridge, balance of time at various digs in Britain. This program is not intended for advanced students.

Accommodations
(1) Student housing.
(2) Student housing for seminars and tour, tents for digs.

Cost
(1) $550–$680 (excluding airfare).
(2) $550, additional charges for international airfare, textbooks, travel to London following dig.
Write for current information.

Further Information
Study Abroad Programs
(212) 883-8266

Irish Georgian Society
455 East 51st Street
New York, New York 10022

Program
Art and culture tours to Ireland, 1–3 weeks throughout the year. The society arranges these tours through its local chapters and in cooperation with other organizations. Participants visit private homes and castles, viewing collections of Irish art and unique architecture.

Accommodations
First-class.

Cost
Write for details.

Comment
The Irish Georgian Society was established in 1959 to protect Georgian buildings of architectural merit. It also encourages research on Irish furniture, silver, and painting and other arts. In-depth lectures are given at many sites by owners or other knowledgeable speakers. Nearly 4000 people have participated in tours; group sizes range from twelve to forty.

Further Information
In the United States:
Joseph D. Ryle
Executive Director
455 East 51st Street
New York, New York 10022
(212) 759-7155

In Ireland:
Leixlip Castle
County Kildare, Ireland

History records are the laboratory data of past experience.
Unknown

New York University
NYU Travel
25 West Fourth Street
New York, New York 10012

Programs
Recent examples:
(1) London, Stratford-upon-Avon, and Oxford; combined theater-sightseeing trip, 1 week, February.
(2) Ireland, 10 days, June.
(3) Spain, Hong Kong, etc.

Accommodations
Deluxe hotels.

Cost
(1) $1249 (airfare from New York and most meals included).
(2) $1849 (airfare from New York and most meals included).
(3) Write for information.

Comment
(1) Hosted by David J. Oppenheim, NYU dean at Tisch School of the Arts. Features lectures by distinguished critics, authors, and actors prior to performances. Also backstage discussions.
(2) Led by L. T. O'Liva, University chancellor and Irish scholar.
(3) Hong Kong trip is designed for business leaders.

Further Information
Alicia Gourino
(212) 598-7988

Questers Tours and Travel, Inc.
257 Park Avenue South
New York, New York 10010

Programs
Worldwide nature tours; varying lengths and destinations throughout year. Examples:

(1) The Everglades, Dry Tortuga, and Southwest Florida, 11 days.
(2) Iceland, 16 days.

Accommodations
First-class or best available twin-bedded rooms.

Cost
(1) $1565.
(2) $2475 (not including airfare).

Comment
Since 1973, Questers has arranged tours enabling nature lovers to observe wildlife and vegetation, mainly in national parks and nature reserves. Tours are often timed to coincide with the blooming of spring flowers or the migrations of certain species. Where applicable, the itineraries include the art, architecture, and archaeology of the areas visited. Tours are led by naturalists from the staff of Questers. Average group size is fifteen.

Further Information
Michael L. Parkin, President
(212) 673-3120

Regent Tours, Inc.
15 Sealy Drive
Lawrence, New York 11516

Program
Art Treasures of Northern Italy and Switzerland, 2 weeks, spring and fall.

Accommodations
First-class and deluxe hotels.

Cost
$2875 (double occupancy), not including airfare.

Comment
Group size limited to twenty-five. Tours, lectures, and museum exploration of works of Old Masters and others (including Rembrandt,

Michelangelo, van Gogh, and Cézanne) by knowledgeable guides.

Further Information
Phoebe Rothkopf
(516) 569-3929

State University of New York at Buffalo
Overseas Academic Programs
D.U.E.
111 Norton Hall
Buffalo, New York 14260

Programs
(1) Programa de Estudios Hispánicos; an annual 5-week Spanish language, literature, and history program held at the University of Salamanca, Spain.
(2) Annual academic year or spring semester in Grenoble, France, at the University of Grenoble. Program includes French language, literature, and civilization, with opportunities for student teaching and work-study.

Accommodations
Private homes.

Cost
(1) $575, room, and board; airfare and tuition extra.
(2) $2500 per academic year, $1319 per semester; airfare and tuition extra.

Comment
(1) Instituted in 1969, the Spanish program is intended for intermediate and advanced undergraduate and graduate students and for prospective teachers of Spanish. It provides an enriched humanistic education in literature, art, and culture. Spanish language is a prerequisite. Credits available.
(2) The French program began in 1971. It is directed toward undergraduates interested in the humanities and social

sciences. French language is a prerequisite. SUNY Buffalo students participating in the full academic year program are eligible to apply for the $500 annual Linda Rock Memorial Scholarship.

Further Information
Director, Overseas Academic
   Programs
(716) 636-2450

> *What we have to learn to do,*
> *we learn by doing.*
>   *Aristotle*

Syracuse University
Division of International
*   Programs Abroad*
119 Euclid Avenue
Syracuse, New York 13210

Program
Study programs abroad, approximately 5 weeks, May–August. A wide variety of locations and subjects that change from year to year. Some recent examples: England—law and retailing internships, British Broadcasting; Italy—Humanism and the Arts in Renaissance Italy, Photography, Environmental Design; Ireland—Cultural Heritage and Current Conditions; Austria—Language, Arts, Culture, and the Alps; Israel—Judaism, the Holocaust, and Modern Israel.

Accommodations
Hotels and pensions rented by the university. The option of living in a private home is sometimes available.

Cost
Varies according to program and credit requirement. Write for information.

Comment
Study programs abroad are designed for students, professionals, and others. Those who do not seek credit may audit courses at a reduced fee. Programs are directed by Syracuse faculty, with occasional guest lecturers and visiting professors from the host country. In 1985, 223 students participated in twenty different programs.

Further Information
Millie Franklin, Program
   Administrator
(315) 423-3471

Tanzania Tourist Corporation
201 East 42nd Street
New York, New York 10017

Program
Tours of various durations and types, including mountain climbing and photographic and walking safaris. Visits to agricultural and industrial areas, coastal tours, and more.

Accommodations
Hotels, lodges, tent camps, as appropriate to tour.

Cost
Write for information.

Comment
The Tanzania Tourist Corporation owns and manages a chain of fourteen hotel/lodges and a tour company. Its tours feature visits to national parks, wildlife reserves, and archaeological sites, as well as to industrial and agricultural sites. Many tours include special boating excursions. Working with the Serengeti Research Institute, the University of Dar es Salaam, and various organizations and governmental ministries, the corporation can arrange programs for

individuals and groups in many areas of special interest, from archaeology to medicine to sports. From time to time, it offers study programs led by professors and naturalists from around the world.

Further Information
Ellison Malekia
(212) 986-7124
Head Office
P.O. Box 2485
Dar es Salaam, Tanzania

University of Salzburg
German Language for
*   Foreigners*
Institute of International
*   Education*
U.S. Student Programs
809 United Nations Plaza
New York, New York 10017

Program
German Language for Foreigners held jointly by University of Salzburg, Austria, and Goethe Institute; 6 weeks, summer. Objective is to provide an opportunity to learn German while in direct contact with Austrian culture, folklore, and way of life. Intensive language lessons at all levels; other subjects offered as well.

Accommodations
Dormitories.

Cost
$907, includes tuition and other program fees, accommodations, and meals.

Cultural Opportunities
Tour of Salzburg, tickets to the Salzburg Festival.

Comment
1986 marks the thirtieth session of the program at the University of Salzburg,

Klessheim campus. In addition to language, there are special courses in German style and Austrian poetry and prose and lectures on related subjects, including Austrian music and history. Guest lectures are given by Austrian professors, diplomats, and politicians. Applicants should be between ages 18 and 50 and have 1 year of college. Credit arranged through participant's own school.

Further Information
In the United States:
(212) 984-5330
In Austria:
University of Salzburg, Klessheim
    Campus
Salzburg, Austria

> *To travel is to discover that*
> *everyone is wrong about*
> *other countries.*
>   *Aldous Huxley*

OHIO

Lake Erie College
Academic Programs Abroad
Painesville, Ohio 44077

Program
Semester and academic-year programs in the language and culture of several countries, conducted at centers in England, France, Spain, Germany, Italy, and Mexico.

Accommodations
Host families, student dormitories.

Cost
Room, board, and tuition: $1900–$3400 per semester; $4200–$6900 per

academic year. Transportation not included. Some grants available.

Comment
For more than thirty years, Lake Erie College has shown its commitment to international education by sending students to foreign institutions for at least a term. These foreign programs have been offered to students of other institutions since 1981.

Further Information
Dr. Lunardi, Director
(216) 352-3361, ext. 370

Ohio University
Athens, Ohio 47501

Programs
Ten-week-semester language studies in Spanish, French, and German:
(1) Spanish, winter semester at Meridan, Mexico.
(2) French, spring semester at Tours, France.
(3) German, spring semester at Salzburg, Austria.

Accommodations
(1) and (2) Private families.
(3) Dormitory.

Cost
Tuition: $690 (Ohio resident); $1390 (nonresident). Room and partial board: $500–$700. Transportation and other fees additional.

Comment
These are annual credit courses that cover a country's culture and language. They are directed by University faculty of the Department of Modern Languages.

Further Information
Department of Modern Languages
(614) 594-5174

Ohio Wesleyan University
Delaware, Ohio 43015

Program
Annual tour. Recent example: Scandinavia, Russia, and the Fjords, 15 days, July–August.

Accommodations
Deluxe cruise ship.

Cost
$3168–$5038 per person (double occupancy), includes airfare.

Comment
All trips feature an educational element. Leader accompanies the group. Background information and a reading list given prior to trip.

Further Information
Laura Newman, Director of Alumni
    Relations
(614) 369-4431

OKLAHOMA

University of Oklahoma
Program Development Services
International Programs
1700 Asp Avenue
Norman, Oklahoma 73037

Programs
Recent examples:
(1) Spanish Language and Latin American Culture, Colima, Mexico; June–July. Credit option.
(2) Other travel/study programs: education, art history, birding, painting, and cultural programs in various locations such as Mexico, Great Britain, Japan, China, and Italy; throughout the year.

Accommodations
Vary with program.

Cost
Example: Mexican Ornithology Field Study at Colima, Mexico, $595 (7-day session), $750 (10-day session). Includes room, most meals, instruction, and local travel. Airfare to and from Guadalajara additional.

Comment
Tour leaders and instructors are university professors or qualified experts.

Further Information
(405) 325-6602

PENNSYLVANIA

Cheltenham Art Centre
439 Ashbourne
Cheltenham, Pennsylvania
   19012

Program
Recent example: cultural exchange tour to China, 22 days, spring. Participants see recent archaeological discoveries, visit two universities, attend juried exhibitions, and hear lectures and see demonstrations by leading Chinese artists. Stops in Tokyo and Hong Kong also included. In summer, three Chinese artist-professors conduct related program in Philadelphia open to all tour participants.

Accommodations
First-class.

Cost
$3400 complete (including all land and air transportation) plus $150 tax-deductible contribution to the Art

Centre. Fee includes summer program in Philadelphia.

Comment
The Chinese cultural exchange tour is led by Merle Spandorfer, artist and educator, who gives background talks. She has lectured on related topics in the Orient.

Further Information
Merle Spandorfer
(215) 379-4660

> *A man knows his companion in a long journey and a little inn.*
>
> *Thomas Fuller*

Eastern College
St. Davids, Pennsylvania 19087

Programs
(1) Summer seminars in Conversational Chinese, Chinese Art and Chinese Life, and Art in Contemporary China; 6 weeks; July–August; offered in collaboration with East China Normal University in Shanghai.
(2) Seminar in Chinese Joint Venture Law, 6 weeks, July–August, with limited number of shorter periods for audit; designed for lawyers and students of business, law, and related areas and offered in collaboration with East China Normal University.
(3) Seminar in Chinese Archaeology, 5 weeks, July–August; offered in collaboration with Northwestern University at Xi'an.

Accommodations
(1) and (2) Residence buildings for foreign students at East China Normal University.

(3) Residence building, Northwestern University of Xi'an.

Cost
$2995 for above examples, including airfare from New York.

Comment
All programs are under the direction and leadership of Dr. Alfonz Lengyel, professor of art history and director of Eastern's Institute for Contemporary Chinese Studies.
(1) and (2) Programs focus on current Chinese culture as it relates to U.S.-Chinese relations; weekend side trips and extended travel to southern China augment studies on campus.
(3) Includes excursions around Xi'an to see archaeologically important sites, along with visits to Beijing, the Great Wall, Nanking, Shanghai, etc. Credit obtainable for all courses and enrollment limited to fifteen participants.

Further Information
Dr. Alfonz Lengyel, Director of China
    Program
200 David Drive, Suite F-1
Bryn Mawr, Pennsylvania 19010
(215) 341-5893 (day, Eastern College)
(215) 525-7680 (evenings)

Franklin Institute
Benjamin Franklin Parkway at
    20th Street
Philadelphia, Pennsylvania
    19103

Program
Trips focusing on science within the United States and abroad.

Cost
Varies with trip.

Comment
The Franklin Institute is a nonprofit institution dedicated to the advancement of science and technology. It is composed of a science museum and planetarium featuring hands-on exhibits and the Bartol Research Foundation. Members are given reduced rates to all events.

Further Information
(215) 448-1200

Joseph Stanley Limited
181 West Bridge Street
Route 202
New Hope, Pennsylvania 18938

Program
Tours in the U.S. and abroad with emphasis on art, architecture, and antiques, fall and spring. Recent examples: New England Ramble, 1 week; Channel Isles, Jersey and Guernsey, 2 weeks; Scotland, 2 weeks.

Accommodations
Hotels, double occupancy.

Cost
Example: for foreign tours above, $2495 plus airfare. Write for information on other trips.

Comment
Joseph Stanley is an established antique dealer. Many tours feature visits to museums and private collections, with lectures, seminars, and field trips. Groups are limited to twenty-five people, many of whom are returning for a second trip. Effort is made to include other cultural experiences such as theater and opera on these trips.

Further Information
Joseph Stanley
(215) 862-9300

> *The use of traveling is to regulate imagination by reality, and, instead of thinking how things may be, to see them as they are.*
> *Samuel Johnson*

Kutztown University of Pennsylvania
Kutztown, Pennsylvania 19530

Programs
Recent examples:
(1) European Art Tour of Belgium, the Netherlands, and France; 2 weeks, July. An in-depth study tour of leading museums.
(2) Pennsylvania Consortium for International Education; courses offered in England, Austria, and Italy. Dates vary. Literature, art, history, and political science courses focusing on their specific location.

Accommodations
(1) First-class hotels.
(2) University dormitories.

Cost
(1) $1900 plus tuition.
(2) $1400–$1800, including tuition, travel, lodgings, most meals, and airfare from New York.

Comment
An excellent opportunity to combine travel and study.

Further Information
Dean, Academic Services
(215) 683-4215

Lehigh University
Alumni Association
Alumni Memorial Building
Bethlehem, Pennsylvania 18015

Program
Thematic tours to various destinations worldwide. Recent example: Passage of the Moors in Morocco and Spain, 15 days.

Accommodations
Vary with tour. For example above, first-class hotels.

Cost
Above example: $2425, including airfare, local transportation, accommodations, and some meals.

Comment
Tours usually attract twenty-five to thirty-five participants and are led by experienced educators. For example, the tour leader of the Morocco-Spain trip was Ricardo Viera, professor of art and architecture and curator of the Lehigh Art Galleries.

Further Information
Leslie A. Brown, Assistant Executive
    Director
(215) 861-3131

University of Pennsylvania
Alumni College Weekends
Special Programs/College of
    General Studies
112 Logan Hall
Philadelphia, Pennsylvania
    19104

Program
Places of historic interest in the United States are the sites of weekend seminars, whose topics reflect the chosen locations. Recent examples:

Thomas Jefferson and His World, Charlottesville, Virginia, April; Three Centuries of American Splendor, motorcoach weekend tour of Newport from Philadelphia, October; 5-day trips to New Orleans (spring), Chicago, and Annapolis, Maryland (fall).

Accommodations
Best available hotels.

Cost
$600–$900 per person, depending on location. Participants arrange own travel to most locations.

Comment
The programs offer participants an opportunity to use the faculty resources of the university in a relaxed vacation setting. Faculty members are selected for their relevant expertise. They lecture and accompany the group throughout each trip. Programs are designed for twenty to thirty adults and are not suitable for children.

Further Information
Joanne M. Hanna, Program
   Coordinator
(215) 898-1390/6479

> *Men are wise in proportion,
> not to their experience, but to
> their capacity for experience.*
>   *George Bernard Shaw*

University of Pittsburgh
Pitt's Informal Program
3804 Forbes Avenue
Pittsburgh, Pennsylvania 15260

Program
Pitt's Informal Program offers a year-round variety of domestic and international tours, 10 days to 3 weeks. Annual tours visit China and Kenya. Pitt also has a 3-month Semester at Sea credit program. Other destinations include: Amsterdam and the Flanders Area; May Day to Moscow; London to Venice on the Orient Express (art). Tours are preceded by a lecture and supplementary reading.

Accommodations
First-class, deluxe.

Children
Children are welcome to join trips appropriate to their interest.

Cost
Varies with tour. Examples: Orient Express, $1720, (all inclusive); Semester at Sea, $9000 +.

Comment
These highly varied tours are led by university professors, skilled professionals, or qualified tour escorts. Groups range in size from fifteen to thirty-five. Airfares can be arranged from the registrant's location. PIP's only restrictions involve the registrant's health or other attributes that might present a problem to other registrants.

Further Information
Betty Goodwin, Travel Coordinator
(412) 624-0812

Victorian Society In America
British Summer School
The Athenaeum
East Washington Square
Philadelphia, Pennsylvania
   19106

Program
Seminars on Victorian architecture, 3 weeks, July. Courses held in London, Birmingham, and Liverpool, England.

Accommodations
Write for information.

Cost
$1080, includes room, breakfast, motorcoach transportation, fees. Travel within London, other meals, and overseas transportation not included.

Comment
The British Summer School was first held in 1975. It concentrates on Victorian architecture but also studies Edwardian architecture and the influences of both on American architecture. Lectures by leading experts in architecture and history (art, social, and religious). Visits to major buildings and monuments throughout England.

Further Information
Johanna Levy
(215) 627-4252

World Affairs Council of
*   Philadelphia*
13th and Market Streets
Philadelphia, Pennsylvania
*   19107*

Program
Recent example: Brazil and Argentina, 2 weeks, March.

Accommodations
First-class hotels.

Cost
$2575 per person from Miami (double occupancy), including $200 tax-deductible contribution.

Comment
World Affairs Council trips feature briefings at American embassies as well as informative meetings with journalists and business leaders.

Further Information
Travel Department
(215) 563-5363

> *A little learning is a*
> *dangerous thing;*
> *Drink deep, or taste not the*
> *Pierian Spring.*
> *   Alexander Pope*

RHODE ISLAND

Brown University
Brown Travelers
Box 1859
Providence, Rhode Island 02912

Program
Trips of various destination and duration worldwide, led by Brown University faculty. Recent examples: Southeast Asia, France, U.S.S.R., the Rhine River, and Christmas in Austria.

Accommodations
Write for details.

Cost
Examples above: Southeast Asia, 13 days, $3960–$4560; Rhine Cruise, 9 days, $1400; Christmas in Austria, 9 days, $2000.

Comment
Brown offers a changing schedule of trips each year led by a specialist on the particular destination visited.

Further Information
Sallie Riggs
(401) 863-2785

> *Each of us is a cultivator of a liberal art.*
>
> *Ovid*

TENNESSEE

TEXAS

*Vanderbilt Alumni Travel
  Program
117 Alumni Hall
Vanderbilt University
Nashville, Tennessee 37240*

Program
Tours emphasizing cultural aspects of destinations both domestic and foreign, throughout the year. Trips are supplemented by prior reading and lectures during the tour. Recent destinations include Paris, the Spoleto Festival in Charleston (South Carolina), the Mediterranean, Alaska, and Hawaii; different tours each year.

Accommodations
Vary; usually first-class or deluxe.

Children
No special programs.

Cost
For examples above: Paris, 7 days, $1130 from Nashville including airfare (meals extra); Spoleto, 4 days, $595 plus airfare (some meals); Mediterranean, 14 days, $3100+ (including cruise) from Nashville.

Comment
The Alumni Travel Program began in 1979 and has in the past included on-campus programs in addition to travel. University professors usually conduct tours and seminars. Average group size is twenty to thirty-five; programs are open to all.

*Baylor University
Waco, Texas 76798*

Program
Recent example: Baylor in the British Isles, 5 weeks, July–August. Historical tours of Ireland, London, Wales, Scotland.

Accommodations
Double occupancy; while in London, participants stay at Westminster School in Westminster Abbey.

Cost
$2400, includes airfare from Dallas, all transportation, rooms, and two meals daily. Optional college credit is $348 per course.

Comment
Program includes free time for sightseeing and other activities.

Further Information
Professor James Vardaman
Department of History
(817) 755-2667

*Lamar University
Division of Academic Services
Box 10126
Beaumont, Texas 77710*

Programs
(1) London Study Program, 3 weeks, usually early June.

(2) Rome Study Program, 4–6 weeks, usually June.

Accommodations
(1) First-class hotel.
(2) Hostels.

Children
With permission; otherwise minimum age is 17 years.

Cost
(1) and (2) $2900, all inclusive.

Comment
Course content varies, but related to countries and sites on itinerary.
(1) Course offerings usually include English, history, art, education, among others. Side trips to Oxford, Canterbury, Stonehenge, Lake Country, Scotland, and more.
(2) Subjects offered usually include Italian, history, art, and more. Side trips include Florence, Venice, Naples, Pisa, and Capri.
Average size of group is thirty-five to fifty people. These trips provide the opportunity to leave the classroom and enter the cultural environment being studied. Write or call about credit possibilities.

Further Information
(1) Nora Leach
(2) Gary Laird
(409) 880-8431

Rice University
Office of Continuing Studies
  and Special Programs
P.O. Box 1892
Houston, Texas 77007

Programs
(1) Passage to Palenque: Crown Jewel of Mayan Art, 4 days, spring.

(2) The Bible on Location, 2 weeks, June.
(3) Aegean Odyssey: The Glory of Ancient Greece, 2 weeks, summer.
(4) East Istanbul: A Journey Across Turkey, 2 weeks, summer.

Accommodations
Hotels.

Cost
(1) $825 (double occupancy), includes round-trip airfare from Houston.
(2) $2450, includes airfare.
(3) $2595, includes airfare.
(4) $2595, includes airfare.

Comment
Tours feature visits of historical interest and include lectures given by professional experts on regional history and historic monuments. College credit obtainable.
(1) Mimi Crossley, art critic.
(2) Dr. Don C. Benjamin, Scanlon Visiting Scholar in Religious Studies.
(3) and (4) Dr. William Neidinger.

Further Information
Dr. Mary McIntyre
(713) 527-4803 or 520-6022

University of Texas at Austin
Department of Classics
Austin, Texas 78712

Program
Recent example: Cruise to classical and medieval sites around the Mediterranean, 2 weeks, May–June; led by two faculty members who provide background briefings and educational commentary.

Accommodations
Cabins on private cruise ship; first-class hotels.

Children
Minimum age: 10.

Cost
$4295–$6795, includes round-trip airfare from Dallas.

Comment
This tour, led by professors of classics and archaeology, visits sites of special significance not normally seen by tourists. Participants need not be university alumni. Maximum group size: 120.

Further Information
Professor Karl Galinsky
(512) 471-5742

Not to know what happened before one was born is always to be a child.
　　　　　　　　Cicero

UTAH

Brigham Young University
310 Harman Continuing
　Education Building
Provo, Utah 84602

Program
Annual Church History Camping Caravan, 10 days, July–August. Journey from Independence, Missouri, to Palmyra, New York, with educational programs along the way.

Accommodations
Participants bring own camper or camping equipment.

Cost
$249 per adult couple; children's price available.

Comment
Since 1978, the Church History Camping Caravan has been led by university professors. The tour is designed to be both informative and relaxing. The number of participants per expedition varies from 30 to 200.

Further Information
James R. Burton, Business Manager
(801) 378-2513

Brigham Young University
Department of Travel Study
310 Harman Continuing
　Education Building
Provo, Utah 84602

Program
Recent example: World of the Bible tour, 10–16 days, December, April, and July. Visits to biblical sites in Israel, with optional tours to Egypt/Athens or Rome. Faculty leaders and other experts provide an educational background.

Accommodations
First-class and deluxe hotel accommodations.

Children
Permitted.

Cost
Base price for Israel tour, 10 days, averages $1600 from New York (includes airfare, local transportation, two meals daily). Egypt/Athens or Rome option is additional $775.

Comment
Experienced faculty directors and religious scholars from Christian and Jewish backgrounds give numerous lectures on the areas visited, adding educational and spiritual dimensions to travel. Informational materials are provided prior to departure, and

college credit is available. Other study programs may be available in Israel; write for more information. Group sizes average thirty to forty-five.

Further Information
Robert C. Taylor, Department
    Chairman
(801) 378-3946

> *Genius is the ability to reduce the complicated to the simple.*
> **C. W. Ceran**

VERMONT

Goddard College
Travel Study Course
Plainfield, Vermont 05667

Program
Travel for Academic Growth is a course designed for students and educators wishing to study during foreign or domestic travel at any time of the year. Registrants arrange their own trips and complete a standard set of course requirements.

Accommodations
Responsibility of participant.

Cost
Tuition: $60 per credit hour (1–6 credits available). All travel costs are responsibility of participant.

Comment
The program allows the participant to develop a travel learning experience and provides a format for completion of a study plan in order to obtain college credit. Intended for students

(undergraduate or graduate), classroom teachers, and educational staff personnel, it is a unique way to further professional development.

Further Information
Dr. Lyle B. Gangsei
    or
Virginia Gangsei
P.O. Box 156
Newbury Park, California
    91320
(805) 499-4656

VIRGINIA

Washington and Lee University
Travel-Study Tours
Office of Summer Programs
Lexington, Virginia 24450

Program
Educational tours to locations around the world. Recent destinations and trip titles include: Greece—Classical Athens, 17 days, June; Ecuador and the Galapagos Islands, 15 days, August.

Accommodations
First-class hotels.

Cost
Above programs: approximately $2500. Write for specific information.

Comment
These university travel programs are led by two experienced faculty members. Emphasis is on exploring the history and culture of countries visited. Program includes readings and lectures. Group sizes are limited to thirty and nineteen adults, respectively.

Further Information
Robert Fure, Ph.D., Director of
    Summer Programs
(703) 463-8723

WISCONSIN

*Foundation for International
    Education
121 Cascade Court
River Falls, Wisconsin 54022*

Program
Overseas counterpart schoolwork for
American teachers in an English-
speaking country, 3 weeks, June–
August. Programs scheduled in
England, Scotland, Ireland, India,
Trinidad and Tobago, Gibraltar, Fiji,
Australia, and New Zealand, among
others.

Accommodations
Usually counterpart teacher's home.
Other arrangements are possible, and
participants should indicate preference
with application.

Cost
Write for information. Participants
make own travel arrangements.

Comment
The Foundation for International
Education was established in 1977. Its
program offers teachers intensive
cultural experiences in a school
setting. Preferences for urban, small-
town, or rural situations can be
accommodated. The program is open to
experienced teachers only, and a
bachelor's degree is required. The
program carries 3 graduate semester
credits.

Further Information
Dr. Ross Korsgaard
(715) 425-2718

*Marquette University
526 North 14th Street
Milwaukee, Wisconsin 53233*

Programs
(1) Language Center in Germany, 7½
weeks, May–July.
(2) Summer Study Program in France
at the University of Limoges, 6½
weeks, June–July.

Accommodations
(1) Family homes and hotels,
depending on location.
(2) Hotels, residence halls at Limoges
University.

Cost
(1) Tuition: $918, 6 credit hours; $1377,
9 credit hours; $1420, room and board
and miscellaneous expenses.
(2) Tuition: $918, 6 credit hours; $1295,
room and board and miscellaneous
expenses.

Comment
(1) The Language Center in Germany
program was first held in 1964. It is for
students with at least 1 year of college
German or 2 years of high school
German. Emphasis is on language and
culture in a German setting; courses
are held in the Rhineland, Berlin,
Hildesheim, and elsewhere. Numerous
excursions to places of cultural
significance are scheduled. Maximum
number of participants is twenty-five;
6–9 credits may be earned.
(2) The Summer Study Program in
France was first held in 1979. It is for
students with 1 year of college French
or 2 years of high school French.
Classes are held in the morning, with
the afternoon kept free for cultural

activities. Schedule includes stay in Paris, other side trips. Average number of participants is twenty; 6 college credits may be earned.

Further Information
(1) Dr. Esther Hudgins
Language Center in Germany
Lalumiere Hall, Room 406
(414) 224-7312
(2) Dr. Brigitte Coste
Summer Study Program in France
Lalumiere Hall, Room 433
(414) 224-6837
Summer session: (414) 224-7506

MEXICO

*International Memorable
    Learning Experience
callejón del Codo no. 6
San Miguel de Allende,
    Guanajuata C.P. 37700
Mexico*

Program
Vacations with a Purpose, a bilingual summer camp for youth ages 8–13, six consecutive weeklong sessions, July and August, in a variety of subject matter, including Spanish, Mexican culture, Mexican cooking, and arts and crafts. Enrollment can be for any or all.

Accommodations
Dormitories.

Cost
$150 per week with 15 percent discounts on each subsequent summer session week. Includes meals, materials, and equipment. Transportation to and from San Miguel, Mexico, and insurance extra.

Recreation
Horseback riding, swimming, hiking, etc.

Comment
Established in 1969, IMLE has served as a study center for hundreds of young students from around the world. Each weekly session is limited to sixteen participants. Supervision by two full-time and several part-time staff members.

Further Information
Richard P. Merrill
2-03-99 and 2-22-76

UNITED KINGDOM

*Embassy Hotels
107 Station Street
Burton-on-Trent DE14 1BZ
England*

Programs
(1) Leisure Learning, more than sixty weekend courses conducted throughout the year at various Embassy hotels in Britain. Topics include canals, churches, opera, famous people, photography, etc.
(2) Embassy Explorers, similar weekend programs designed for groups. Longer tours are also available.

Accommodations
Hotels of Embassy chain.

Cost
(1) From £70.

Comment
Leisure Learning weekends were first offered in 1977. Instructors are professors, lecturers, and other experts; programs include informal

talks, films, slide presentations, and guided tours. Average class size is forty.

Further Information
In England:
Tony Winslade
(0293) 67713
Booking agent in the United States:
Utell International
119 West 57th Street, 3rd Floor
New York, New York 10019
(800) 223-9868
    or
(212) 757-2981

> *Many receive advice, only the wise profit from it.*
> *Publilius Syrus*

University of Cambridge
Board of Extramural Studies
Madingley Hall
Madingley, Cambridge
CB3 8AQ
England

Program
Courses in British history, literature, art history, etc., for beginners and advanced students; 2–6 weeks, July–September.

Accommodations
University residential center.

Cost
Write for information.

Comment
Courses available for specialists (lawyers, literature teachers, etc.), though to be admitted one must only be at least 18 years old and have a good knowledge of English.

Further Information
In England:
Course Registrar
(0954) 210636
In the United States:
AIFS (USA)
102 Greenwich Avenue
Greenwich, Connecticut 06830
(There are others in the United States as well.)

University of Exeter
Residence and Conference
*   Office*
Devonshire House, Stocker
*   Road*
Exeter EX4 4PZ
England

Programs
(1) Annual International Summer School in English life, literature, and art; 3 weeks.
(2) Twenty-four 1-week courses in a variety of academic and recreational subjects.

Accommodations
University residence halls.

Cost
Write for information.

Recreation
Social programs are scheduled, and the surrounding area offers numerous touring opportunities.

Comment
The International Summer School has been conducted for over 50 years. All of Exeter's programs are designed to give participants a broad introduction to British culture and are open to college and university students, former students, teachers, and others interested in learning more about

English life and thought. Individuals and groups are wlcome.

Further Information
Residence and Conference Office
(0392) 215566

University of Kent at Canterbury–Rutherford College
School of Continuing Education
Canterbury CT2 7NX
England

Programs
(1) English Heritage, a series of four linked 1-week summer schools concerning visual evidence of past centuries, from the Roman presence to the present day, July–August.
(2) Summer Academy, thirty-four 1-week courses at nine universities in Britain where art, literature, and history are taught, August.

Accommodations
University facilities.

Cost
(1) £170 per week, full board, tuition, social events, and excursions.
(2) From £159 per week, full board, tuition, social events, and excursions.

Comment
Groups are welcome. Lectures and extensive visits are provided with all programs.

Further Information
(1) Booking Agents: A. Riley
Rutherford College
(0227) 66822, ext. 663
(2) Peter Jordan
(0227) 69186

University of Warwick Summer School
Coventry CV4 7AL
England

Program
British Studies Programme, 1 month, July–August. Courses in archaeology, history, literature, politics, art history, and theatre studies.

Accommodations
University single study-bedrooms.

Cost
$1020–$1300, tuition, room and board.

Comment
Courses include formal class work, field trips, and educational excursions to a variety of sites. Instructors are from the University.

Further Information
Dr. D. Mervin, Director
(0203) 24011, ext. 2303

3 *ARCHAEOLOGY, SCIENCE, AND HISTORY*

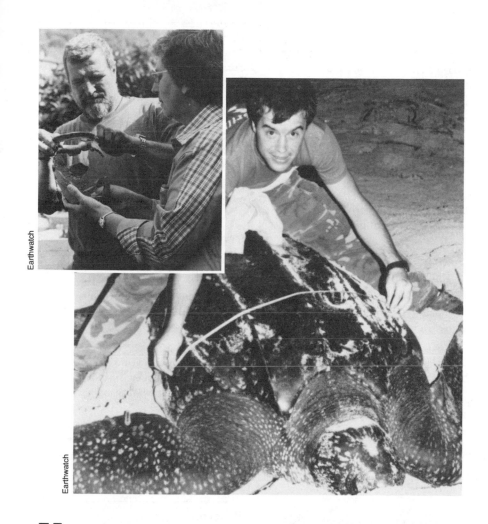

Earthwatch

Earthwatch

*V*iewing historic sites or exploring the past by digging its relics provides fun, excitement, and adventure while offering the reward of an enhanced knowledge of history and science.

> *The Stone Age may return on the gleaming wings of Science.*
> **Winston Churchill**

ARIZONA

Arizona State University
Tempe, Arizona 85287

Program
Archaeological research project at Shoofly Village Ruins (near Payson, Arizona, and at Tonto National Monument), 5 weeks, June–July.

Accommodations
Rustic housing in tents; meals and major field equipment provided.

Cost
Tuition: $318 per credit hour; room and board: $300.

Comment
Course open with limited enrollment to undergraduate and graduate students and has prerequisite of course in anthropology or archaeology. Stresses use of research designs and investigation of anthropological problems. Graduate students are expected to conduct original research after program. 6 credits obtainable.

Further Information
Dr. Charles A. Redman, Director
(602) 965-6213

> *Few of us take the pains to study the origin of our cherished convictions.*
> **J. H. Robinson**

CALIFORNIA

California Polytechnic State University
Department of Social Sciences
San Luis Obispo, California 93407

Program
Archaeological field school at Mission San Antonio de Padua, 6 weeks, June–July. Includes research, fieldwork, lab analysis, and evening lectures. The site is Spanish colonial (1771–1834).

Accommodations
Single rooms in mission; cooperative housekeeping.

Cost
$600, includes tuition (6 credits), room, and board.

Comment
The Mission San Antonio program has been offered since 1976. Thirty college students or high school graduates are accepted each year. Interested persons outside of academia are also encouraged to apply. College credit is available.

Further Information
Dr. Robert L. Hoover
Department of Social Sciences
(805) 546-2260

Foundations for Field Research
787 South Grade Road
Alpine, California 92001

Program
Participation in a scientific research expedition for nonspecialists; varying durations and destinations. Some examples: Excavation of Frontier Trading Post, Southern California, 5

days, March; Marine Biology, Sea of Cortez, Mexico, 5 days, April; Israel Archaeology, 3 weeks, June–July. Other expeditions study wildlife, rock art, different cultures.

Accommodations
Outdoor tent camping, lodges, hotels as appropriate.

Cost
For the examples above: Trading Post, $400; Marine Biology, $375; Israel, $1750. These figures do not include long-distance transportation or equipment or other items that may be required. NOTE: Most costs of the expeditions are considered contributions to basic research and are tax deductible.

Comment
Foundations for Field Research is a nonprofit corporation. Participants work on the research project of an active scientist. No special training or skills are required, although they may be of benefit on particular expeditions. Most expeditions involve outdoor work; some include primitive camping. Preparatory materials and a reading list are provided for each expedition.

Further Information
Thomas J. Banks, Director
(619) 445-9264

University of California,
Berkeley
University Research
Expeditions Program
Berkeley, California 94720

Programs
Year-round programs in archaeology, anthropology, plant and animal ecology. Recent examples:
(1) Patagonia, Argentina, 2 weeks.

(2) Goa Carnival, India, 2 weeks.
(3) Tropical Rain Forest, 2 weeks.

Accommodations
Vary with program, but usually camping.

Cost
Costs, which exclude airfare, are usually considered tax-deductible contributions to the University. For examples above:
(1) $1285
(2) $1635
(3) $1135

Comment
These programs are open to adults (18 and older) to assist field director and staff on projects throughout the world. Founded in 1975, the Research Expeditions Program has been supporting over one hundred field programs in fifty countries. Participants actively contribute to major research projects by lending a hand in the field and making a financial contribution. Special skills and previous experience are useful but not necessary. Groups range from three to twelve. Credit may be obtained for certain expeditions.

Further Information
Program Director
(415) 642-6586

COLORADO

Colorado State University
Department of Anthropology
Fort Collins, Colorado 80537

Program
Archaeological field school at pre-Columbian site; 4–8 weeks, May–July.

Accommodations
Vary from personally arranged quarters in Fort Collins to rustic field camps.

Cost
Tuition for Colorado residents: $230.50, 4 weeks; tuition for nonresidents: $750.50, 4 weeks. Write for more information.

Comment
The Colorado State University archaeology program was first offered in 1968. It is for college students; the number of participants is limited to twenty to twenty-five. Local transportation and equipment are provided. Academic credit is available; units earned depend upon duration of stay.

Further Information
Dr. Calvin H. Jennings
Chair, Department of Anthropology
(303) 491-5447

ILLINOIS

*Center for American
    Archeology
Kampsville Archeological
    Center
Box 365
Kampsville, Illinois 62053*

Program
Join with archaeologists in excavation of important prehistoric settlements, 2–5 weeks, summer. Programs for high school and college students as well as adults.

Accommodations
Dormitories, shower house.

Cost
$240–$310 per week, including tuition, room, and board.

Cultural Opportunities
Center Museum has both outdoor and indoor exhibits, with a significant collection from CAA research in the Lower Illinois Valley.

Comment
The CAA was founded in 1957 as the Foundation for Illinois Archaeology; it moved all operations to the Kampsville site in 1985. It is the oldest and largest archaeological research and teaching center in the United States. Its staff consists of specialists in archaeology, geology, botany, zoology, computer programming, and biological anthropology. Archaeological experience is not necessary for the program. High school and college credit available.

Further Information
Director of Admissions
(618) 653-4316

*Illinois State Museum
Springfield, Illinois 62706*

Program
Domestic and foreign trips with emphasis on geology, archaeology, and similar fields; summer and fall. Recent examples: Colorado River Trip, through Grand Canyon, 12 days, late spring; East African Geological Safari, 3 weeks.

Accommodations
Domestic trips: example above, camping; foreign trips: deluxe or best available hotels.

Cost
For above examplse: Colorado River Trip, $800, not including travel to site;

East African Geological Safari, $3500, complete.

Comment
Sponsored by the State Museum since 1978. Trips and excursions are led by museum education expert, Christopher J. Schuberth. Minimum age for participants is 21.

Further Information
Christopher J. Schuberth, Curator of
    Education
(217) 782-5955

> *Engineering is the art of doing that well with one dollar, which any bungler can do with two after a fashion.*
> *Arthur M. Wellington*

INDIANA

Ball State University
Muncie, Indiana 47306

Program
Five-week field school in archaeological excavation procedure, summer. Methods of excavation and recording will be taught in east-central Indiana. Field camp will be at reservoir site about twelve miles from Peru, Indiana.

Accommodations
Students are responsible for their living expenses and camping equipment.

Cost
$42 per undergraduate hour of credit; $47 per graduate hour of credit.

Comment
Methods of excavation and recording will be taught; field observation and cultural interpretation are stressed.

Further Information
Donald Cochran
Department of Anthropology
(317) 285-5385

KENTUCKY

Western Kentucky University
Department of Anthropology
Bowling Green, Kentucky 42101

Program
Volunteers needed to work in archaeology laboratory on various Indian projects or reports, throughout the year.

Accommodations
University dormitories.

Cost
No charge for program. Dormitory rooms approximately $30 per week. Volunteers provide own food and other incidentals.

Comment
The Western Kentucky archaeology program was first offered in 1980. It provides equipment, instruction, and training. Participants must be high school graduates, over 21 years of age, and must agree to stay at least 2 weeks.

Further Information
Dr. Jack Shock
(502) 745-2193

LOUISIANA

Northeast Louisiana University
700 University Avenue
Monroe, Louisiana 71209

Program
Archaeological field school and
volunteer program at Poverty Point
State Commemorative Area (1500–700
B.C.), June–July.

Accommodations and Cost
Write for information.

Comment
Field school for high school students,
college undergraduates, or graduate
students, who earn college credit.
Volunteers also needed. Instruction,
on-site training, local transportation,
and equipment are provided. Field
school is limited to twenty-five people.

Further Information
Dr. Glen S. Greene
Department of Geosciences
(318) 342-4100

MAINE

Norlands Adult Live-In
Program
Washburn Norlands
RD 2, Box 3395
Livermore Falls, Maine 04254

Program
Weekend-long "living history"
experience. Participants live as rural
citizens of Maine in 1870; monthly,
year-round except December and
January.

Accommodations
1870 farmer's cottage; participants
must bring own sleeping bag and
pillow.

Cost
$160 per person, including meals and
handbook.

Comment
The program was started in 1975 at the
request of the Maine State Department
of Education and is designed to give
recertification credit to teachers but
open to others as well. Cottages have
no running water, electricity, or
modern plumbing. Food for meals
comes from animals and vegetables
raised on the farm. Participants spend
1 day doing "women's work" and 1 day
doing "men's work." Activities vary
with season and are done as in 1870.
College credit offered upon completion
of research paper.

Further Information
Mrs. Alfred Q. Gammon
(207) 897-2236

MARYLAND

Baltimore Zoological Society
Druid Hill Park
Baltimore, Maryland 21217

Program
Trips worldwide with emphasis on
animal habitats and wildlife, 2–4
weeks, throughout year.

Accommodations
Vary with trip; safari lodges, tents, etc.

Cost
$1000 (domestic) to $4000 (foreign).

Comment
Zoological Society staff, local naturalists, and park rangers have been conducting trips for the Baltimore Zoo since 1981. Size of groups usually ranges from ten to fifteen participants.

Further Information
Craig Sholley
(301) 467-4387

> *The first rule of intelligent tinkering is to save all the parts.*
> *Paul Ehrlich*

Historic Annapolis, Inc.
Old Treasury Building
State Circle
Annapolis, Maryland 21401

Programs
(1) Archaeological Heritage Tour, October. Scholars give interpretive lectures and answer questions.
(2) Preservation and advanced preservation tours, year-round. Emphasis placed on preservation theory, techniques, and practice in Annapolis.
(3) Art and Architecture Tours, 1 or 2 days, by reservation. Emphasis placed on various arts and crafts.
(4) Tours for special interest groups made by arrangement.

Accommodations
Responsibility of participants; write for information.

Cost
(1) $35, including reception.
(2) $10, preservation tour; $25, advanced preservation tour and lunch.
(3) $25, 1 day, including lunch; $50, 2

days, including lunch and evening program.

Recreation
Annapolis offers a wide variety of recreational opportunities, including sailing and tennis.

Cultural Opportunities
Slide lectures given in the William Paca House.

Comment
Historic Annapolis, Inc., was established in 1952 to protect and restore the Colonial character of Maryland's capital. Because of the city's many historic buildings and streets, Annapolis has been described as "a museum without walls." Historic Annapolis tour guides are experts in the fields covered. In addition to the above programs, daily walk-in tours are available throughout the year, as are foreign language tours and tours for the handicapped.

Further Information
Director
(301) 267-8149

National Aquarium in
Baltimore
Pier 3, 501 East Pratt Street
Baltimore, Maryland 21202

Programs
Recent examples:
(1) Whale watching, Baja California, Mexico; 10 days; March.
(2) Coral-reef biology at St. Croix, 1 week, January.

Accommodations and Cost
Write for information.

Comment
The National Aquarium in Baltimore has been offering 1-day, 1-week, or 10-

day science excursions for several years, led by staff members or outside naturalists.

Further Information
Nancy Hotchkiss
Department of Education
(301) 576-3875

St. Mary's City Museum
St. Mary's City, Maryland 20686

Program
Historical Archaeological Field School, a 10-week course in archaeological methodology sponsored by the Saint Mary's City Commission and the Maryland Historical Trust in conjunction with St. Mary's College; mid-June to August.

Accommodations
Vary; write for information.

Cost
$500–$600.

Comment
Primarily for students; limited enrollment. Seminars supplement practical experience and field trips. Final weeks spent in Colonial living. College credit given.

Further Information
Henry Miller, St. Mary's City
    Commission
(301) 862-9889

Towson State University
Towson, Maryland 21204

Program
Annual geographical and field anthropological trip to the American Southwest, 20 days, winter.

Accommodations
Motels and hotels.

Cost
$1100, inclusive.

Comment
First offered in the late 1970s, this program emphasizes studies of pre-Columbian petroglyphs, pueblo structures, Navajo remains, and the like. Beginning in Los Angeles, the itinerary includes areas adjacent to Palm Springs and Las Vegas, plus Death Valley and sites in Arizona. Participants return from San Diego. There are excellent photographic opportunities; 3 college credits are available.

Further Information
G. Franklin Mullen, Director of
    Academic Affairs
(301) 321-2032
    or
Dr. Marshall Stevenson, Professor of
    Geography
(301) 321-2963

University of Maryland
School of Architecture
College Park, Maryland 20742

Program
Educational travel programs emphasizing architecture, summer. Recent examples include hands-on preservation and reconstruction work at Cape May, New Jersey; explorations in Sri Lanka; and European Studio and Seminar programs in Paris, Rome, and Denmark. Also archaeological digs.

Accommodations and Cost
Write for information.

Comment
All programs led by distinguished scholars, practitioners, and visiting

architectural critics. Trips are part of the School's Master of Architecture program, but others may participate.

Further Information
John A. Steffian, Dean
(301) 454-3427

> *The hostility between science and technology ... really can't be true.*
> *David Hilbert*

MASSACHUSETTS

Bridgewater State College
Department of Sociology and Anthropology
Bridgewater, Massachusetts 02324

Program
North River Archaeological Project, annual, 2–6 weeks, summer.

Accommodations
Write for information.

Cost
$47 per credit hour.

Comment
The North River Archaeological Project, which began in 1983, is part of a series of such programs sponsored by the College. The project's goals are the reconstruction of cultural history and processes of change beginning with the Paleo-Indians of 13,000 years ago through the years of European settlement and American development to 1900. High school seniors through graduate students may earn 2 to 6

college credits while developing field excavation and laboratory processing skills working with artifacts taken from the North River drainage area in eastern Massachusetts.

Further Information
For program information:
Dr. Curtiss Hoffman
(617) 697-1262
For registration:
Programs of Graduate and Continuing Education
(617) 697-1262

Earthwatch
10 Juniper Road
Box 127N
Belmont, Massachusetts 02178

Program
Research expeditions conducting scientific field study, worldwide, 2–4 weeks. Participants are nonspecialist volunteers. Recent expeditions: archaeology in Majorca, Bermuda, and Wisconsin; whale research in Hawaii and California; bird studies in Panama, Arizona, and France. Numerous other projects throughout the year.

Accommodations
Vary with expedition.

Cost
Range: $600–$2000. Example: Prehistoric Man of Majorca, 2 weeks, $1345, including meals, accommodations, and equipment; transportation to site is additional. NOTE: Costs are considered contributions to the project and are tax deductible.

Comment
Earthwatch is a nonprofit clearinghouse, providing funding and

volunteer assistance for scholars doing field research in sixteen states and thirty-six countries. In 1971, it began sponsoring expeditions to support these research projects. Expeditions feature studies of diverse cultures, wildlife, ecosystems, and archaeology. Each is led by a prominent scholar. There are six to fifteen persons per group. Membership in Earthwatch is a prerequisite.

Further Information
Mary Blue Magruder
Director of Communications
(617) 489-3030

Massachusetts Archaeological Society
c/o Bronson Museum
8 North Main Street
Attleboro, Massachusetts 02703

Programs
Meetings and fieldwork through affiliated chapters. Write address above for newsletter giving addresses of various chapter headquarters, names of directors, meetings, and work in progress.

In addition, the Massachusetts Archaeological Society conducts annual and semiannual meetings at Clark University Academic Center, Worcester, Massachusetts.

Further Information
Tom Lux, Director
(617) 222-5470

*Everything which we think
has already happened.*
                    Unknown

MISSOURI

Missouri Botanical Garden
P.O. Box 299
St. Louis, Missouri 63066-0299

Programs
Trips to England and South America emphasizing botanical and horticultural aspects.
(1) The Gardens and Stately Homes of England, 16 days, spring.
(2) Costa Rica National Parks, 2 weeks, spring.

Accommodations
(1) Deluxe hotels.
(2) Moderate (including 2 nights in bunkroom).

Cost
(1) $4245, includes airfare from St. Louis and $250 tax-deductible donation to Missouri Botanical Garden.
(2) $2900, includes airfare from St. Louis and $200 tax-deductible membership.

Comment
The Missouri Botanical Garden was founded in 1958.
(1) Led by Alan Godlewski, chairman of horticulture, Missouri Botanical Garden; trip also features visits to elegant homes.
(2) Led by Dr. Tom Croat of museum staff and Dave Whitacre, a zoologist and professional naturalist. It is designed for nature enthusiasts willing to do some leisurely hiking. Must also have the ability to withstand hot temperatures and humid conditions in lowlands, as well as elevations as high as 10,000 feet. Binoculars are essential.

Further Information
Dana Hines, Membership Coordinator
(314) 577-5108

> *... No empire, no sect, no star seems to have exerted greater power and influence in human affairs than these mechanical discoveries.*
> *Francis Bacon*

NEW YORK

Archaeological Tours
30 East 42nd Street
Suite 1202
New York, New York 10017

Programs
Tours to various archaeological sites around the world including Asia, the Mediterranean, and Peru. Some recent trips include:
(1) Thailand and Burma, 23 days.
(2) Indonesia, 22 days.

Accommodations
Write for information.

Children
Children are generally not permitted. Special requests are handled on an individual basis.

Cost
(1) $3635, including transportation.
(2) $4100, including transportation.

Comment
Led by noted scholars, the tours visit the most important historical and archaeological sites in each country. Average group size is twenty to thirty.

Further Information
(212) 986-3054

Hebrew Union College
Jewish Institute of Religion
One West Fourth Street
New York, New York 10012

Program
Archaeological excavations at Tel Dan, Israel. Recent sessions were 6 weeks, mid-June to late July.

Accommodations
Youth hostels.

Cost
$1950, includes group travel, registration, tuition, room, and board; $950 base program cost excluding travel. Weekend expenses extra.

Comment
Fieldwork for volunteers, age 18 and up, with an interest in anthropology, ancient history, Near Eastern or biblical studies. Excavations are directed by Dr. Avraham Biran. Academic credit available.

Further Information
Dr. Paul M. Steinberg
(212) 674-5300

Hebrew University of
* Jerusalem*
Rothberg School for Overseas
* Subjects*
11 East 69th Street
New York, New York 10021

Programs
(1) Excavating Jerusalem, 3 weeks, July; 1-week class precedes 2-week dig.
(2) Other short courses, varied topics. (See Chapter 1.)

Accommodations
Hebrew University dormitories; transportation to excavation site provided.

Cost
$295, tuition; $140, housing.

Comment
Formal classroom instruction precedes excavating on archaeological site in the Jerusalem area. Dig is under the supervision of the Israel Department of Antiquities and Museums and involves strenuous work 6–7 hours per day. Credit available.

Further Information
(212) 472-2288

New York Botanical Gardens
200th Street and Kazamiroff
*   Boulevard*
Bronx, New York 10458

Programs
Foreign trips, air and sea, with horticultural emphasis as per examples:
(1) Island World of Britain, 17 days, June; air and cruise by chartered ship.
(2) Galapagos Islands, air and sea, 10 days to 2 weeks, February.
(3) The Amazon, air and sea, 10 days to 2 weeks, July or October.

Accommodations
Varied shipboard and first-class hotels.

Cost
(1) Write for information.
(2) $2000–$3500, depending on shipboard reservation.
(3) $2000–$3500, depending on shipboard reservation.
Portion of fees for (2) and (3) may be considered tax-deductible contribution to Botanical Gardens.

Comment
Founded in 1901, the New York Botanical Gardens is devoted to the scientific study of plants and the education of the public. Trips are led by professional botanists and staff instructors and focus on plant identification and the role of plants in unique habitats.

Further Information
Carol Gracie
(212) 220-8736

New York Zoological Society
Travel Department
185th Street and Southern
*   Boulevard*
Bronx, New York 10460

Program
Trips to the eastern United States and other areas worldwide. Duration of these adventures, which focus on natural history, ranges from 1 day to 4 weeks, throughout the year. U.S. sites include Cape Cod for whale watching, Brigantine National Wildlife Refuge, and the Society's Wildlife Survival Center on St. Catherine's Island, Georgia. More distant expeditions include special participatory conservation trips to Argentina and Costa Rica. Other destinations are Papua New Guinea, Peru, Kenya and Tanzania, Australia, and China.

Accommodations
As appropriate to type of trip, including first-class hotels when available, yachts, tents, field stations.

Children
Children 12 or older are welcome, but those under 18 must be accompanied by an adult.

Cost
Wide ranges, from $60 for a 1-day excursion to $6500 for an expedition to Papua New Guinea, including airfare and all expenses; tours available to groups of ten to forty people.

Membership in the Society is required. Write for details.

Comment
The Zoological Society, founded in 1890, is an educational, cultural, and research organization that supports numerous scientific and conservation projects in addition to administering the Bronz Zoo and New York Aquarium. Trips are led by professional scientists and naturalists and are oriented toward nature study (bird watching, animal-plant ecology, etc.). They also offer firsthand contact with rare and endangered species in their natural habitats.

Further Information
Travel Department
(212) 220-5085

State University of New York at Binghamton
Archaeological Field School
Department of Anthropology
Binghamton, New York 13901

Program
Field training in archaeology and cultural resource management, 8 weeks, July and August. Field investigations vary from year to year but are generally in nearby areas of New York State.

Accommodations
Participants provide their own accommodations.

Cost
Tuition: $450 (New York State resident); $1070 (nonresident of New York State). Books and miscellaneous fees, extra.

Comment
This program is designed for extensive training in field archaeological techniques and offers experience in cultural resource management. Initial classroom instruction at the site is followed by extensive fieldwork, controlled mapping and excavation, and the recovery and recording of raw archaeological data. The program is limited to fifteen participants and is led by university professors. Class is in session Monday through Friday from 8 a.m. to 5:30 p.m. Preference is given to early applicants; 10 college credits can be earned.

Further Information
Dr. Vincai Steponaitis
(607) 777-2738

Wisdom may be secured painlessly if we will only turn to the past.
Unknown

OHIO

Cincinnati Zoo
3400 Vine Street
Cincinnati, Ohio 45220

Program
One or two tours abroad annually, with emphasis on animal life. Recent examples: Indonesia, 4 weeks, including 15-day cruise; shikar in India, a 17-day game viewing tour to many of the major game parks, visiting major cities also (6-day extension, optional, for those wishing to visit game parks in the south of India).

Accommodations
Write for information.

Cost
Varies with tour. Examples above:
Indonesia, $6585 (minimum),
including airfare, land travel, and
cruise; India, $4800 (double
occupancy), round trip from
Cincinnati.

Comment
Since the early 1960s, the Cincinnati
Zoo has been offering tours to areas of
the world that are rich in animal life.
Participants are escorted by the zoo
director or curator general; there are
ten to thirty persons per trip. Cost
includes a required tax-deductible
contribution to the zoo.

Further Information
Lee F. Mando
Provident Travel
1000 Provident Tower
One East Fourth Street
Cincinnati, Ohio 45202
(513) 621-4900

Cuyahoga Community College,
Western Campus
Archaeological Field School
11000 Pleasant Valley Road
Parma, Ohio 44130

Program
Archaeological Field School at
prehistoric Indian site (1050–1650
A.D.); 8-hour days, 5 days a week; late
June to late July.

Accommodations
Dormitories at nearby college.

Cost
Tuition: $126–$168, Ohio residents;
$336, nonresidents. Dormitory: $70 per
week.

Cultural Opportunities
Summer plays and concerts in the
Cleveland area, Cleveland Orchestra,

Cleveland Museum of Art, Cleveland
Museum of Natural History.

Comment
Proper methods of archaeological
fieldwork are emphasized. Average
size of group is ten; minimum age 16.
Six quarter credits available from
Cuyahoga Community College.

Further Information
Daniel A. Grossman
Department of Behavioral Sciences
(216) 845-4000, ext. 5960

OREGON

Northwest Christian College
Lachish Excavation
828 East 11th Street
Eugene, Oregon 97401

Program
Archaeological excavation at the
biblical site of Lachish, Israel; 8 weeks;
summer. Courses in field and biblical
archaeology. Daily digging from 6 a.m.
to 2 p.m.; balance of day cleaning and
cataloging. Scheduled lectures and
slide shows.

Accommodations
Kibbutz Gat.

Children
Minimum age is 18.

Cost
Tuition: $70 per credit hour; room and
board: $120 per week.

Comment
Excavation at Lachish started in 1973.
Since then the site has become one of
the largest, most fully documented
archaeological sites of ancient Israel
and Canaan. The program is conducted

jointly by the Institute of Archaeology, Tel-Aviv University, and the Israel Exploration Society. Average size of group is 140. Minimum stay for credit students is 4 weeks, 2 weeks for noncredit students. Up to 6 hours of credit, graduate or undergraduate, available.

Further Information
Dr. Song Nai Rhee, U.S. Project
   Coordinator
(503) 343-1641

> *One man with courage makes a majority.*
> *Andrew Jackson*

PENNSYLVANIA

West Chester University of Pennsylvania
West Chester, Pennsylvania 19380

Program
Archaeological research and field school at Printzhoff site (Swedish-American settlement, 1643–55 A.D.) in Essington, Pennsylvania; 2 weeks; late July.

Accommodations
On-campus housing for students; motel at site for others.

Cost
$225, tuition for University students. $150–$250, tuition for volunteers (see Comment).

Comment
Site is near Philadelphia airport. Twenty-eight students work and study

with six university faculty members, earning up to 9 credits in anthropology. Through the American Swedish Historical Society, volunteers may participate for $150–$250.

Further Information
Marshall J. Beckler
Anthropology
(215) 436-2884

SOUTH DAKOTA

Black Hills Natural Sciences
   Field Station
South Dakota School of Mines
   and Technology
Rapid City, South Dakota 57701

Program
Courses in various natural sciences, 1–5 weeks, summer. Among subjects are biology, archaeology, geology, and paleontology.

Accommodations
Lodges, dormitory rooms, or tents (bring own gear), depending upon course.

Cost
Tuition: $50–$60 per semester, undergraduate and graduate; laboratory and travel fees extra.

Recreation
Backpacking, mountain climbing, swimming, canoeing.

Cultural Opportunities
Libraries, Museum of Geology, Mount Rushmore, and Badlands nearby; plays and concerts; seminar lectures by faculty and visiting scientists.

Comment
The Black Hills Natural Sciences Field Station was established in 1970.

Located on the campus of the School of Mines and Technology, its summer program attracts between 100 and 150 students annually with an enrollment of 25 to 30 people per course. These courses are offered in cooperation with colleges in the area from which the faculty is drawn. The environment and climate of the Black Hills afford unique opportunities for the observation of natural habitats and of man's interaction with them. Most courses require 8 hours of attendance per day to fulfill requirements. College credit is available.

Further Information
Dr. James E. Martin, Director
(605) 394-2494

TEXAS

University of Texas at Austin
Department of Oriental and
*   African Languages and*
*   Literature*
2601 University Avenue
Austin, Texas 78712

Program
Research and field school at Tel Yin'am, Israel; mid-July to late August. Excavations cover Bronze and Iron ages; Persian, Roman, and Byzantine occupations.

Accommodations
Tents.

Cost
Tuition: $177–$207 for 3–6 credits (residents of Texas); $437–$827 for 3–6 credits (nonresidents). Room and board: $110 per week. Airfare not included.

Comment
A limited number of volunteers are needed for a minimum stay of 2 weeks. Must be 18 years old. Instruction and training provided. Field school for limited number of college students; college credit is available.

Further Information
Dr. Harold Liebowitz
(512) 471-1365

Witte Museum of History and
*   Natural History*
P.O. Box 2601
San Antonio, Texas 78299

Programs
(1) Archaeology of the Yucatán, 7 days, January.
(2) Marine Biology for Scuba Divers, Monterey, California; 5 days; May.
(3) Texas Independence Trail, 3 days, June.

Accommodations
Sometimes simple, but always of high quality.

Children
(1) and (2) Adults only.
(3) Children over 12, accompanied by an adult.

Cost
(1) $930, includes transportation, hotel, fees, and breakfast.
(2) $884, includes transportation, equipment, hotel, and fees.
(3) $175, includes transportation, hotels, and fees.

Comment
The focus of the Witte Travel Program is in-depth interpretation of the nature, archaeology, and history of Texas, Latin America, and beyond. Education is its primary goal. Trips are developed and led by museum curators

and guest lecturers who are experts in their fields. Group sizes average ten on longer trips; twenty to thirty-five on Texas trip.

Further Information
Sara Kerr
Associate Curator, Natural Sciences
(512) 226-5544, ext. 248

UTAH

College of Eastern Utah,
San Juan Campus
White Mesa Institute
639 West 100 South (50-1)
Glading, Utah 84511

Program
Wide variety of 1-week public participation field research programs on archaeology, archaeoastronomy, ethnography, botany, zoology, geology, and history. All programs take place in the Four Corners region of the American Southwest, primarily in southeastern Utah and southwestern Colorado.

Accommodations
Variable, depending on specific program. Range from comfortable indoor accommodations to temporary field camps. Some programs involve backpacking. Write for specific details.

Cost
Variable, depending on program. Costs generally range from $150 to $500 per person. Write for specific details.

Comment
The White Mesa Institute developed out of a commitment on the part of the College of Eastern Utah's San Juan Campus and the local community to provide opportunities for lay citizen involvement in research and study of the region's unique but threatened resources. All programs emphasize the concept of the outdoors as a vast but fragile living museum and an unbounded laboratory/classroom. Arrangement can be made for academic credit through the College of Eastern Utah for most programs. Instructors are expert consultants who design the program, its research focus, its structure, etc.

Programs are kept small (generally five to twenty persons), and informal. Free brochures providing program information are available on request.

Further Information
Nancy Bradford, Secretary-Treasurer
(801) 678-2201
Fred Blackburn, Director of
  Interpretive Programs
(801) 678-2201
Winston Hurst
(801) 678-3305 (evenings)

> *We can take no comfort in the belief that what appears to be the whole truth will be the whole truth tomorrow.*
> *Barnaby Keeney*

WASHINGTON

Society Expeditions
723 Broadway East
Seattle, Washington 98102

Programs
(1) In-depth archaeological and cultural trips. Examples:

(A) Burma/Thailand, 18 days, November and winter; includes stays at Bangkok and Rangoon, with lectures en route. (November departures include elephant roundup).

(B) Tunisia, 16 days, spring; highlighting Roman ruins and Phoenician civilization.

(C) Turkey via Orient Express, 14 days, spring and fall; an archaeological expedition exploring ruins of Troy and other landmarks.

(2) Cruises, various destinations.

(A) Antarctica, 3 weeks, winter; *Society Explorer* and *World Discoverer* trips.

(B) New Zealand, Great Barrier Reef, Bali, and Milford Sound special cruises, 18–37 days, winter; aboard *World Discoverer.*

Accommodations
(1) Comfortable hotels.
(2) Aboard luxury cruise ships *World Discoverer* and *Society Explorer.*

Cost
(1) (A) $3490, land arrangements only.
    (B) $2390, land arrangements only.
    (C) $2390, land arrangements only.
(2) (A) $4750–$7920, depending on cabin.
    (B) $3990–$9790, depending on cabin.

Comment
Society Expeditions was established in 1974. It is a travel organization whose programs focus on the conservation and preservation of archaeological monuments. Tour leaders are members of the society staff. Lecturers and escorts are ornithologists, botanists, anthropologists, historians, explorers, adventurers, or others with special knowledge of areas visited and topics to be emphasized. Group size averages 20 people for land expeditions, with a maximum of 140 people on the cruises.

Further Information
(800) 426-7794

. . . Reasoning consists in finding arguments for going on believing as we already do.
            J. H. Robinson

WISCONSIN

University of Wisconsin System
Pigeon Lake Field Station
315 North Hall
UW–River Falls
River Falls, Wisconsin 54022

Programs
(1) Interim session, 1- to 3-week classes, May–June. Recent examples: Plant Taxonomy, Herpetology, Wreck Diving, Advanced Outdoor Pursuits.
(2) Recreation classes, 3 days to 2 weeks, June–August. Recent examples: Canoe Technique, Camp Leadership, Sports Liability, Basketball Theory.
(3) Art classes, 1 week, June–July. Recent examples: Landscape in Pigment and Pencil, Primitive Claywork and Firing, Blacksmithing.
(4) Science classes, 2 days to 3 weeks, June–August. Recent examples: Entomology, Aquatic Biology.

Accommodations
Cabins accommodating eight students each; participants with families make own arrangements in nearby villages or campgrounds.

Cost
Tuition: $45 per undergraduate semester credit and $81 per graduate semester credit for Wisconsin residents; $155 per undergraduate semester credit and $253 per graduate semester credit, for nonresidents. Room and board: $83.50 per week.

Recreation
Swimming, volleyball, softball, basketball, fishing, canoeing, and more.

Comment
Pigeon Lake Field Station is situated in Bayfield County, Wisconsin, thirty miles southeast of Superior, Wisconsin, and has been operated as a combined instructional research facility since 1960. The station serves as a center for study, teaching, and research in a variety of fields, where learning is augmented by utilizing a natural wilderness environment. Emphasis is placed on knowledge of and familiarity with local Wisconsin flora and fauna. Well-equipped laboratories provide instructional facilities when courses are not in the field.

Further Information
Don C. Aabel
(715) 425-3333

> *[In] every good laboratory [there] is an unsociable, wrong-headed fellow working on unprofitable lines, and in his hands lies the hope of discovery.*
> *Lord Rutherford*

CANADA

University of British Columbia Center for Continuing Education
5997 Iona Drive
Vancouver, British Columbia V6T 2A4
Canada

Programs
(1) Exploring Johnstone Strait, 4 days, August. Study of marine mammals and inhabitants of northeast coast of Vancouver Island.
(2) Queen Charlotte Islands Field Study Cruise, 1 week, June.

Accommodations
(1) Shared accommodations in guest house; sleeping bag also required.
(2) Cruise ship MV *Edgewater Fortune.*

Cost (Canadian dollars)
(1) $495, includes $150 tax-deductible tuition portion; does not include miscellaneous transportation fees.
(2) $2150, includes $375 tax-deductible tuition portion.

Comment
(1) Part of trip by boat; participants require sleeping bags; also features lectures and slide shows. Led by Michael Bigg, marine mammalogist, and Peter McNair, anthropologist.
(2) Part of trip spent ashore visiting small islands, museum, etc. Limited enrollment. Led by botanist, anthropologist, and marine biologist.

Further Information
(604) 222-2181

4 THE GREAT OUTDOORS

Outward Bound

*L*earning vacations for the adventurous of all ages who enjoy the natural environment. Programs include backpacking, sailing, wilderness experiences, and related courses. Learn outdoor skills and survival techniques while discovering more about ecological systems and the wildlife they support.

> *Far away there in the sunshine are my highest aspirations. I may not reach them, but I can look up and see their beauty, believe in them and try to follow where they lead.*
>
> *Louisa May Alcott*

ALASKA

Kachemak Bay Wilderness Lodge and Chenik Wilderness Camp
Box 956
Homer, Alaska 99603

Programs
(1) Kachemak Bay Wilderness Lodge provides the base for hiking and boat expeditions throughout the summer; certified and licensed wilderness naturalist guides lead groups in observing marine mammals, birds, and flora.
(2) Chenik Camp is a remote camp especially noted for its proximity to the McNeil River Brown Bear Sanctuary; visitors can observe and photograph the bears in pristine surroundings.

Accommodations
The camps are located on either side of the entrance to Cook Inlet, Alaska; the lodge is one hundred air miles southwest of Anchorage; Chenik Camp is an additional one hundred miles.
(1) Guest bedroom in lodge, private cabins nearby. Shared baths; meals in lodge.
(2) Tent-cabins with outside bath; meals and activities in lodge.

Children
Children are welcome at the Kachemak Lodge; write for details.

Cost
(1) Rates per person: from $595 (for 3 days) to $1480 (for 6 days), including room and board, guide services, and transportation to lodge from Homer.
(2) Per person, $1500 for 5 days, including all above. A combined 10-day package for both locations is $2250.

Recreation
Fishing, canoeing, kayaking, hiking, climbing, photography.

Cultural Opportunities
Art Studio of Diana Tillion, Halibut Cove. Ms. Tillion paints with octopus ink.

Comment
Hosts are Mike and Diane McBride. He is a registered guide, naturalist, and former bush pilot, who has lived in Alaska for 20 years. She is a biologist and gourmet cook. The McBrides have entertained such well-known figures as actress Estelle Parsons and Prince Rainier of Monaco. Groups are limited to twelve.

Further Information
Mike or Diane McBride
(907) 235-8910
Mail is preferred.

ARIZONA

Desert Botanical Garden
1201 North Galvin Parkway
Phoenix, Arizona 85008

Programs
Field trips to desert, mesa, and mountain areas, monthly to changing

destinations, overnight to 4 days, spring and summer. Examples:
(1) Three-day hike into Tsegi Canyon to visit ancient Indian ruins and see forest with sage, wildflower, and cacti.
(2) Four-day adventure down the upper portion of the San Juan River.

Accommodations
The Garden provides participants with the use of a van and sleeping bags.

Cost
Example: $30 for overnight hike. Advance registration and payment of fees required; write for information.

Comment
Since its founding in 1935, the Garden's threefold purpose has been study, conservation, and education. Its field trips, led by staff members, are designed to serve these ends.

Further Information
Education Director
(602) 941-1225

> *These trees shall be my books.*
> *William Shakespeare*

Expeditions, Inc.
Route 4, Box 755
Flagstaff, Arizona 86001

Program
Rafting trips down the Colorado River through the Grand Canyon, 5–18 days, April to October. Kayaking trips and custom-designed expeditions also available.

Accommodations
Outdoor camping, meals provided.

Children
Children are permitted on all trips. No minimum age, but should have appropriate outdoor and water experience. Suggested minimum age is 16 for long trips.

Cost
$525–$1350 per person, including round-trip transportation from Flagstaff on most trips, meals, and sleeping bag. Discounts available.

Comment
Expeditions, Inc., is an authorized National Park Service concessioner in Grand Canyon National Park. Dick and Susan McCallum, the proprietors, conduct most trips personally. They are educators and experienced outdoor explorers who since 1969 have taken more than 3000 people of all ages through the canyon.

Groups range in size from fifteen to twenty-two. Safety, as well as adventure, is emphasized. All necessary gear other than personal items is furnished.

Further Information
Dick or Susan McCallum
(602) 774-8176 or 779-3769

CALIFORNIA

Baja's Frontier Tours
3683 Cactus View Drive
San Diego, California 92105

Programs
Natural history expeditions up to 21 days to Baja California, Mexico, including:
(1) Sea of Cortez, 8 days.
(2) Introduction to Baja, 8 days.

(3) Whale Watching Air Safari at San Ignacio, 8 days.

Accommodations
Vary from luxury hotels to camping with a basic 8-by-10-foot tent.

Children
No minimum age requirement.

Cost
(1) $1285.
(2) $985.
(3) $1485.

Recreation
Excellent fishing opportunities; fishing tackle available for use.

Comment
Founded in 1966, Baja's Frontier Tours cover the entire peninsula with personalized programs designed for between two and twenty people. All tours focus on the natural environment and feature whale watching along with the exploration of old missions and mines, islands, bays, and beaches. On some tours, transportation is by mule and small boat. Generally, there is one guide for every two to four participants. All tours emphasize photographic opportunities; a full range of professional services for photographers and filmmakers is available.

Further Information
Piet Van de Mark
(619) 262-2003

ECHO: The Wilderness Company, Inc.
6529 Telegraph Avenue
Oakland, California 94609

Program
White-water rafting trips in California, Idaho, and Oregon. Different trips emphasize bird

watching, paddling, extended camping, and white water. Trip lengths: California, 1–3 days; Oregon, 3–5 days; Idaho, 5–6 days; Grand Canyon, 13 days.

Accommodations
Camping.

Children
Minimum age is 7. A few trips are reserved for adults.

Cost
Some examples: Kern River California, 1 day, $80; Snake River/Birds of Prey Idaho, 5 days, $524; Grand Canyon, 13 days, $1200. Youth rates (ages 7–17) are lower. Group discounts available. Write for specific details.

Comment
ECHO, founded in 1971, has designed river trips for all ages and for individuals, families, and groups. Its trips feature exploration of remote areas, wildlife, and native cultures as well as training in river skills, safety procedures, and care and maintenance of equipment. It has over sixty licensed guides, and its equipment is Coast Guard approved. Average group size ranges from fifteen to twenty.

Further Information
Reservations Manager
(415) 652-1600

Mountain Travel
1398 Solano Avenue
Albany, California 94706

Program
Numerous wilderness tours in more than fifty countries—hikes, safaris, climbing, kayaking; year-round. Some examples: Backpacking on Mt. McKinley (Alaska), 14 days;

Australian Outback Camel Safari, 33 days; Touring in Norway, 11 days. Trips are graded from easy to extremely difficult.

Accommodations
Outdoor camping, huts, and cabins.

Cost
For above examples: McKinley, $1590; Outback, $2490; Norway, $1090, not including airfare or some meals.

Comment
Founded in 1967, Mountain Travel arranges tours to all parts of the world; it specializes in adventure tours to remote areas. The tours seek "discoveries which fall outside the normal scope of travel itineraries." Leaders of the tours are explorers and adventurers with strong outdoor credentials; native guides and porters are also used where appropriate. Average group size is ten.

Further Information
Pam Shandrick, Promotions Director
(415) 527-8100 or (800) 227-2384

Oceanic Society Expeditions
Fort Mason Center, Building E
San Francisco, California 94123

Program
Various learning adventures, focusing on wildlife and habitat exploration. Programs are worldwide throughout the year. Example: dolphin research in the Bahamas, 5 days, August.

Accommodations
Hotels, cabins, tent camps, sailboats, and motor yachts.

Cost
Example: Dolphins in the Bahamas, $595. Write for information.

Comment
Established in 1969 as the research and expedition arm of the Oceanic Society, Oceanic Society Expeditions provides unregimented tours for adventurous people of all ages and backgrounds. They are led by experts in marine biology, ecology, and natural history. Group sizes range from four to thirty.

Further Information
Expeditions Manager
(415) 441-1106

Pacific Exploration Company
Box 3042
Santa Barbara, California 93130

Program
Annual nature hiking tour of New Zealand, featuring the country's national parks; 23 days, November–March. Also, year-round independent tour programs to the countries of the South Pacific.

Accommodations
Range from tent camping to first-class hotels.

Cost
New Zealand Walkabout, $1790 for land arrangements. Round-trip airfare from Los Angeles, $1190–$1340 (depending on season).

Comment
Since 1977, Pacific Exploration has arranged tours to the South Pacific for small groups and individuals on an escorted and independent basis. It specializes in arrangements emphasizing nature, hiking, safari, and outdoor activities in New Zealand and Australia with extensions available to Tahiti, Fuji, Rarotonga, and Papua New Guinea. Experienced specialists accompany group tour

programs, assisted by local guides. College credit can be arranged through university extension programs.

Further Information
Ronald Richardson, Director
(805) 687-7282

Pacific Sea Fari Tours
Agent for H&M Landing
2803 Emerson Street
San Diego, California 92106

Programs
(1) Natural history expeditions to Baja California, Mexico's whale-breeding lagoons (San Ignacio and Scammons), winter and spring home for the California gray whale; 9–11 days; winter and spring.
(2) Seagoing excursions exploring the Baja offshore islands, home to elephant seals, sea lions, and harbor seals; 5 days; early winter.

Accommodations
Private and semiprivate cabins aboard two diesel boats, *Tradition* (78 feet) and *Spirit of Adventure* (88 feet).

Cost
$610–$1395 per person, complete.

Comment
H&M Landing has been in business since 1935. Pacific Sea Fari Tours are leisurely and average twenty-four to thirty participants. All groups are accompanied by two or more professional naturalists. Informal briefings and slide lectures prepare participants for each day's activities; "whale petting" is a highlight of many tours. Pacific Sea Fari has been instrumental in working with the Mexican government to keep the whale-mating and -calving lagoons of Baja California free from unregulated traffic.

Further Information
Dale Sydenstricker, Natural History
  Coordinator
(619) 226-8224

> *Nature and books belong to the eyes that see them.*
> *Ralph Waldo Emerson*

Sierra Club
730 Polk Street
San Francisco, California 94109

Program
Approximately 300 outings to every region of the United States, Canada, Mexico, and other countries worldwide; generally 1–2 weeks; year-round. Base camp of operations is common to all trips, which encompass fishing, photography, biking, study, nature walks and hikes, skiing, rafting, etc. Outings are described in detail in catalog, including information on physical stamina and experience required.

Accommodations
As appropriate to trip; participants must bring their own sleeping bags.

Cost
Write for information.

Comment
Founded in 1892 by John Muir, the Sierra Club has grown to become a nationwide organization of over 350,000 members in fifty-seven chapters. All trips are led by naturalists, photographers, and others who know the outdoors and are skilled campers. Trips emphasize conservation and protection of the environment. Participants are of all ages; groups range in size, being purposely kept

small to minimize destructive impact on land. Also featured are special service trips at minimum fees for those wishing to participate in clean-up and restoration projects and trail maintenance.

Further Information
Sierra Club Outing Department
(415) 776-2211

Yosemite Institute
Box 487
Yosemite National Park,
California 95389

Programs
(1) Sierran Summer I, ecology backpacking trip for high school students through mountainous regions of Yosemite National Park; 5 days; June–August. Emphasis on natural history, geology, astronomy, and orienteering.
(2) Sierran Summer II, program of daily hikes and classes for organized high school–aged groups at Crane Flay, Yosemite National Park; 5 days; June–August. Hikes and classes emphasize natural history, geology, and astronomy.

Accommodations
(1) Camping.
(2) Dormitories.

Cost
(1) $169 per week, all inclusive.
(2) $154 per week, all inclusive.

Recreation
Time allowed for swimming, fishing, photography.

Cultural Opportunities
Pioneer and Indian cultural museums.

Comment
(1) Trip covers approximately five miles daily; participants should be able

to carry twenty-five to sixty pounds. Usually fourteen people per trip.
(2) Average twelve people per class. The programs of Yosemite Institute, incorporated in 1971, are geared toward increased awareness and improved understanding of the environment. The highly qualified staff communicates scientific and environmental concepts effectively. Some college credit and adult courses available.

Further Information
Vincent P. Kehoe, Vice President
(209) 372-4441

COLORADO

American Wilderness
Experience, Inc.
P.O. Box 1486
Boulder, Colorado 80306

Program
Numerous outdoor trips, 3–6 days, year-round. Schedule includes backpacking, horsepacking, canoeing, sailing, and white-water rafting trips. Custom outings for groups or individuals also available. Destinations include most of the western United States, Minnesota, and Hawaii.

Accommodations
Usually primitive camping.

Children
Minimum age is 8 (10 for rafting); those under 16 must be accompanied by an adult.

Cost
Depends on program. Examples: Colorado backpacking trip, 6 days, $350; horsepacking trips, $70–$95 per day.

Comment
Since 1971, American Wilderness Experience has involved more than 2500 people in its numerous programs. Trip leaders have at least 15 years' experience in the back country. Most programs include outdoor lectures and instruction in survival, shelters, plant and animal identification, and more. No previous experience is needed, but participants should be in good physical condition.

Further Information
Dave Wiggins, President
(303) 444-2632

CONNECTICUT

Audubon Ecology Workshop in Connecticut
Audubon Center in Greenwich
613 Riversville Road
Greenwich, Connecticut 06830

Program
Several annual sessions for adults, 1 week, June–August. Introductory Field Ecology and Field Ecology for Educators offer in-depth study of natural history; workshops in citizen activism.

Accommodations
Modern lodge (485-acre Greenwich Center, thirty-five miles north of New York City), twin-bedded rooms with private baths.

Cost
$385 per session. Write for details; college credit additional.

Cultural Opportunities
Library, auditorium.

Comment
The Connecticut Workshop is one of four operated by the National Audubon

Society, a conservation organization. The program includes hikes, lectures, optional classes, and a field trip to Long Island Sound. Instructors are professional naturalists, educators, and research biologists. College credit is available from Fairfield University.

Further Information
Registrar, Northeast Camp/Workshops
(203) 869-2017

> *One could do worse than be a swinger of birches.*
> *Robert Frost*

National Audubon Society Expedition Institute
Northeast Audubon Center
Sharon, Connecticut 06069

Program
Expeditions of varying duration to unique wilderness areas throughout North America, summer. All expeditions include outdoor living, travel, and investigation of a variety of natural and social environments. Recent examples: Pacific Northwest Expedition, 28 days; New England Expedition, 21 days; Northwest Mountain Semester, June–August.

Accommodations
Outdoor camping; travel by van, canoe, foot, etc.

Cost
For the examples above: Pacific Northwest, $850; New England, $650; Northwest Mountain, $3390. Financial aid is available for some programs. Write for details.

Comment
Audubon summer expeditions raise awareness of global and environmental

concerns, studying people and things in their natural environment. The varied itineraries expose participants to aspects of ecology, outdoor skills, geology, astronomy, history, and group dynamics. Each group of eight to ten is led by two experienced leaders trained by the institute. Many leaders have master's degrees in environmental education. Some programs are offered in cooperation with other institutions; all offer college and/or high school credit.

Further Information
Sheryl Crockett, Summer Coordinator
(203) 364-0522

Outward Bound
384 Field Point Road
Greenwich, Connecticut 06830

Program
Wilderness and outdoor programs for people of all ages. Standard programs, 21–30 days, and short programs, 4–15 days, in the United States and Canada, all seasons. Subjects include skiing, dogsledding, mountaineering, backpacking, sailing, rafting, canoeing, cycling, and more. In addition, there are semester-long programs; several programs are designed for special groups, e.g., over age 30 or under age 16.

Accommodations
Usually camping in the wilderness but varies with program; restrictions on pets.

Cost
$1125 average for standard 21-day course, includes everything but transportation to and from site and personal clothing. Write for specific program costs.

Comment
Outward Bound was organized in the United States in 1962. Its program develops self-reliance, confidence, and a spirit of cooperation. Each program has five phases: physical and skills training; extended journey; individual reflection; organizing another expedition; and group discussion and evaluation. Instructors are trained to work with people in stressful situations. Average number per course is eight to twelve. Credit available through many high schools and colleges.

Further Information
Director, Public Relations
(800) 243-8520 or (203) 661-0797

DISTRICT OF COLUMBIA

National Wildlife Federation
Conservation Summits
1412 Sixteenth Street, N.W.
Washington, D.C. 20036

Program
Conservation Summits: Blue Ridge Summit, Black Mountain, North Carolina, late June; Rocky Mountain Summit, Estes Park, Colorado, early June; Coastal Summit, Brunswick, Maine, early August. Workshops focus on natural history and conservation and discuss more than twenty-five topics, including plant identification, folk history, backpacking, and wildlife ecology.

Accommodations
Vary with location: motel-style rooms, dormitory rooms, campsites. No pets allowed, except for Rocky Mountain, where they must be leashed.

Children
Ranger Rick Youth Program (ages 5–12); Teen Adventure Program (ages 13–17); children under 16 must be accompanied by an adult.

Cost
Tuition: $170 adult, $90 teen, $90 youth; lodging and meals: $335–$600 per couple. Special arrangements for children and single adults. Membership: $12.

Recreation
Swimming, tennis, hiking, crafts, and many more activities.

Comment
Established in 1936, the National Wildlife Federation sponsors these annual workshop/vacations as part of its education program in conservation. They are designed for entire families. Average group size is 550. Federation membership required for participation. College credit is available for University of Bridgeport (Connecticut) and Colorado State University.

Further Information
John Stone
Senior Director, Conservation Education
(703) 790-4363

Knowledge is one.
Halford John Mackinder

GEORGIA

Wilderness Southeast, Inc.
711-LV Sandtown Road
Savannah, Georgia 31410

Program
Natural adventure courses, usually 3–7 days, year-round. Wilderness explorations provoke new understanding of nature and oneself. Leaders are experts in biology, ecology, and human and geologic history of the destinations. Expeditions include Okefenokee Swamp, Bahamas–Dry Tortugas Snorkeling and Sailing, Great Smoky Mountains, and more.

Accommodations
Vary with outing; tent camping, sailboat bunks, etc.

Children
Minimum age varies with difficulty of expedition, but unaccompanied children must be at least 15. Some regular programs appropriate for families. Also two summer camp programs: Coastal Experience (ages 11–14) and Mountain Trek (ages 13–17).

Cost
Varies with course. Some examples: Okefenokee/Suwannee River Canoeing, 6 days, $315; Cumberland Island Day Hiking, 4 days, $170; Snorkeling and Sailing, 7 days, $570.

Comment
Established in 1973, Wilderness Southeast is a nonprofit school of the outdoors with a unique emphasis and style. Each course goes out as a completely outfitted learning expedition into one of the Southeast's wild areas. Wilderness Southeast provides two experienced leader/naturalist interpreters, tents, food, safety equipment, and all necessary arrangements. No experience is needed—just good general health and a sense of adventure. Maximum number of participants is sixteen, usually 25–70 years of age.

Further Information
Richard Murlless, Director
(912) 897-5108

IDAHO

University of Idaho
Idaho Educational Adventures
Moscow, Idaho 83843

Program
Weekly rafting trips throughout the summer on the Salmon River in Idaho and the Grande Ronde River in Oregon, 5 days; feature natural history and/or instruction in river-running skills.

Accommodations
Motels prior to trip; camping on the river.

Children
Minimum age is 10.

Cost
$424, includes all river and camping equipment, transportation from Moscow, and meals (including pre-trip banquet).

Comment
The trips offer an exciting white-water experience and the opportunity to explore ancient Indian grounds, abandoned homesteads, and miners' diggings. The geology of the river canyons is particularly interesting. Trip leaders are university faculty and staff; the director has led groups for over 10 years. Average group size is fourteen. Children 10 and over are permitted.

Further Information
Director, Outdoor Program

> *The better part of every man's education is that which he gives himself.*
> **J. R. Lowell**

> *It is one of the most beautiful compensations of this life that no man can sincerely try to help another without helping himself.*
> **Ralph Waldo Emerson**

MAINE

Audubon Ecology Camp in
* Maine*
Keene Neck Road
Medomak, Maine 04551

Programs
(1) Ecology Camp, four 2-week sessions, June–August; daily field classes for adults in island, pond, forest, and estuary ecology.
(2) Youth Ecology Camp, one 12-day session, June; geology, biology, energy, flora, and fauna of the Maine coast for ages 10–14.
(3) Field ornithology in Maine for beginning or experienced birders, two 1-week sessions, August–September; emphasis on field identification and biology; peak time for migrations.

Accommodations
Wood-frame dormitory; singles share rooms, couples have private rooms. Shared baths; meals served in restored nineteenth-century farmhouse.

Cost
(1) $625.
(2) $525.
(3) $385.
Write for details.

Recreation
Swimming, hiking, boat trips, cultural library.

Comment

The Maine camp was established in 1936 at the 333-acre Todd Wildlife Sanctuary on Hog Island at the head of Muscargus Bay, sixty miles northeast of Portland. It was the first of four camps now operated by the National Audubon Society, a conservation organization founded in 1905. The program goes beyond observation to explore habitats and ecological niches of the many animals nearby. Classes, lectures, and field trips round out the educational experience. College credit available from the University of Maine.

Further Information

Registrar, Northeast Camps/
 Workshops
Audubon Center in Greenwich
613 Riversville Road
Greenwich, Connecticut 06830
(203) 869-2017

Chewonki Foundation, Inc. RFD #3 Wiscasset, Maine 04578

Programs

(1) One-day teacher workshops on various subjects. Recent examples: Winter Ecology workshop in February; Spring Natural History workshop in April; Trip Leaders workshop in May.
(2) Natural History of the Maine Coast, workshop for families, adults, and educators; one week; August.
(3) Family Wilderness Trips: canoeing on the Allagash Wilderness Waterway, canoeing on the St. Croix River, sea-kayaking and sailing on the Maine coast, hiking Maine's Mount Katahdin; 7–10 days; mid- to late August.
(4) Chewonki Wilderness Trips, summer-long; write for information on dates and locations.

Accommodations

(1) and (2) Simple cabins.
(3) and (4) Tents.

Cost

(1) $10 per person, all inclusive (discounts available for teams of teachers from the same school system).
(2) $285, all inclusive (adults); $200 (children under 12).
(3) $350–$550, depending on duration and destination of trip.
(4) $1150–$2000.

Recreation

(1) and (2) Waterfront, boats, kayaks, and canoes; tennis courts.

Cultural Opportunities

(1) and (2) Concerts, plays, museums in nearby communities of Wiscasset, Bath, and Brunswick.

Comment

Established in 1963, the Chewonki Foundation is an educational corporation promoting personal growth, community awareness, and sensitivity to the natural world.
(1) The workshops are designed to increase teacher awareness of the subjects treated and are kept small to encourage the development of a close-knit community where the sharing of ideas, techniques, knowledge, and experience becomes the heart of the program.
(2) Program opens with field trips and evening lectures. Emphasis is on field trips relating to subjects treated on a day-to-day basis. A maximum of 3 Maine recertification credits for educators are obtainable.
(3) Each group is small (about ten) with two Chewonki leaders. Responsibility and work are shared, so that everyone can learn woodcraft and camping skills. Participants should be good swimmers. No previous hiking or canoeing experience is necessary.

Participants bring their own personal equipment (sleeping bag, pack, etc); Chewonki provides all general camping gear.
(4) Trips offer opportunity to deal with the wilderness and are designed to increase awareness of the natural environment. Some days are given over to instruction and preparation prior to each trip.

Further Information
Tim Ellis, Executive Director
(207) 882-7323

*I'm a great believer in luck,
and I find the harder I work
the more I have of it.*
Thomas Jefferson

MARYLAND

Annapolis Sailing School
601 Sixth Street
Annapolis, Maryland 21403

Program
Sailing courses for all levels, aptitudes, and ambitions in the following categories: basic, cruising, racing, and advanced auxiliary. Sessions vary from 1 weekend to 10 days, seasonally or year-round, depending on location.

Accommodations
For cruising courses, tuition includes on-board accommodations. Certain vacation packages combine sailing instruction with hotel accommodations.

Cost
$125–$225, beginners courses; $250–$1245, cruising courses, many including on-board living expenses.

Comment
The Annapolis Sailing School, founded in 1959, is the first institution of its kind. Highly trained instructors lead courses using specially designed boats and materials, as well as proven teaching methods in the art and sport of sailing. The headquarters of the school is in Annapolis, Maryland. Branches are at St. Petersburg, Florida; Marathon, in the Florida Keys; San Diego, California; St. Croix, United States Virgin Islands; Galveston Bay, Texas; Stamford, Connecticut; Lake of the Ozarks, Missouri; and Norfolk, Virginia.

Further Information
(800) 638-9192 (outside Maryland)
(301) 267-7205 (in Maryland)

Anne Arundel Community
College
Chesapeake Bay Cruise
101 College Parkway
Arnold, Maryland 21012

Program
Chesapeake Bay cruise aboard the *Aquarius,* a 70-foot estuarine research vessel; 2 weeks.

Accommodations
Dormitories or tents.

Cost
$400, including food, lodging, and all scientific equipment.

Comment
The objective of this cruise is to focus on the ecological problems of Chesapeake's waterways. Group limited to twenty-one people. Trip led by Professor Hugo Germignani, chairman of the science division; 3 credits obtainable from Anne Arundel Community College.

Further Information
Professor Hugo Germignani
(301) 269-7260

The Backpacking Institute
Hivernan Wilderness Guide
501 Milford Mill Road
Sudbrook Park
Baltimore, Maryland 21208

Programs
(1) Gourmet Wilderness Backpacking
Adventures for small groups; weekend
trips for all ages and abilities; year-
round except August. Fall color treks
and winter treks are specialties.
(2) Backpacking classes and
workshops: certified teachers conduct
hands-on courses in minimal-impact
wilderness living and travel. Annual
equipment-overhaul workshops
included.

Accommodations
Tents. Guests provide own
transportation, sleeping bags, etc.;
meals are provided. Special diets can
be accommodated. Mobility-impaired
individuals, seniors, and children over
4, accompanied by a parent, are
welcome.

Cost
Weekend Adventure Trek: $80
(adults); $75 (children under 12);
workshops included with membership
(write for information).
Extended Treks (3 days or more): $35
per day (adults); $32 per day (children).
Group Treks (for six or more people in
the same party): $30 per day (adults
and children).

Comment
Hivernan treks on over fifty different
mid-Atlantic trails in Maryland,
Pennsylvania, Virginia, and West
Virginia, including the Appalachian

Trail, the George Washington and
Monongahela National Forests, etc.
Classes and workshops are conducted
in the Baltimore area. The Hivernans
have been teaching and leading
minimal-impact, gourmet backpacking
expeditions since 1980. Treks are led
by trained professional trail guides.
Classes in minimal-impact
backpacking and travel techniques,
guide training, and a speaker service
are also available.

Further Information
Reed Hellman
(301) 484-4583

St. Mary's College of Maryland
St. Mary's City, Maryland 20686

Programs
(1) Summer Institute in Aquatic
Biology, 2 weeks, July–August.
Program for high school students.
(2) Sailing Camp, two consecutive 2-
week sessions, designed for youth ages
11–17.

Accommodations
St. Mary's College dormitories.

Cost
(1) $425, room and board.
(2) $650, all inclusive.

Recreation
College gymnasium, tennis courts,
swimming pool; volleyball, basketball,
other sports.

Cultural Opportunities
College library, musical and theatrical
events. St. Mary's was the first capital
of Colonial Maryland, so there are
many places of historic interest
nearby.

Comment
(1) The Summer Institute in Aquatic
Biology began in 1978. Courses stress

field study and laboratory work using the natural laboratories of rivers, marshes, and the Chesapeake Bay. High school students, college students, and adults must have had 1 year of biology. Class size is limited to forty to ensure individual attention.

(2) The Sailing School program is divided into on-shore and on-water phases, and emphasis is placed on sailing skills and boating safety. Instruction in windsurfing also included. Participants in the program must be able to swim fifty yards.

Further Information
Director of Summer Sessions
(301) 862-0200

MASSACHUSETTS

School for Field Studies
196 Broadway
Cambridge, Massachusetts
*   02139*

Program
Fourteen expeditions, 1 month, summer and January; three semester-long courses, spring, summer, and fall. Topics of expeditions include wildlife biology and management, rain forest and freshwater ecology, primate social behavior, and more. Locations range from Kenya to Alaska to Ecuador. Two levels of courses are offered: A (introductory) and B (advanced).

Accommodations
Tents, semipermanent basecamps. All courses include primitive camping.

Cost
Month-long programs: $950–$1800; semester programs: $4600–$5400. Personal gear and airfare are additional.

Comment
The School for Field Studies was founded in 1980. It is a private, nonprofit organization for field research, training, and education in the environmental sciences. Programs give high school and college students firsthand experience in conductng field research and detailed knowledge of a critical environmental issue or problem. Groups of fifteen to twenty students work with two or three faculty members, who are selected from universities and colleges across the country for research expertise, knowledge of subject and site, and teaching and interpersonal skills. Academic credit available.

Further Information
(617) 497-9000

NEW HAMPSHIRE

Appalachian Mountain Club
Pinkham Notch Camp
Gorham, New Hampshire 03581

Program
A series of guided overnight hikes in the White Mountains, summer.

Accommodations
Camping, alpine huts.

Cost
$100–$150 per hike, including meals and lodging.

Comment
Established in 1876, the Appalachian Mountain Club is a nonprofit organization with nearly 30,000 members. Hikes are led by two guides thoroughly familiar with the White Mountains; participants are of all ages

and backgrounds. The program's emphasis is on the natural and social history of the area, hiking safety, and a friendly sharing of the mountain experience.

Further Information
(603) 466-2727

NEW MEXICO

Southwest Safaris
P.O. Box 945
Santa Fe, New Mexico 87504

Program
Natural history treks through the American Southwest, 1–5 days, throughout the year. Travel is mostly by plane but also by jeep, horse, car, and raft.

Accommodations
Camping or lodges, depending on the trip.

Cost
Varies with length of tour. Examples: $899 (3 days), $1595 (5 days); prices include tour, accommodations, and meals.

Comment
Southwest Safaris, established in 1971, conducts natural history expeditions that combine outdoor adventure with field study of geology, archaeology, botany, and western history. Bruce Adams, pilot and lecturer (with degrees in philosophy and English), is in charge of all trips. Small groups of three to five people ensure personal attention.

Further Information
Bruce Adams
(505) 988-4246

> *The creation of a thousand forests is in one acorn.*
> **Ralph Waldo Emerson**

NEW YORK

Offshore Sailing School, Ltd.
East Schofield Street
City Island, New York 10464

Programs
Examples:
(1) Learn to Sail, 1-week course at deluxe resort, year-round or seasonal, depending on location.
(2) Bareboat Cruising Preparation, 1-week course at deluxe resort, year-round or seasonal, depending on location.
(3) Sailing and Cruising, Racing and Intensive Racing, Live-Aboard Cruising for Bareboat Certification, Coastal Cruising, Sail and Dive, and Passage Making courses at different locations; call or write for information.
(4) Day, weekend, and holiday courses at City Island, New York, April–October; call or write for information.

Accommodations
(1) Deluxe accommodations for singles, couples, or families.

Children
Minimum age for instruction is 12.

Cost
(1) $495 tuition only; accommodation packages available.
(2) $525 tuition only; accommodation packages available.
(3) $525–$1095; accommodation packages available.

Recreation
Tennis, golf, swimming, bicycling, horseback riding, fishing, and hiking are available at most locations.

Comment
The Offshore Sailing School was founded in 1964 by Olympic competitor Stephen Colgate. Its purpose is to teach beginners how to sail and to enable experienced sailors to improve at cruising and racing. The introductory course uses 27-foot Olympic-class Solings; the advanced courses use 28- to 50-foot boats. The school's locations are City Island, New York; Newport, Rhode Island; Captiva Island, Florida; Tortola, British Virgin Islands; Bar Harbor, Maine; and Bay Point, Florida. Nonsailing family and friends welcome.

Further Information
(800) 221-4326 or (212) 885-3200

Suffolk County Community College
Speonk Riverhead Road
Riverhead, New York 11901

Program
Various cruises studying marine plant and animal life are offered throughout the year. Examples: cruise off coast of New England, 1 week, August; weekend cruises throughout the Long Island area, summer.

Accommodations
Sleeping facilities aboard ship.

Cost
New England cruise, $250, including lodging. Write for information on weekend trips.

Recreation
Swimming, snorkeling, scuba diving, underwater photography, fishing, sailing.

Comment
Cruises have been offered since 1977. The program includes biological sampling and field techniques, collecting and preserving marine organisms, and the study of marine habitats. Scuba diving optional; nondivers are welcome. All cruises are aboard the 55-foot *Wahoo*, a twin-diesel-powered research vessel. College credit is available with extra tuition charge.

Further Information
Professor Henry Keatts
(516) 369-2600, ext. 251

NORTH CAROLINA

North Carolina State University
Sport Fishing School
Division for Lifelong Education
Box 7401
Raleigh, North Carolina 27695

Program
Annual sportfishing course, 1 week, June. Demonstrations and lectures in basics of saltwater and freshwater fishing, with emphasis on tackle, lures, rods and reels, baits, and fish identification. Also 2-day Gulf Stream fishing trips.

Accommodations
Selected motels and cottages.

Cost
$500, includes classroom and surf instruction, fishing trips, bait, seafood buffet, and course materials.

Recreation
Swimming, boating, sailing, camping, hang gliding nearby; sightseeing.

Cultural Opportunities
Cape Hatteras and Ocracoke lighthouse, Wright Brothers Memorial, Fort Raleigh, Elizabethan Garden, historic play *The Lost Colony.*

Comment
Headquartered at the Community Center in Hatteras, North Carolina, the Sport Fishing School was first offered in 1957. It appeals to veteran fishermen and novices. Program leaders include university faculty members, marine biologists, professional fishermen, and other experts. Enrollment is limited to forty.

Further Information
Alice Strickland Warren, Continuing Education Specialist
(919) 737-2261

TEXAS

Austin Nature Center
401 Deep Eddy Avenue
Austin, Texas 78703

Program
Year-round classes in natural science; cross-country skiing, backpacking, canoeing, and other trips.

Accommodations
Provided; write for details.

Cost
Varies from free to $350, with most in the $5–$30 range.

Comment
Two instructors staff each trip. Trips to Big Bend National Park region, New Mexico, and Colorado; average size of group is fifteen people. These trips are designed for novices and emphasize skills, safety, environmental impact, and natural history information.

Further Information
Scott Schrage, Program Supervisor
(512) 472-4523

Nothing in the world can take the place of persistence.
Calvin Coolidge

Texas Tech University
Department of Biological
Sciences
Box 4149
Lubbock, Texas 79409

Program
Course in coral reef biology, 2 weeks, June. Classroom instruction combined with observations of natural coral reef and turtle grass communities near Key Largo, Florida. Most diving is within Pennekamp Coral Reef State Park and Key Largo National Marine Sanctuary.

Accommodations
Camping (tents furnished); meals in local restaurants.

Cost
$570, includes meals, lodging, transportation, equipment, and course materials; tuition, travel to Florida, and personal gear not included.

Comment
This is a course designed for both majors and nonmajors; nonmatriculated adults have completed it in the past, as have college students. Prerequisites: introductory course in zoology and scuba certification; course must be taken for credit. The instructor has many years' experience, and a certified diving instructor supervises all diving. Investigating a protected reef system

that abounds in coral and tropical marine life, the course is designed for those who wish to understand the biology of this fascinating and beautiful habitat. Maximum enrollment: twenty.

Further Information
Larry S. Roberts, Professor
(806) 742-2730

UTAH

Canyonlands Field Institute
P.O. Box 68
Moab, Utah 84532

Program
Canyonlands EDventures, 1–7 days, spring–fall. Seminars and outings in natural history, geology, prehistoric cultures, art, literature, and outdoor education. Travel by raft, horse, or jeep.

Accommodations
Combination of motel and camping, as appropriate to trip.

Children
Welcome on most programs.

Cost
$35 per person on day trips, $50–$100 per person per day on longer trips; includes meals, rooms, and outfitter fees where appropriate.

Comment
Canyonlands is a nonprofit educational organization. Its EDventures take people into the heart of canyon country with a congenial specialist in the natural sciences or humanities. Group sizes average eight to fifteen; special outings can be arranged. College credit is available for some seminars.

Further Information
Karla Vander Zanden, Program
  Director
(801) 259-7750

Learning is the eye of the mind.
                    Thomas Draxe

VIRGINIA

The Cousteau Society's Project
  Ocean-Search
930 West 21st Street
Norfolk, Virginia 23517

Program
Project Ocean-Search is a series of intensive field-study programs conducted by the Cousteau Society in association with the University of Southern California College of Continuing Education. Programs take place in varying locations, both near and far. Projects are designed for both divers and nondivers.

Accommodations and Cost
Vary according to location; write for information, addresses given below.

Comment
The projects, which began in 1973, are adventures in every sense of the word. They are led by Jean-Michel Cousteau (son of the noted undersea explorer Jacques-Yves Cousteau) and his associates. Minimum age for participation is 16; a physician's certificate is required. College credit is available from the University of Southern California.

Further Information
In eastern United States:
Sandy Bond

930 West 21st Street
Norfolk, Virginia 23517
(804) 627-1144

In western United States:
Jeri Betts or Pam Stacy
The Cousteau Society's Project Ocean-
Search
8440 Santa Monica Boulevard
Los Angeles, California 90069
(213) 656-4422

Eastern Mennonite College
Harrisonburg, Virginia 22801

Program
Learn to Ski at Massanutten, 1
evening weekly, January and
February.

Accommodations
College dormitories.

Cost
$74, including instruction; equipment
rental and lift tickets additional.

Comment
For skiers of all abilities (minimum
age: 13); college credit available.

Further Information
Marie Horst
College of Continuing Education
(703) 433-2771

WASHINGTON

Special Odysseys
Special Interestours, Inc.
P.O. Box 37
Medina, Washington 98039

Program
Tours to various arctic regions, mostly
in Canada, Greenland, and South
Pacific; 1 3 weeks. Examples:

(1) Worlds of the High Arctic, 12 days,
August.
(2) Nova Scotia Odyssey, 7 days,
September.
(3) Dog Sled Treks (from Ellsmere and
Baffin islands in arctic Canada).

Accommodations
Igloos, tents, yachts, hotels, according
to tour. Write for details.

Cost
(1) $3450, inclusive, from Yellowknife,
Northwest Territories, Canada.
(2) $965 (double occupancy) from
Boston.
(3) Write for information.

Comment
Special Odysseys was incorporated in
1977. Its programs offer unique travel
experiences and chances to encounter
native cultures and wildlife, as well as
excellent opportunities for
photographers. The tours are geared to
healthy, self-reliant people but are not
strenuous. Tour leaders are
knowledgeable about the natural
history and inhabitants of regions
visited. Local guides are used. Groups
range in size from one to fifteen.

Further Information
Susan Voorhees
(206) 455-1960

WISCONSIN

Audubon Ecology Camp in
Wisconsin
Hunt Hill Sanctuary
Sarona, Wisconsin 54870

Programs
(1) Ecology Camp for adults, 1- and 2-
week programs, June–August.
Instruction in plant and animal
ecology, field trips, photography, and

individual pursuits.
(2) Family Ecology Camp, 1 week, August; camping, canoeing, photography, and nature study for families only; schedule allows families to spend time together and to work individually.

Accommodations
Wood-frame buildings; singles share large rooms, couples have private rooms; shared baths.

Children
(1) Ages 10–14 may enroll at the youth program of nearby Northwoods Audubon Center.
(2) Children age 6 and up, with their parents or guardian. Parents supervise meals and bedtimes. Special programs for youngsters.

Cost
(1) $385 for 1 week, $625 for 2 weeks.
(2) $385 for age 10–adult; $230 for children under 10.

Recreation
Snorkeling, canoeing, hiking, fishing,

Comment
The Wisconsin Ecology Camp is one of four operated by the National Audubon Society, a conservation organization founded in 1905. The camp is located on the 339-acre Hunt Hill Sanctuary, near four lakes in northwestern Wisconsin (117 miles northeast of Minneapolis and 80 miles south of Superior, Wisconsin). It provides a variety of ecological experiences: bogs, lakes, forests, and prairies. College credit through University of Wisconsin–Superior.

Further Information
National Audubon Society
Lumber Exchange Building, Suite 920
10 South Fifth Street
Minneapolis, Minnesota 55402
(612) 375-9140

> *When he has learnt that bottinney means a knowledge of plants, he goes and knows 'em.*
> **Charles Dickens**

WYOMING

Audubon Ecology Camp in the West
Trail Lake Ranch
Dubois, Wyoming 82513

Programs
(1) Field Ecology for adults, 2 weeks, June–August. Field experiences and discussions emphasize ecological relationships and a variety of natural history subjects.
(2) Youth Ecology Camp, 12 days, August. For children ages 11–15; subjects include local wildlife, mountain ecology, Native American culture, and contemporary issues. Field trips add to the learning experience.
(3) Nature Photography, 8 days, June. Field seminar led by professional photographers; discussions of technique, explorations of Whiskey Basin and Yellowstone. The final 3 days are spent at Canyon Village in Yellowstone.

Accommodations
Original homestead cabins; singles share cabins, couples have private room; shared baths.

Cost
(1) $625.
(2) $525.
(3) $625.

Recreation
Hiking, fishing, rock climbing, canoeing.

Comment
The Wyoming Camp is the most remote of four operated by the National Audubon Society, a conservation organization founded in 1905. It is located in a glaciated valley at an altitude of 7500 feet and is surrounded by the Wind River Range (13,000 feet), Fitzpatrick Wilderness, and the Whiskey Basin Bighorn Sheep Winter Range. Participants choose activities consistent with their interests, academic level, and physical condition. College credit is available through the University of Wyoming.

Further Information
National Audubon Society
4150 Darley Avenue, Suite 5
Boulder, Colorado 80303
(303) 499-5409

---

*National Outdoor Leadership
   School
P.O. Box AA, Department LV
Lander, Wyoming 82520*

Program
Expeditions in Wyoming, Utah, Washington, Alaska, Mexico, and Kenya; 2 weeks to 3 months; throughout the year. Comprehensive wilderness and mountaineering curriculum stresses awareness of nature and training in outdoor skills, as well as the development of leadership qualities.

Accommodations
Wilderness camping.

Cost
$1440, basic 5-week course, $3700, semester courses, including tuition and

rations. Additional equipment rental deposit: $125–$250.

Comment
Founded in 1965, the National Outdoor Leadership School is an educational institution dedicated to teaching people how to enjoy and conserve the outdoors. Professional staff give instruction in mountaineering, outdoor leadership, nature study, survival, medical emergency techniques, and minimum-impact camping. Minimum age is 16 for most courses; special courses for 14–15 year olds and those over 25. Average class size is seventeen, faculty-student ratio is one to five. College credit available through University of Utah.

Further Information
Paul Calver, Admissions Director
(307) 332-6973

---

*Yellowstone Institute
P.O. Box 117
Yellowstone National Park,
   Wyoming 82190*

Programs
Field courses in Yellowstone Park, primarily in summer, occasionally in winter. Topics include wildflowers, bears, geology, Indian history, wildlife photography, women and wilderness, archaeology, artists in Yellowstone, canoeing, hiking and camping, fly-fishing, and many other subjects related to the history and natural history of the Yellowstone region. Courses vary from 2 to 6 days.

Accommodations
Rustic cabins are available for courses held at the Institute's headquarters. A few classes encamp in tents in the backcountry; others use hotels and lodges within the park.

Cost

For most classes, tuition averages $35 per day plus cabin fees of $6 per night per person. For backcountry classes, the average is $70 per day, including meals, canoes or horses, and other outfitting costs.

Comment

The Institute is located in the Lamar Valley, a wildlife haven in the northeast corner of Yellowstone. Enrollees represent all ages and backgrounds. There are special classes for families and youngsters. Instructors are tops in their fields. Many courses carry optional academic credit and can be used for teacher recertification. A course catalog is available by February 1 of each year. Most classes are limited to fifteen.

Further Information

Gene Ball, Director
(307) 344-7381, ext. 2384

> *Division (of knowledge) into subjects is a concession to human weakness.*
>   *Halford John Mackinder*

CANADA

Federation of Ontario Naturalists
355 Lesmill Road
Don Mills, Ontario M3B 2W8
Canada

Programs

Trips to remote North American wilderness areas by horse, canoe, boat, bus, or foot; March–November. Recent examples include:

(1) Pacific Rim, backpacking the rain forests of Vancouver Island; 10 days.
(2) Paddling the Kinogama River in northern Ontario by canoe, 7 days.
(3) Observing polar bears along the shores of Hudson Bay, 4 days.

Accommodations

Camping on some trips, lodges or hotels on others.

Cost (Canadian dollars)

$425–$1950, all inclusive from point of origin, with reservations held by required deposit ($100–$300).
Examples:
(1) $840, some meals extra.
(2) $425.
(3) $1075, inclusive.
Individual membership in the two sponsoring organizations (see Comment) ranges from $15 to $25. Membership is required for participation.

Comment

The Federation of Ontario Naturalists and the Canadian Nature Federation are the largest conservation organizations in Canada and have been offering nature tours since the 1930s and 1975, respectively. Their tours are led by experienced travelers and naturalists with a participant-to-leader ratio of approximately five to one on wilderness trips. Required skill levels vary, but no naturalist experience is necessary. Minimum age is 16, with parent or guardian approval needed for ages 16–18; there is no upper age limit. Canoes, most camping equipment, and food are provided. Most trips originate in Ontario or western Canada.

Further Information

FON Conservation Centre
355 Lesmill Road
Don Mills, Ontario M3B 2W8
Canada
(416) 444-8419

5 ARTS, CRAFTS, AND PHOTOGRAPHY

Chatauqua Institution

Shaping and capturing the world with your hands and eyes, you work with many different media to exercise your talents—on your own and with others. These programs offer both the beginner and the professional a chance to improve skills and demonstrate creativity.

> *The hand is the cutting edge of the mind.*
>
> *Jacob Bronowski*

ARKANSAS

Ozark Arts and Crafts Fair Association, Inc.
War Eagle Mills Farm
Route 1
Hindsville, Arkansas 72738

Program
Annual Ozark Arts and Crafts Seminar, 2 weeks, June. A 60-hour, learn-by-doing experience for artists ranging from beginning to highly experienced. Subjects include painting, carving, weaving, pottery, and more.

Accommodations
Campsites, housekeeping motels. Write for details.

Cost
$75, one class only.

Recreation
Swimming, fishing, hiking, photography.

Cultural Opportunities
Historic sites.

Comment
The seminar offers an opportunity for the amateur or professional to improve technique in an informal atmosphere. Instructors are distinguished artists from the region. War Eagle Mills Farm is in the Ozarks near Beaver Lake, close to the major towns of northwest Arkansas.

Further Information
Blanche H. Elliot, Executive Director
(501) 789-5398

CALIFORNIA

Garendo Gallery
12955 Ventura Boulevard
Studio City, California 91604

Program
Annual tour of kiln sites, craft centers, and artisans' studios of Japan; approximately 3 weeks; departing Los Angeles in mid-October.

Accommodations
Hotels and inns with twin-bedded rooms and private bath.

Cost
$3880, includes tour, accommodations, meals, and round-trip airfare from Los Angeles; price based on group rate for fifteen or more.

Comment
These tours visit a variety of craftsmen and craft sites. They are led by Masako Sadler, owner of the Garendo Gallery, who began them in 1977 for craft-oriented people who share common interests and goals. Her qualifications include knowledge of the language, country, and craftsmen of Japan.

Further Information
Masako Sadler
(213) 489-5191

> *Industry without art is brutality.*
>
> *John Ruskin*

> *A student who can weave his technology into the fabric of society can claim to have a liberal education.*
> *Eric Ashby*

Montalvo Center for the Arts
P.O. Box 158
Saratoga, California 95070

Programs
(1) Classes, workshops, and lectures in all subjects related to the arts, including literature, drama, painting, sculpture, and music; varied lengths throughout the year. The annual Montalvo Summer Music Festival is a highlight.
(2) Artist-in-residence program for those with approved creative projects, 1–3 months; maximum of six artists at one time.

Accommodations
(2) Furnished apartments for selected artists-in-residence are available by application. Other accommodations nearby.

Cost
(2) Information given on application for fellowship.

Comment
Montalvo is a historic country park built in 1912 by James D. Phelan, a former United States Senator; it became an arts center in 1930 following his death. It is a community resource combining the development of skill in the arts with the opportunity to enjoy outdoor experiences.
Surrounding its 5 acres is a 170-acre arboretum separately maintained. In 1978, Villa Montalvo mansion was named to the National Register of Historic Places.

Further Information
Villa Montalvo Office
(408) 741-3421

COLORADO

Anderson Ranch Arts Center
P.O. Box 5598
Snowmass Village, Colorado 81615

Program
Annual workshops in painting, printmaking, clay, wood, fibers, and photography; 1–3 weeks; summer.

Accommodations
Shared condominiums with kitchen facilities. Students make own arrangements.

Children
Programs offered.

Cost
Tuition: $150–$300 per workshop.

Recreation
Swimming, hiking, rock climbing, backpacking, fishing, kayaking, ballooning, golf, tennis, bicycling.

Cultural Opportunities
Aspen Music Festival concerts, Ballet West performances, International Design conference, lectures, craft fairs, theaters; Aspen Institute for Humanistic Studies. Snowmass, Colorado, is approximately 110 miles west of Denver and 15 miles northwest of Aspen.

Comment
Established in 1971, the center currently offers workshops designed for approximately fifteen participants. Students are given the opportunity to explore new media, supplement previous training, and expose themselves to different methods and philosophies in a close community of artists. Workshops are conducted by nationally prominent craftsmen.

Further Information
Director
(303) 923-3181

Colorado Mountain College
Art In The Rockies
P.O. Box 117
Minturn, Colorado 81645

Program
Year-round workshops, 1–3 weeks. Courses include ceramics, glass, metalsmithing, jewelry making, fibers, printmaking, photography, drawing, and painting.

Accommodations
Limited camping. Write for information on nearby lodging.

Cost
$125–$400 per week.

Recreation
Tennis, golf, fishing, hiking, horseback riding, rafting, bicycling, and more.

Cultural Opportunities
Vail Institute for Performing Arts, Eagle Valley Arts Council Exhibitions, Colorado Ski Museum and Hall of Fame.

Comment
Established in 1971, the Minturn Center is located on 110 acres of land adjacent to Holy Cross Wilderness area, eight miles west of Vail,

Colorado. It currently offers a year-round artist-in-residence program, Associate in Arts degree, and intensive art workshops. Facilities include studios, meeting rooms, a gallery, cafeteria, and gymnasium.

Further Information
Director of Art Programs
(303) 827-5703

> *What sculpture is to a block of marble, education is to the soul.*
>
> *Joseph Addison*

CONNECTICUT

Brookfield Craft Center
286 Whisconier Road (Route 25)
P.O. Box 122
Brookfield, Connecticut 06804

Program
Year-round craft school conducts weeklong, weekend, and evening classes in all media at all interest levels; summer, spring, fall.

Accommodations
Numerous motels and hotels in area. Write for list of rooms in private homes.

Cost
Write for information.

Recreation
Near Candlewood Lake area; picnicking, walks.

Cultural Opportunities
Many music and drama productions nearby.

Comment
Founded in 1954 and located on the banks of Still River, a rural area of Connecticut, the school occupies four buildings, including a restored gristmill and nineteenth-century barn. Nationally known craftsmen-instructors teach over 250 separate classes.

Further Information
John I. Russell, Executive Director
(203) 775-4526

Wesleyan Potters, Inc.
350 South Main Street
Middletown, Connecticut 06457

Programs
(1) Classes in various crafts, taught on a continuing basis; quarterly registration.
(2) Intensive workshops, 1–2 days or 1 week, at various times.

Accommodations
Responsibility of participant.

Children
Special classes on general art for grades 2–4 and 5–7 and for teens.

Cost
(1) $20–$200.
(2) Depends on teacher and length of workshop.

Recreation
Skiing, swimming.

Cultural Opportunities
Harriet Beecher Stowe House, Mark Twain Memorial, Wadsworth Atheneum, Wesleyan University, and New Haven.

Comment
Wesleyan Potters was established in 1948. Crafts include pottery, weaving, jewelry, basketry, and others. The school has fully equipped pottery, weaving, and jewelry studios. Average group size is fifteen.

Further Information
Business Office
(203) 347-5925

> *It is no tragedy to have just one talent, but not using it is.*
> *Unknown*

GEORGIA

Hambidge Center for Creative Arts and Science
P.O. Box 33
Rabun Gap, Georgia 30568

Program
Courses in pottery, weaving, painting, writing, nature studies, astronomy, photography; 1 day to 2 weeks; April–October. Participants must be at least 15 years old. The Hambidge Center also operates a working artist retreat.

Accommodations
Two comfortable old houses in 700-acre mountain setting; excellent food. No camping or pets permitted on premises. Nearby motels, lodges, cabins, and campsites.

Cost
$200–$350 for 1 week, all inclusive; varies according to course and time. Write for information.

Recreation
Mountains, valleys, streams, woods. Property includes walking and hiking trails, a gristmill, and nearby lakes and waterfalls.

Cultural Opportunities
Concert series, monthly performances, May–October; monthly exhibitions at Hambidge Center Concert Hall; lectures, slide shows.

Comment
The Hambidge Center, a nonprofit foundation, was established in 1934. Located in the foothills of the Appalachian Mountains, it is on the National Register of Historic Places. While maintaining its original concentration on weaving and self-sufficiency, the center has broadened its scope, initiating many new educational programs.

Further Information
(404) 746-5718 or (404) 746-2491

> *The future belongs to those who believe in the beauty of their dreams.*
> *Eleanor Roosevelt*

MAINE

Haystack Mountain School of Crafts
Deer Island, Maine 04627

Program
Sessions in selected craft media, 2–3 weeks, summer. Each session has a different emphasis; among subjects covered are clay, metals, paper, fibers, blacksmithing, and photography.

Accommodations
Bunkhouse (limited availability); cabins with single, double, or triple rooms.

Cost
Tuition: $125 per week. Room and board (per week): $95, bunkhouse; $150, double; $290, single. Competitive scholarship grants available.

Recreation
Maine coast, small beach; woods nearby.

Cultural Opportunities
School library, gallery; evening slide presentations, lectures, music.

Comment
Haystack was founded in 1950. It caters to the beginning craftsman as well as the advanced professional. Some classes are limited to experienced artists; slides of recent work are requested. Instructors are college professors (M.F.A.'s) and professional craftsmen. Minimum age is 18; enrollment is limited to sixty-five resident and ten day students per session. College credit available.

Further Information
Howard M. Evans, Director
(207) 348-6946

> *It is the attitude of mind developed in the student which determines the character and extent of his education.*
> *Luther Eisenhardt*

Maine Photographic Workshops
Rockport, Maine 04856

Programs
(1) Summer Workshops, a series of master classes and workshops on all aspects of photography; 1–2 weeks;

June–September. Basic and intermediate workshops; classes on specific topics with leading artists, craftsmen, and teachers. Annual Photographer's Market Conference. (2) Travel Programs, trips to various destinations throughout the world, led by skilled photographers; 2–4 weeks; summer. Recent destinations include Florence, Italy; Ecuador; and the Caribbean. Admission by portfolio.

Accommodations
(1) On campus in restored Victorian homes; motels and inns nearby.
(2) Write for information.

Children
Young Photographers Workshop, 2 weeks, July. For teens already possessing skill in photography; same format as regular intermediate course. Admission by portfolio.

Cost
(1) Workshops: $275–$1000, plus lab fees; on-campus room and board: $180–$350 per week. Some financial aid available.
(2) $1600–$2895, includes room and most meals, local transportation, instruction, and fees; airfare additional.

Comment
Maine Photographic Workshops began in 1973. Topics include photographic technique, darkroom work, color and black-and-white, photojournalism, and more. Courses are for both amateurs and professionals. Some advanced sessions require submission of a portfolio for admission. More than 1000 people attend annually; average class size is 15. College credit available.

Further Information
Carol Stevens
Public Relations
(207) 236-8581

MARYLAND

The Ward Foundation
655 South Salisbury Boulevard
Salisbury, Maryland 21801

Program
The Summer Seminar, a variety of waterfowl carving, sculpting, and painting classes taught by different craftsmen; two 1-week sessions; June. Full-day hands-on sessions including lectures and critiques. Recent examples: Carve and Paint a Goldfinch, Choice of Summer and Winter Plumage, and Clay Sculpting (Sparrow Hawk, Saw-Whet Owl, and Cardinal).

Accommodations
Air-conditioned dormitories on campus of Salisbury State College, Maryland; participants can make own arrangements.

Cost
$540, tuition, room, and board; $430, tuition only. NOTE: Membership in Ward Foundation required; $20 individual dues.

Comment
Comprehensive instruction covers anatomy, pattern considerations, texturing, coloration, use of washes, brush techniques, and more. Participants have choice of numerous seminars, each with a different instructor.

Further Information
Summer Sessions Registrar
(301) 742-4988 or 749-6104

Art is the paper and string of life . . .
Anne Morrow Lindbergh

> **Well done is better than well said.**
>
>   **Ben Franklin**

MASSACHUSETTS

Heartwood Owner-Builder School
Johnson Road
Washington, Massachusetts 01235

Program
Residential house building courses, 3 weeks; also 1-week courses in renovation, timber framing, contracting, cabinetmaking; May–September.

Accommodations
Single and double rooms, cabins, and camping at houses and nearby resort.

Cost
Tuition: $600 per person, 3 weeks; $1100 per couple, 3 weeks; $275 per person, 1 week; $500 per couple, 1 week.

Cultural Opportunities
Located in the Berkshire Mountains, near Tanglewood Performing Arts Center and other cultural activities.

Comment
The Heartwood house-building program was first offered in 1978. No previous experience is necessary to enroll. Academic credit is often available to college students. The 3-week course covers house building and design plus training in use of tools and carpentry practices. There are six instructors; average group size is twenty per session. Twenty-five

percent of "graduates" build their own home within 2 years of taking course.

Further Information
Will Beemer, Director
(413) 623-6677

Irish Photographic Workshop
c/o Ron Rosenstock
91 Sunnyside Avenue
Holden, Massachusetts 01520

Program
Photographic field trips to western Ireland; seven times annually; 2 weeks; spring, summer, and fall. Instruction emphasizes black-and-white photography and covers camera skills, zone system, filters, darkroom, and development of individual vision and techniques.

Accommodations
Hillcrest House, Westport, County Mayo, Ireland.

Cost
$1875, includes instruction, shared lodgings, some meals, local transportation, and round-trip airfare from Boston.

Cultural Opportunities
Concerts, art exhibits, Irish traditional music in local pubs, and more.

Comment
Ron Rosenstock began leading photographic trips to England in 1970; 5 years later he moved the program to Ireland, where it has remained. He is an experienced professional and has been teaching since 1968. Persons of all skill levels with a sincere commitment to photography are welcome; maximum number of participants per trip is ten. There will be time for extracurricular activities.

College credit is available through Clark University in Massachusetts.

Further Information
Ron Rosenstock
(617) 829-6052

> *A great pleasure in life is doing what people say you cannot.*
>
> *Walter Gagehot*

Nantucket Island School of Design and the Arts
Waiunet Road
Nantucket, Massachusetts 02554

Program
Graduate and undergraduate interdisciplinary studies relating to art and the environment, with courses in visual and performing arts; 8 weeks.

Accommodations
Housekeeping cottages available.

Cost
Varies according to credit hours and length of stay; write for information.

Recreation
The island and its beaches offer many outdoor pursuits.

Comment
Originally established in 1974, the Nantucket School of Design and the Arts became affiliated with the Massachusetts College of Art (which co-sponsors certain courses) in 1978; credit is obtainable through them.

Further Information
Kathy Kelm, Director
(617) 228-9248

MINNESOTA

Danebod Folk School
Tyler, Minnesota 56178

Programs
(1) Family recreation camps; 1 week; June, July, August. Singing, crafts, folk art, recreational activities.
(2) Fall folk meeting, 4 days, September. Lectures, singing, folk dancing, fellowship.

Accommodations
Folk School dormitory; electrical hookups for campers, tent space available.

Children
Children's program of crafts and games.

Cost
(1) $100 full program (adults); $35–$77 (children).
(2) Write for information.

Recreation
Swimming, hiking, golf, field trips.

Comment
(1) The family camp has been held annually since 1948. It features poetry writing, woodcarving, pewter casting, and rosemaling, with offerings varying from year to year. Average number of participants is 135.

Further Information
Elsie Hansen, Registrar
(507) 247-5422

> *Fine art is that in which the head, hand, and heart go together.*
>
> *John Ruskin*

> *The painter should not paint what he sees, but what will be seen.*
>
>   *Paul Valéry*

Grand Marais Art Colony
P.O. Box 626
Grand Marais, Minnesota 55604

Program
Courses in various aspects of visual fine arts, traditional and experimental, July–September. Subjects include: oil, acrylic, and watercolor painting; drawing; and printmaking. Sculpture and art taught by college-level instructors.

Accommodations
Resorts, tourist cabins, hotel, and trailer park campground located on the harbor.

Children
A special class is offered for ages 7–12 Saturday mornings.

Cost
$155 per week (adults).

Recreation
Sailing, windsurfing, golf, swimming, fishing, tennis, hiking, canoeing.

Cultural Opportunities
Library, theater, music, museum.

Comment
The Grand Marais Art Colony was established in 1947. Its summer courses annually attract 150 people, who take advantage of its excellent studio, small-town atmosphere, and picturesque surroundings on the north shore of Lake Superior.

Further Information
Sharon Roberts Macy, Administrator
(612) 387-2737

> *The reward of a thing well done is to have done it.*
>   *Ralph Waldo Emerson*

Minneapolis College of Art and Design
Extension Programs
133 East 25th Street
Minneapolis, Minnesota 55404

Program
Summer program of courses in traditional and experimental techniques; fine arts, media arts, and design; 6 weeks, days and evenings; June–July. Available to students pursuing a degree, professionals seeking further training, or other interested individuals.

Accommodations
Campus residence.

Children
Summer art classes for ages 13–16 in painting, drawing, design, sculpture, photography, video, and more.

Cost
Write for information.

Cultural Opportunities
Minneapolis Institute of Arts, Walker Arts Center, Guthrie Theatre, smaller galleries and performing arts groups, summer festivals.

Comment
The college is a division of the Minneapolis Society of Fine Arts, a membership organization established in 1883. Classes cover a wide range of subjects at beginning and advanced

levels. College or continuing education credit available; noncredit courses also offered.

Further Information
(612) 870-3065

___

University of Minnesota, Duluth
Continuing Education and
*   Extension*
403 Darland Administration
*   Building*
10 University Drive
Duluth, Minnesota 55812

___

Program
Chinese painting and watercolor painting at the Zhejiang Academy of Fine Arts, city of Hangzhou, People's Republic of China; 6 weeks; June–July. Instruction in Chinese painting and other arts, Chinese art history, theory, and other subjects. Tours of Guilin, Shanghai, Nanjing, and Beijing.

Accommodations
Double rooms at International Student Residence Hall, Zhejiang Academy.

Cost
$4100 includes program, room and board, travel within China, international airfare, and fees.

Comment
The purpose of the tour is to introduce American painters to Chinese painting and other art forms. Twenty-eight participants are selected for the program. Students must have basic training in painting or have a general background in the visual arts. Due to the restrictions of the Zhejiang Academy, elderly people and those in poor health are advised not to apply. Instructors are from the academy, with an accompanying instructor from the University of Minnesota. The Zhejiang Academy, founded in 1928, is one of the

most prestigious in China. Program includes studio instruction, field trips, entertainment, and touring. Early registration is essential.

Further Information
Terry Anderson, Program Director
(218) 726-8113

NEVADA

___

Tuscarora Pottery School
Box 7
Tuscarora, Nevada 89834

___

Program
Several 2-week summer sessions, July–August; month-long session, May; fall semester, September–December. All cover various aspects of pottery: wheel throwing, raw glazing, kiln building, etc.

Accommodations
Nineteenth-century rooming house, single or double occupancy.

Cost
$455, 2-week session (10 percent off if attending more than one session); $830 per month, May or autumn. Includes room, board, and instruction; clay extra.

Recreation
Fishing, swimming, hiking, backpacking, cross-country skiing.

Cultural Opportunities
Public library, museum of local history.

Comment
Tuscarora is an International Ceramic Arts Study Center established in 1966. Past participants have come from throughout the U.S. and abroad,

ranging in skill from advanced
beginner to professor of art. Limited
enrollment (eight students) allows
personal instruction on a tutorial
basis. Courses are directed by Dennis
Parks, resident artist, member of the
International Academy of Ceramics,
and former curriculum chairman of the
National Council on Education for
Ceramic Arts. College credit available.

Further Information
Dennis Parks, Director
(702) Tuscarora toll station 6598
   (operator assisted)

NEW HAMPSHIRE

*Appalachian Mountain Club
Pinkham Notch Camp
Gorham, New Hampshire 03581*

Program
Seminars in various types of
photography, 1 week, autumn.

Accommodations
Camping, alpine huts.

Cost
$270–$290 per seminar, including
tuition, lodging, and meals.

Comment
Established in 1876, the Appalachian
Mountain Club is a nonprofit
organization with nearly 30,000
members. The seminars explore the
photographer's use of natural light in a
wide variety of setting. Program
combines a learning experience with
the enjoyment of hiking in the White
Mountains.

Further Information
(603) 466-2727

*The MacDowell Colony
100 High Street
Peterborough, New Hampshire
   03458*

Program
The MacDowell Colony provides
residence for artists, writers,
composers, and filmmakers; open
throughout the year. It is especially
suitable for those with works in
progress.

Accommodations
Thirty-one separate residential
studios, twenty of which can be used in
the winter.

Cost
From free to $75 per day.

Recreation
Swimming in nearby lakes and ponds;
nature walks and observations.

Comment
The MacDowell Colony, incorporated
in 1907, is the first retreat of its kind in
the United States. To date, it has
attracted more than 2000 creative
people (including 42 Pulitzer Prize
winners). The rural New England
solitude ("a sustained quietness seldom
available elsewhere" in the words of a
former participant) is conducive to
uninterrupted creative work.
Participants are selected by a
committee.

Further Information
Admissions Secretary
(603) 924-3886
In New York:
(212) 966-4860

> *Our chief want in life is
> somebody who will make us
> do what we can.*
>   *Ralph Waldo Emerson*

> *Happiness lies in the joy of achievement and the thrill of creative effort.*
> **Franklin Roosevelt**

NEW JERSEY

Madison-Chatham Adult School Creative Learning Vacation
P.O. Box 125
Madison, New Jersey 07940

Program
Annual summer art program for adults, 1 week, late June. Daily courses in painting, sculpture, photography, and more.

Accommodations
Ralph Waldo Emerson Inn or nearby motels.

Cost
Tuition: $80 per course; additional fees; write for information.

Recreation
Swimming, deep-sea fishing, sailing, tennis, golf.

Cultural Opportunities
Art galleries, historic sites, shops, museums, evening programs.

Comment
Madison-Chatham Adult School is one of the oldest schools of its kind in New Jersey, marking its fiftieth anniversary in 1987. The summer program at Rockport, Massachusetts, has been held since 1974. Small classes are geared for both beginning and advanced artists. Instructors are award-winning professional artists.

Further Information
Kathryn J. Memoli, Director
(201) 635-6500

Peters Valley Craft Center
Layton, New Jersey 07851

Program
Fall and spring weekend workshops; other workshops, up to 2 weeks, July–August. Subjects include ceramics, jewelry, photography, textiles, woodworking, and blacksmithing.

Accommodations
Off-campus youth hostel, motels, or limited campus housing. Write for information.

Cost
Varies according to duration; materials are additional. Write for information.

Recreation
Center located in the Delaware Water Gap National Recreation Area.

Comment
Peters Valley Craft Center was established in 1970. Class size averages four to twelve people. Minimum age is 16.

Further Information
(201) 948-5200

NEW MEXICO

La Romita School of Art, Inc.
1712 Old Town Road, NW
Albuquerque, New Mexico 87104

Program
Instruction in various aspects of art in Umbria, Italy; 4 weeks; June–July. Topics include painting, drawing, photography, art history, and more.

Accommodations
Double occupancy in La Romita, a sixteenth-century monastery, with modern living quarters, situated on a hillside above the town of Terni, Italy.

Cost
$2000, includes room and board, local transportation; airfare not included.

Cultural Opportunities
School library, visits to monasteries and churches, medieval towns, Spoleto Festival; trips to Florence and Sienna or to Venice and Ravenna.

Comment
Instruction is combined with work in the studio and the countryside. Program is open to both beginners and professionals; an average of fifteen people attend each session. Instruction in Italian may be available.

Further Information
Paola Quargnali, Director
(505) 243-1924

Las Palomas de Taos
P.O. Box 3400
Taos, New Mexico 87571

Program
Workshops of various durations covering numerous aspects of the art and culture of the Southwest: crafts, foods, religion, language, architecture, and history of the region. Also, institutes and seminars on international development issues. Programs held year-round.

Accommodations
Rooms and meals at the Mabel Dodge Luhan House, a national historic site and art center.

Cost
Varies with program and length of stay. Examples: Art and Culture of the Southwest, 3 days, $165; Creative Photography, 8 days, $485. Costs include room and board, instructional materials; college credit additional.

Recreation
Skiing, fishing, hiking, whitewater rafting, horseback riding nearby.

Cultural Opportunities
The Millicent Rogers Museum, Taos Pueblo, the Harwood Gallery, Kit Carson Foundation historic sites; Fort Burgwin archaeological excavation.

Comment
Las Palomas is a private, nonprofit membership organization that encourages and supports the preservation and study of the diversity of southwestern art, culture, and history. The director is Dr. George G. Otero Jr.; staff members include nationally known artists and writers and long-time community residents.

Further Information
(505) 758-9456

> *Art is not an end in itself, but a means of addressing humanity.*
> *M. P. Mussorgsky*

Travel Photography Workshop
in Santa Fe
P.O. Box 2847
Santa Fe, New Mexico 87501

Programs
(1) Three consecutive 1-week workshops, September.
(2) On Location Tours to Britain, other West European countries, and India; generally 2–3 weeks.

Accommodations
(1) Provided; write for details.
(2) First-class hotels.

Cost
(1) $785 per week, includes program, room and board, and related fees; $485, program only.
(2) $2985–$4980, according to destination and trip's duration, airfare included.

Comment
The Travel Photography Workshop stresses development of a personal photographic style. On Location Tours are led by Lisl and Landt Dennis, proprietors of the Travel Photography Workshop; in addition to on-location demonstrations, photo critiques are given frequently.

Further Information
Lisl Dennis
(505) 982-4979

NEW YORK

Catskill Center for
*   Photography*
Woodstock Photography
*   Workshops*
59A Tinker Street
Woodstock, New York 12498

Program
Workshops, lectures, and exhibition; weekends; July–September. Recent courses: Hand Coloring, Reality and Photography, The Nude as a Portrait, and others. Recent guest artists: Duane Michals, Stephen Shore, Art Kane, Lucien Clergue.

Accommodations
Local campgrounds, hotels, motels, inns.

Cost
$55, 1-day workshop; $100, 2-day workshop; $2, lecture fee.

Cultural Opportunities
Woodstock is a historic arts community, 2 hours from New York City. The area is rich in visual arts, music, and theater. The region provides the scenic beauty of the Catskill Mountains and Hudson River Valley.

Comment
The Woodstock Photography Workshops were first held in 1978. A variety of topics are scheduled annually, and different guest artists lead workshops on each. Workshop enrollment averages between ten and twenty people.

Further Information
Bil Jaeger, Director
(914) 679 9957

Long Island University,
*   Southampton Campus*
Master Workshop in Art
Southampton, New York 11968

Program
In-depth studio workshop for the artist who has mastered the basic techniques of painting, drawing, and sculpture; 5 weeks; July–August. Instruction by full-time faculty members and guest artists.

Accommodations
Dormitories.

Cost
$1600, includes tuition, room and board, college credit.

Recreation
Swimming, tennis, fitness trail, university facilities.

Cultural Opportunities
Campus library, art galleries, summer theater, museums, botanical gardens.

Comment
Students work with renowned artists, participating in individual critiques, demonstrations, discussions, and visits to the artists' studios. Admission is limited to thirty-five, selected by slide portfolio.

Further Information
Alice Flynn
Summer Office
(516) 283-4000, ext. 114

New York University
Film Production Workshop
School of Continuing Education
126 Shimkin Hall
New York, New York 10003

Program
Annual workshop, 5 weeks, summer. Features an overview of the film industry, focusing on cinematography, sound, lighting, editing, and other technical aspects of film production.

Accommodations
Responsibility of participants, who are encouraged to live on campus due to the demands of the program.

Cost
Tuition only: $2000.

Recreation
Parks, athletic fields, tennis courts nearby.

Cultural Opportunities
New York City has a wealth of cultural institutions and events.

Comment
Film Production Workshop offers more than 275 hours of classroom and workshop study with a faculty of professional filmmakers. The curriculum combines theory with hands-on practice. Fully equipped facilities include cutting rooms and a soundstage. Faculty and students work together on 16mm silent films and advanced sound-film projects.

Further Information
Dorothy Durkin
Director, Public Relations
(212) 598-2026

> *Art is the stored honey of the human soul, gathered on wings of misery and travail.*
> *Theodore Dreiser*

Skidmore College
SIX Summer Art Program
Saratoga Springs, New York
*   12866*

Program
Annual summer art program, two consecutive 6-week sessions during the College Summer School. Topics include drawing, painting, printmaking, ceramics, architecture, design, and art history.

Accommodations
Campus dormitories, single or double rooms.

Cost
Tuition: $150–$960, depending on number of credits and state of residence. Room and board: $870 per session.

Recreation
Tennis, horseback riding, campus athletic facilities.

Cultural Opportunities
Saratoga Performing Arts Center,
Newport Jazz Festival (weekends);
theater, concerts, other events nearby.

Comment
The SIX Summer Art Program is an
intensive learning experience that
provides an opportunity to explore and
develop ideas in depth in a community
of artists and students from various
backgrounds. The sessions feature
critiques, workshops, and lectures, led
by nationally known visiting artists.
College credit is available; graduate
courses are offered in cooperation with
State University of New York at
Albany.

Further Information
Dean of Special Programs
(518) 584-5000

---

*Thousand Islands Craft School
and Textile Museum
314 John Street
Clayton, New York 13624*

Program
Craft courses in various media, 1 week
and 2 weeks, July–August, also
evenings and weekends. Course
offerings include weaving, metals,
drawing, pottery, carving, lace,
quilting, painting on fabric, and Early
American decoration.

Accommodations
Responsibility of participant. Write for
information.

Children
Program in pottery for elementary
school pupils and others.

Cost
Tuition: $30, evening course, to $150,
2-week course; registration fee: $10–
$20. Materials fee in some courses.

Recreation
Thousand Islands recreational
facilities.

Cultural Opportunities
Textile Museum, Berta Frey Library
(weaving and textiles), Helene Cobb
Gallery.

Comment
Thousand Islands is a private,
nonprofit educational institution
whose purpose is to promote and
encourage public interest in crafts. The
school was founded in 1967; usually
200 students attend annually. Average
class size is ten; some class sizes are
limited. Volunteers are always
welcome in various aspects of the
school's operation. College credit is
available.

Further Information
Jane Gillett, Director
(315) 686-4123

NORTH CAROLINA

---

*John C. Campbell Folk School
Brasstown, North Carolina
28902*

Programs
(1) Weekend workshops in crafts; 1
week and 2 weeks; spring, summer,
fall. Many traditional and modern
crafts courses available.
(2) Work-study program; 3 months;
spring, summer, fall. Students take
variety of short courses and participate
in ongoing community programs. Work
covers room and board expenses.
(3) Residential Middle/High School
Programs, 5 days, spring. Experience
in crafts or cultural history.
(4) Elderhostel.

Accommodations
Double and single rooms, plus campground. All meals, if desired. No pets allowed, except on leash in campground.

Cost
(1), (2), and (3) Tuition: $120, 1 week; $210, 2 weeks. Lodging: $42–$60 per week.
(4) $195, 1 week, inclusive.

Recreation
Folk dancing, hiking, fishing, rafting, and more.

Comment
Founded in 1925, the John C. Campbell Folk School is located in the western North Carolina Mountains. Students nationwide come to study crafts, self-sufficiency skills, music, and dance. An important part of the Brasstown community, the school serves as a meeting place for community organizations. It also operates a cottage industry for local woodcarvers, whose creations are available in the school's craft shop.

Further Information
(704) 837-2775

TENNESSEE

Arrowmont School of Arts and
  Crafts
Box 567
Gatlinburg, Tennessee 37738

Programs
(1) Workshops; 1 week and 2 weeks; March, June, July, and August. Subjects include ceramics, fiber, fabric, drawing, painting, photography, wood,

metal, stained glass, and papermaking.
(2) Other workshops, Elderhostel classes, conferences, exhibitions, and more; throughout the year. Write for details.

Accommodations
Room and board on campus. No dogs allowed.

Cost
Tuition: $155 per week; room and board: $105–$160 per week; materials extra.

Recreation
Volleyball, hiking, fishing, skiing, and swimming in the area.

Cultural Opportunities
Lectures, musical programs, slide-film programs, year-round, changing exhibitions in the Arrowmont Gallery.

Comment
The Arrowmont School was founded in 1945 and since 1975 has been attracting 1000 students annually. During the spring and summer, instruction is provided by more than fifty artists and craftsmen. Courses are offered at beginning, intermediate, and advanced levels, in all arts and crafts media. Classes limited to twenty students; minimum age 13. College credit obtainable from the University of Tennessee, Knoxville.

Further Information
Program Coordinator
(615) 436-5860

You must treat a work of art like a great man: stand before it and wait patiently till it deigns to speak.
    Arthur Schopenhauer

> *Nothing is more useful to
> man than those arts which
> have no utility.*
>
>   *Ovid*

VERMONT

Fletcher Farm Craft School
Ludlow, Vermont 05149

Program
Intensive 1-week, 2-week, and
weekend classes for beginner through
advanced adult students. Traditional
and contemporary arts and crafts:
weaving, rug making, quilting,
needlework, rosemaling, pottery, Early
American decorating, fine arts, and
more. Program varies yearly.

Accommodations
Single and double motel-type units on
premises. Public camping nearby. No
pets.

Children
A few classes available for students
ages 8–17.

Cost
Tuition: $120–$130 average weekly;
room and board: $150 weekly.

Recreation
Hiking, swimming, fishing, tennis;
jogging trail nearby.

Cultural Opportunities
Summer theater, antique shops, early
New England village, museums, art
galleries, craft centers nearby. Society
of Vermont Craftsmen shop on
premises.

Comment
Historic Fletcher Farm is southeast of
Rutland, in central Vermont in the
heart of the Green Mountains. The
school was established in 1948 and is
sponsored by the Society of Vermont
Craftsmen, Inc. Classes are small,
averaging five to ten students per
class. Instructors are mainly
professionals, many certified.

Further Information
Cyrena Persons
(802) 228-8770

WEST VIRGINIA

Augusta Heritage Center
Davis & Elkins College
Elkins, West Virginia 26241

Programs
(1) Classes in traditional skills and
crafts, 1–3 weeks, July–August.
Subjects include playing and making
musical instruments (fiddle, dulcimer,
and banjo); also folklore and nearly
twenty-five crafts (including weaving
and basketry).
(2) Evening and weekend workshops;
subjects include clogging, music,
broom making, wild mushrooms, and
natural dyeing.
(3) Winter Augusta Workshop: A week
of workshops in Appalachian and
British traditional dance, music, and
crafts; the week of New Year's Day.
Topics include ballads, fiddle, and
square and big circle dances.

Accommodations
Modern dormitory facilities at Davis &
Elkins College; camping nearby;
motels and tourist homes.

Children
Special programs for teens; other
children's activities available. Some
day care available in Elkins.

Cost
Tuition: $23 per day, materials extra.
Room and board: $21 per day
(semiprivate); vegetarian option
available.

Recreation
Tennis, fishing, rafting, backpacking,
climbing, golf, skiing, other sports.

Cultural Opportunities
Festival events both summer and
winter: square dances, concerts, special
exhibits, lectures, and more.

Comment
The Augusta Center was established in
1973. Its programs are open to both
beginners and professionals. In 1985,
total enrollment was over 1000; typical
class sizes are six to twelve for crafts,
seventy-five to ninety for some
weeklong musical events. College
credit is available from Davis & Elkins
College; extra tuition charge.

Further Information
Doug Hill, Publicity Coordinator
(304) 636-1903

Crafts Center
Cedar Lakes Conference Center
Ripley, West Virginia 25271

Program
Weekend and weeklong workshops in
arts and crafts for beginners and
professionals; July–August. Topics
include painting, calligraphy,
weaving, blacksmithing, and more.

Accommodations
Dormitory or semiprivate room, meals
in dining hall.

Cost
Registration: $85, week-vacation
residents; $100, out-of-state residents.
Studio fee: $10–$40. Housing: $7.50–
$13 per night; meals: $8.50 per day.

Comment
The Crafts Center was founded in
1975. Programs emphasize technique
and design fundamentals through
hands-on experience. Instructors are
experienced craftsmen in their fields.
Class size is ten to fifteen; college
credit available.

Further Information
(304) 372-7005

> *The test of the artist does not
> lie in the will with which he
> goes to work, but in the
> excellence of the work he
> produces.*
>
> *Thomas Aquinas*

WISCONSIN

The Clearing
P.O. Box 65
Ellison Bay, Wisconsin 54210

Program
Week-long courses in art, crafts, study
of nature, and culture, including
landscape with watercolors, weaving,
spring birds of northern woods and
waters; May–October.

Accommodations
Dormitories and rooms with private
baths.

Cost
$303–$325 per week, including tuition,
room, and board.

Recreation
Sailing, fishing, swimming, hiking,
golf, and tennis nearby.

Cultural Opportunities
Peninsula Music festival, Door County
Historical museums, Peninsula
Players, art galleries.

Comment
Established in 1935, The Clearing is a
place where one can feel the true
importance of nature to living or, as its
name suggests, can clear one's mind in
a woodland setting. Classes are kept
small; there is a knowledgeable
faculty.

Further Information
(414) 854-4088

University of Wisconsin–
Madison
Rhinelander School of Arts
722 Lowell Hall
610 Langdon Street
Madison, Wisconsin 53706

Program
One-week session, late July.
Workshops include drawing, painting,
writing, photography, self-publishing,
dance, and more.

Accommodations
Responsibility of participant.

Cost
Tuition: $100 per week.

Recreation
Northwoods lake country, with
camping, swimming, boating, fishing,
and golf.

Cultural Opportunities
Logging Museum; theater productions.

Comment
The Rhinelander School was
established in 1964 to offer summer
programs in the arts in northern
Wisconsin. Workshops are offered at
all levels, and the program is open to
all persons interested in the arts.
Sponsors include the Wisconsin
Regional Writers' Association and the
Northern Arts Council. Continuing
Education Units (CEUs) are available.

Further Information
Gene Lewis
(608) 263-3494

CANADA

B. Allen Mackie School of Log
Building and Environmental
Centre
P.O. Box 1238
Prince George, British
Columbia V2L 4V3
Canada

Program
Sessions on various aspects of building
with logs, 1 day to 4 weeks, March–
November.

Accommodations
Responsibility of students, who usually
live on campus.

Cost (Canadian dollars)
Tuition: $160–$275 per week,
depending on course.

Recreation
Small lake with wood-burning sauna
at its shore; horseshoe pit, volleyball
court, and children's playground;
within easy driving distance of
mountains, lakes, and rivers with
opportunities for swimming, hiking,
boating, and fishing.

Cultural Opportunities
Prince George, the third-largest city in
British Columbia, offers a variety of
sights and activities.

Children
Children are welcome if supervision is
provided by family.

Comment
The school, established in 1975, is a
wilderness workshop located twenty-
four miles west of Prince George in
British Columbia. The majority of
enrollees are owner-builders. The wide
range of programs are directed to both
owner-builders and potential
contractors.

Further Information
(604) 563-8738

Lilly Bohlen's Studio
1021 Government Street
Victoria, British Columbia
*   V8W 1X6*
Canada

Program
Weaving workshops, 1–3 weeks, year-
round. Techniques of weaving rugs, art
weavings, fabrics, and linens; tapestry,
draw loom, damask, and other
traditional methods are taught.

Accommodations
Responsibility of participant.

Cost (Canadian dollars)
$91, 1 week; $256, 3 weeks; $73–$146,
materials.

Comment
Students work individually with the
instructor, experimenting with color
mixing and form. Lilly Bohlen's
background includes many years of
teaching in Scotland and Ireland and 4
years of managing the Weaving
Department of the Banff School of Fine
Arts. She opened her Victoria studio in
1973. Class size is limited to five;
minimum age 18.

Further Information
(604) 388-5982

Sunbury Shores Arts and
*   Nature Center, Inc.*
P.O. Box 100
139 Water Street
St. Andrews, New Brunswick
*   E0G 2X0*
Canada

Programs
Courses on painting, sculpture,
printmaking, pottery, marine ecology,
etc.; 1–2 weeks.

Accommodations
Hotels, motels, inns, camping.

Children
Weekly art and nature workshops for
children ages 6–12, 8 weeks during the
summer.

Cost (Canadian dollars)
$210 for nonstudents, $140 for
students taking July courses in art.

Recreation
Sailing, swimming, tennis, golfing,
hiking.

Cultural Opportunities
Continuous exhibitions by Canadian
artists, special interest shows on
subjects such as archaeology and boat
building. Illustrated talks, films,
concerts, and library.

Comment
The arts and handcrafts programs
were first offered in 1964 when
Sunbury Shores opened. Their purpose
is to help participants enjoy and
appreciate fine art and craft work.
There are also programs on natural
history and conservation education.
All courses are taught by expert
instructors.

Further Information
Nancy Aiken, Director
(506) 529-3386

UNITED KINGDOM

Mounts Bay Arts Center
Trevatha, Faugan Lane
Newlyn, Penzance TR18 5DJ
England

Program
Residential holiday art center
specializing in landscape painting, 1 or
more weeks, late May to early October.

Accommodations
Main house or nearby bed-and-
breakfast.

Cost
£153 per week, full program, lodging,
and meals.

Comment
Program includes illustrated talks on
aspects of painting and daily painting
trips to the Cornwall coast. Large
studios are available. Maximum group
size is ten.

Further Information
Bernard Evans
Penzance
(0736) 66284

New Academy for Art Studies
3 Albion Street
London W2
England

Program
Annual diploma course in history and
appreciation of fine and decorative

arts, three 10-week terms, October–
June. Emphasis on painting, sculpture,
architecture, interior decoration,
furniture, ceramics, glass, and
metalwork.

Accommodations
Arranged by students, but the
academy will make recommendations.

Cost
£2450 ($3480) plus Value Added Tax
(VAT) for program. (Equivalent
exchange rate at time of publication.)

Comment
The academy course provides firm
groundwork in the history and
practices of the arts and assists
students who seek more permanent
involvement or employment in the
academic or commercial fields. The
program includes study of taste and
patronage in England, visits to
museums and private collections, and
opportunities to travel to continental
Europe in order to study works of art in
their original context. The academy
faculty is supplemented by
distinguished visiting experts.

Further Information
In North America:
Margo Donahue, Representative
118 East 82nd Street
New York, New York 10028
(212) 288-3603

Work thou for pleasure—
paint, or sing, or carve
The thing thou lovest, though
the body starve . . .
Kenyon Cox

6 MUSIC, DANCE, AND DRAMA

Stratford Festival

Music in the Mountains

*E*xperience the arts through a fascinating variety of worldwide educational and entertainment opportunities as either participant or spectator.

*There is nothing more
notable in Socrates than that
he found time to learn music
and dancing, and thought it
time well spent.*
                                    Montaigne

ALABAMA

*Birmingham Festival of the Arts
Suite 910, Commerce Center
2027 First Avenue North
Birmingham, Alabama 35203*

Program
Annual spring festival highlighting a
different country each year, 10–12
days. Features dance, theater,
Birmingham Symphony, lectures,
cooking demonstrations, and more.

Accommodations
Festival Committee will assist in
finding accommodations.

Cost
Tickets required to some events; others
free.

Comment
The Birmingham Festival, established
in 1951, is the oldest and largest
continuing arts program of its kind. It
promotes international understanding
through cultural, artistic, and
educational exchange.

Further Information
(205) 323-5461

ARIZONA

*Tucson Festival Society, Inc.
8 West Paseo Redondo
Tucson, Arizona 85701*

Program
Annual Tucson Festival in April
includes twenty or more events
celebrating the Indian, Spanish,
Mexican, and pioneer American
heritage of the Tucson community.

Cost
Free.

Comment
The Tucson Festival was first held in
1951. It usually features a torchlight
pageant, arts festival, children's
parade, traditional Mexican fiesta,
pioneer living history, mission tours,
walking tours of Tucson, programs at
the desert museum and planetarium,
and more.

Further Information
Jarvis Harriman, Executive Director
(602) 622-6911

CALIFORNIA

*California State University,
   Chico
Chamber Music Workshop
Music Department
Chico, California 95929*

Program
Two 1-week sessions, August.

Accommodations
University dormitories.

Cost
$215, including tuition, accommodations, meals.

Recreation
Swimming, tennis.

Comment
The Chico Chamber Music Workshop was first offered in 1970. Its program provides an opportunity for amateur musicians to receive coaching by the artist-teachers from California universities who staff the workshop. Participants are divided into ensembles of various numbers; time is also available for independent informal playing. Approximately eighty to ninety people attend each weekly session. Academic credit obtainable.

Further Information
(916) 895-6116

Idyllwild School of Music and the Arts
P.O. Box 38
Idyllwild, California 92349

Program
Summer courses in creative writing, dance, music, theater, and fine arts for both adults and children (ages 9–18). Specially featured are courses, workshops, and exhibitions in Native American arts. Sessions are generally 1–3 weeks (some longer).

Accommodations
Housing: tent ($40 per week) and trailer sites ($80 per week), a few with electrical, water, and sewer hookups; motel-like residence hall; and motels or homes rented in the Idyllwild community.

Cost
Tuition for most individual courses: $85–$295; lab fees extra. Room and board: $195 per week per person. Financial aid available.

Recreation
Hiking, mountain climbing, swimming in pool, nature walks.

Cultural Opportunities
Folk dancing, folk music, recitals, lectures, and films.

Comment
Founded in 1950, the 200-acre campus is located on the western slopes of the San Jacinto Mountains. The campus is 2½ hours from Los Angeles and San Diego by car. There is no public transportation to Idyllwild. Completion of a health history form is required for enrollment.

Further Information
Registrar
(714) 654-2171

Opera Education International
400 Yale Avenue
Berkeley, California 94708

Program
Annual operatic tours: Great Summer Festivals of Germany and Austria, Autumn in New York, A Lifetime of Christmases (in Europe), and Spring Festivals of Italy. Travel programs also scheduled to opera in Sante Fe, San Francisco, and elsewhere.

Accommodations
Choice of deluxe or no frills (moderately priced first- or second-class).

Cost
Domestic tours average $150–$200 per day; European tours average $275 per day (not including air transportation).

Comment
Established in 1969 (as Opera Education West) by Professor Michael Barclay, opera scholar and critic, Opera Education International tours are designed for "opera freaks," with daily performances on the itinerary, though some trips may be organized with only two or three performances a week. All tours allow participants to go backstage to meet opera stars and feature daily background lectures by Professor Barclay and other experts. Side trips to related cultural and historic sites are also scheduled.

Further Information
Professor Michael D. Barclay, Founder
    and Director
(415) 526-5244

---

*Young Artists Peninsula Music
    Festival
6931 Vallon Drive
Palos Verdes Peninsula,
    California 90274*

Program
Annual weekend music festival, June. Provides performance opportunities to young artists from the United States and abroad. Soloists, ensembles, choruses, youth orchestras. Admission by audition.

Accommodations
Rooms in private homes provided for out-of-state performers along with practice facilities.

Cost
Application fee: $15.

Comment
The festival was established in 1977 by Erika Chary, concert pianist and teacher, and takes place in the Norris Theatre for the Performing Arts,

overlooking the Pacific on Palos Verdes Peninsula, California, thirty miles south of Los Angeles. Performers selected receive an honorarium; maximum age is 25. A special prize is awarded for chamber ensemble performance. Each festival features a theme, honoring a composer or style of music.

Further Information
Erika Chary, Director
(213) 377-8891

> *Come and trip it as you go
> On the light fantastic toe.*
>   *John Milton*

COLORADO

*Aspen Music Festival and
    School
Box AA
Aspen, Colorado 81612*

Programs
(1) Annual Aspen Music Festival, 9 weeks, usually beginning in late June; featuring a wide variety of musical performances including orchestral, chamber music, opera, choral, and jazz. (2) Aspen Music School, concurrently with the festival; sessions of 4, 5, and 9 weeks scheduled in the following areas: strings, woodwinds, brass, percussion, conducting, piano, opera, choral, composition, guitar, and audio recording. Special master classes given by guests and faculty artists.

Accommodations
Contact Aspen Chamber of Commerce for information. Lodges available in the town of Aspen.

Cost
(1) $5–$17.50 for single-performance tickets (series tickets available). (2) Tuition: $950–$1550; room and board: $810–$1450, depending on length of session.

Recreation
Hiking, climbing, fishing, golf, horseback riding, tennis, swimming, bicycling, skating.

Comment
The Aspen Music Festival was first held in 1949 as part of the Goethe Bicentennial. Since then it has attracted more than 80,000 visitors. Each year there are musical groups including the Festival Orchestra, the Concert Orchestra, the Philharmonic, and the Jazz Ensemble; along with opera and Young Artists Concerts that rotate nightly performances throughout the 9-week summer season. Intermixed with these are recitals by the school's faculty and visiting guest artists. An annual feature is the Aspen Music Festival Conference of Contemporary Music. The Aspen Music School began operation in the early 1950s as an outgrowth of the festival. Currently, it enrolls 1000 students annually, selected by competitive examination. Its 189 faculty members and guest artists represent major conservatories throughout the world. College credit may be obtained through the University of Colorado.

Further Information
From June 1 to August 31:
Director of Public Relations
(303) 925-3254
From September 1 to May 31:
Director of Public Relations
Aspen Musical Festival and School
250 West 54th Street
New York, New York 10019
(212) 581-2196

CONNECTICUT

Music Mountain
P.O. Box 506
Falls Village, Connecticut 06031

Programs
(1) Adult Amateur Chamber Music Conferences, 1 week in June and 2 weekends in August; coaching sessions, master classes, and concerts for forty participants. No audition required.
(2) Young Professional Quartet Seminar for four quartets, 3 weeks, July–August; studies the art of the string quartet, including daily coaching, master classes, workshops, student recitals, and performances in churches, camps, cultural centers, and schools. Audition required, either on tape or in person.

Accommodations
(1) Indian Mountain School in nearby Lakeville.
(2) Free housing on Music Mountain.

Cost
(1) Full week (except Sunday evening): $300 double; $350, single, with meals. Weekend: $150 double; $175, single, with meals, except as above.
(2) $120 for cooperative food buying and preparation; tuition and housing free.

Recreation
Swimming, boating, canoeing, fishing, hiking, golf.

Comment
An opportunity to spend a week or long weekend in the Berkshires playing chamber music at Music Mountain. Conferences are dedicated to the development of the amateur musician as chamber-music player and listener.

Music Mountain combines a program of coaching and master classes with workshops, concerts, and other activities. Participants are matched according to ability and experience and are encouraged to form their own ensembles in their spare time.

Further Information
Elizabeth Kihl, Registrar
P.O. Box 506
Kent, Connecticut 06757
(203) 927-4125

FLORIDA

New College Music Festival
5700 North Tamiami Trail
Sarasota, Florida 34243

Program
Intensive master classes, workshops, and seminars, under the guidance of distinguished guest faculty artists; first 3 weeks of June. Open on an auditing basis to the public, as observers only.

Accommodations
Dormitories of New College of the University of South Florida.

Cost
Registration: $75, participants; $15, auditors. Tuition: $75, 3 weeks; $35, weekly. Tuition scholarship grants available.

Cultural Opportunities
Asolo State Theatre, Florida West Coast Symphony, Ringling Museums.

Comment
New College is one of the country's outstanding chamber music festivals. Students, selected by audition, enjoy close contact with an internationally renowned guest faculty and also have

an opportunity to perform publicly in ensembles. A series of weekend concerts by the guest faculty performing in solos and ensembles highlights the festival.

Further Information
(813) 355-2116/8886

A dance is a measured pace as verse is a measured speech.
Francis Bacon

GEORGIA

Copecrest Square Dance Resort
P.O. Box 129
Dillard, Georgia 30537

Program
Continuous 1-week square dance programs, March–November.

Accommodations
Inns, colleges, campgrounds.

Cost
$259 per person (double occupancy), includes meals, dance workshops, and activities; $85, children.

Recreation
Fishing, hiking, white-water rafting, climbing in the northeast Georgia mountains.

Comment
For square- and round-dance enthusiasts, with each week geared to a specific skill level. Professional staff of nationally known callers and cuers. Formerly called Square Dance Resort at Andy's Trout Farms.

Further Information
Jerry and Becky Cope
(404) 746-2134

> *Music exalts each joy, allays each grief, expels diseases, softens every pain, subdues the rage of poison, and of plague.*
>
> *John Armstrong*

ILLINOIS

Northwestern University School of Music
Evanston, Illinois 60201

Program
Workshop, master classes, and courses covering various types of music: classical, popular, and jazz. Workshops and master classes, 1–2 weeks; courses, 2–6 weeks.

Accommodations
Dormitory rooms available on campus.

Cost
Write for information.

Recreation
Beach, pool, gymnasium, tennis courts.

Cultural Opportunities
Museums, theater, concerts, and more in nearby Chicago.

Comment
Northwestern's Summer Session music courses have been offered for many years. They are taught by resident faculty and visiting experts and are designed for the amateur or professional. Class size ranges from ten to one hundred; program flexibility allows interested persons to attend single lectures. Several master classes are held in conjunction with the Ravinia Festival. College credit available.

Further Information
James Moore
Director, Summer Session, School of Music
(312) 492-3141

Ravinia Festival
22 West Monroe Street
Chicago, Illinois 60603

Programs
(1) Annual Ravinia Festival, June–September. Classical music performances by the Chicago Symphony, visiting orchestras, celebrated soloists, and chamber ensembles; popular music; and theatrical and dance performances. Also, a full schedule of piano master classes conducted in cooperation with the Northwestern University School of Music.
(2) Young Artists Institute; beginning in 1987; 8-week session during the festival offering special training and performance opportunities to young artists who have demonstrated their potential.

Accommodations
Responsibility of participant.

Cost
Write for information.

Comment
The Ravinia Festival was established in 1936; James Levine has been its music director since 1973. The festival regularly attracts leading figures in international music, e.g., Leonard Bernstein, Leontyne Price, Andre Watts, Mischa Dichter, and Ella Fitzgerald.

Further Information
Communications Department
(312) 728-4642

For information on master classes:
School of Music
Northwestern University
Clark and Orrington Streets
Evanston, Illinois 60201
(312) 492-7575

> *On with the dance! let joy be*
> *unconfined;*
> *No sleep till morn, when*
> *Youth and Pleasure meet*
> *To chase the glowing hours*
> *with flying feet.*
> *George Gordon, Lord Byron*

University of Chicago
Division of Continuing
Education
5835 South Kimbark Avenue
Chicago, Illinois 60637

Program
Stratford (Ontario) Theater Trip, 5
days, summer.

Accommodations
Guest houses and motels.

Cost
$350–$400.

Comment
Trip (by bus) offers an opportunity to
meet performers backstage. It is
conducted by University of Chicago
faculty, and there is an orientation
seminar preceding the trip as well as
one following it. Maximum group size
is forty-four.

Further Information
Pam Knerr
(312) 962-1722

LOUISIANA

Fine Arts Foundation of
Lafayette, Inc.
Celebration of the Fine Arts
Festival
P.O. Box 53320
Lafayette, Louisiana 70505

Program
Celebration focusing on the works of a
leading classical composer, 1 month,
August–September. Features young
artists in various programs:
workshops, master classes, and
lecture-demonstrations.

Accommodations
Hotels and motels nearby.

Cost
Varies with program.

Recreation
Golf, tennis, horse racing, hunting, and
fishing nearby.

Comment
The Celebration of the Fine Arts
Festival has developed from a single
performance in 1972 into an annual
festival. In addition to instruction,
numerous concerts and art exhibitions
are featured. The Fine Arts
Foundation of Lafayette is a nonprofit
organization that sponsors almost
twenty performances every year.

Further Information
Michael Curry, Executive Director
(318) 233-2045

> *Every man is a damn fool for*
> *at least five minutes every*
> *day; wisdom consists in not*
> *exceeding the limit.*
> *Elbert Hubbard*

New Orleans Jazz and Heritage Festival
P.O. Box 2530
New Orleans, Louisiana 70176

Program
Jazz and Heritage Festival, annually, last weekend in April through first weekend in May. The festival features a wide variety of music, including jazz, blues, rock, gospel, and more. There are crafts exhibits, the Afro-American Market, parades, and evening jazz concerts.

Cost
For information, send self-addressed stamped envelope, marked "Attention: Public Relations" to the address above.

Comment
The festival is a national event and one of the outstanding cultural celebrations in the world. It is presented each year by the Jazz and Heritage Foundation and dedicated to preserving the traditions of New Orleans's music and Louisiana's heritage. The festival draws 250,000 people annually and presents more than 3000 musicians who perform at a fairgrounds racetrack, local clubs, concert halls, and aboard the Riverboat President, all in New Orleans.

Further Information
(504) 522-4786

Live neither in the past nor in the future. Let each day's work absorb your entire energies and satisfy your widest ambition.
                    William Osler

MARYLAND

Baltimore Opera Company
527 North Charles Street
Baltimore, Maryland 21201

Program
Musical and cultural tours in the United States and foreign countries. Past trips: a Royal Viking cruise to a Mediterranean musicale, the Santa Fe Opera Festival, and a musical tour of South America.

Accommodations and Cost
Write for information.

Comment
All Baltimore Opera Company tours stress the commitment to musical education that began when Metropolitan Opera Diva Rosa Ponselle established the company in 1950. Trips are led by Jay Holbrook, general manager of the company and an afficionado of this musical genre. Participants are given lectures prior to tours by Mr. Holbrook, other members of the company, and guest artists and are provided with related study materials.

Further Information
Kathleen Laughery
(301) 727-0592

MASSACHUSETTS

Jacob's Pillow Dance Festival
Box 287
Lee, Massachusetts 01238

Programs
(1) Jacob's Pillow Dance Festival School; 2-, 3-, and 5-week sessions, late

July to late August. Intensive courses for serious dance students.
(2) Annual season of performances of ballet in the Ted Shawn Theater, both modern and ethnic dance; also instrumental music concerts, June–September.

Accommodations
(1) Four-room cottages, double occupancy.
(2) Write for information.

Cost
(1) $765, 2-week session; $1145, 3-week session; $1180, 5-week session.
(2) Tickets: $15–$22.50.

Comments
Jacob's Pillow, established in 1931 by choreographer Ted Shawn, occupies one hundred wooded acres in the Berkshire Hills, in Beckett, about eight miles east of Lee on Route 20 and 150 miles from both Boston and New York City.

Further Information
Artistic Director
(413) 637-1322
Box Office
(413) 243-0745

Pines Theatre
Look Memorial Park
300 North Main Street
Northampton, Massachusetts
01060

Program
An outdoor program of music, theater, and children's events, summer and early fall.

Accommodations
Responsibility of participant.

Children
Theater series for children; train rides and zoo on park grounds.

Cost
Tickets: $1–$7; many programs free.

Recreation
Swimming, paddleboats, picnicking, and Pancake Cabin restaurant on park grounds.

Comment
Regular programming includes the Pickin' in the Pines bluegrass festival, popular artists series, and Sunday evening concerts.

Further Information
(413) 584-5457

The Tanglewood Music Center
Lenox, Massachusetts 01240

Programs
(1) Listening and Analysis Seminar, two consecutive 4-week sessions, late June to late August.
(2) Seminars for singers and conductors, 8 weeks, summer; write for information.

Accommodations
Dormitories, double occupancy.

Cost
(1) Tuition: $475 per 4-week session; accommodations and meals: $775 per 4-week session.

Recreation
Resort facilities and activities in the Berkshire Hills.

Cultural Opportunities
Berkshire Theatre Festival, Jacob's Pillow Dance Festival, and more nearby.

Comment
These seminars are designed for music lovers who wish an intensive music experience and the opportunity to become a part of the musical community surrounding the Boston

Symphony Orchestra at Tanglewood. Some prior background in classical music is necessary, but anyone over 16 years old may apply. An average of fifteen to twenty-five participants attend each seminar; enrollment in both sessions is allowed. Established in 1940 and formerly called the Berkshire Music Center, the Tanglewood Music Center provides an environment in which young performers can continue their professional training under the guidance of eminent musicians.

Further Information
Richard Ortner, Administrator
c/o Symphony Hall
Boston, Massachusetts 02115
(617) 266-5241

University of Massachusetts at Amherst
Historical Dance and Music Institute
P.O. Box 351
Amherst, Massachusetts 01004

Programs
(1) Annual Historical Dance Week covering varied dance types from fifteenth through nineteenth centuries.
(2) Intensive dance seminars.
(3) Dance Musicians Seminar.
(4) Marion Verbuggen Recorder Master Class.
All programs are 1 week during July.

Accommodations
Amherst College dormitories.

Cost
Tuition: $175; room and board: $175 (state resident participants). Write for information about nonresident fees and credit fees.

Comment
Historical Dance Week provides an opportunity for scholars, teachers, and

serious students to gain experience in a wide range of historical dance styles; special performances highlight the week. The Dance Musicians Seminar provides a week of ensemble and improvisatory experience; the Recorder Master Class is an intensive week of classes and lessons with an eminent virtuoso. Graduate and undergraduate credit obtainable for dance programs at additional cost.

Further Information
(413) 545-0111

MICHIGAN

Interlochen Center for the Arts
Chamber Music Conference
Interlochen, Michigan 49643

Program
Annual Chamber Music Conference for adults, 1 week, late August. Ensembles, master classes, repertory classes in piano, string, and chamber music; nightly concerts by renowned artists.

Accommodations
Housing on campus with private baths; housekeeping cottages for families.

Cost
Registration: $110; housing: $225–$325 (single), $400–$490 (double); $260–$500 (cottages). All except cottages include meals. University credit additional.

Recreation
Tennis, boating, swimming on campus; two lakes and golf course nearby; borders state park.

Comment
The Interlochen Chamber Music Conference was first held in 1950. It is

geared to amateur and semiprofessional musicians and features professional coaching in a structured program. Placement auditions are held for string players at the start of the conference. Instructors are university professors and professionals. Guest artists present nightly concerts. Average attendance is over 200.

Further Information
Special Events Office
(616) 276-9221, ext. 440

> *Civilization implies the graceful relation of all varieties of experience to a central humane system of thought.*
>
> *Robert Graves*

MONTANA

Montana State University
Adult Chamber Music Festival
Bozeman, Montana 59717

Program
Annual festival, comprising a workshop, concerts, and activities; 9 days; late June. Workshops are assigned by skill level and various ensemble combinations; coaching by professional musicians. Credit available.

Accommodations
Dormitory rooms, single and double.

Cost
Registration: $150 (partial programs available); rooms: $10–$12.50 per person per night; meals extra.

Recreation
Hiking, biking, fishing, tennis, swimming, mountain picnics.

Cultural Opportunities
Concerts, art exhibits, Museum of the Rockies, Shakespeare in the Parks, Loft Theatre.

Comment
The Adult Chamber Music Festival was first offered in 1971; approximately one hundred people attend annually. The atmosphere is relaxed and friendly. Playing groups are rotated daily with playing opportunities for student performances. An excellent chamber music library is available.

Further Information
Mary C. Sanks, Director
(406) 587-8220 or 944-3561

NEW HAMPSHIRE

Apple Hill Center for Chamber
*   Music*
East Sullivan, New Hampshire
*   03445*

Program
Chamber music group courses; three short sessions of 10 days each, followed by a 1-month session; summer. Sessions are designed for musicians of all skill levels.

Accommodations
Rustic cabins on property.

Cost
Tuition: $485, short session; $1285, long session. Application fee: $10.

Recreation
Swimming, mountain climbing, soccer, volleyball.

Cultural Opportunities
Faculty recitals and concerts; dances, movies.

Comment
The Apple Hill Center was founded in 1968. Forty-five to fifty students attend each session and are matched in carefully chosen ensembles including strings, woodwinds, voice, and piano. In short sessions, participants are assigned to at least two ensembles; in the long session, two per week. Core faculty are members of the Apple Hill Chamber Players; guest faculty are chosen for their communications skills and are graduates or affiliates of such schools as Juilliard, Oberlin, Brandeis, and the Tchaikovsky Conservatory in Moscow. College credit available.

Further Information
(603) 847-3371

*Merrimack Valley Music and
   Art Center
2500 North River Road
Manchester, New Hampshire
   03104*

Program
Annual seminars, master classes, and coaching for amateur chamber musicians; three weeklong sessions; July. An art program, in a variety of media for students at all levels, is conducted at the same time.

Accommodations
Dormitories and apartments.

Cost
$290–$485 per week, depending on type of accommodations, all inclusive.

Recreation
Tennis, swimming, racquetball, golf, and more.

Cultural Opportunities
Staff concerts, weekly student art exhibits, films, library.

Comment
The Merrimack Valley Center was established in 1975 as part of New Hampshire College. The chamber music program offers a wide variety of options. String and woodwind players and pianists are scheduled daily in compatible groups, with or without professional coaching. Participants play in the Merrimack Valley Chamber Music Orchestra, which gives informal performances. The art program provides individual instruction. The Center can accommodate one hundred people per week.

Further Information
Director of Summer Programs
(603) 669-1831

> *Profound truths [are] recognized by the fact that the opposite is also a profound truth.*
>
> *Niels Bohr*

NEW JERSEY

*Westminster Choir College
Princeton, New Jersey 08540*

Programs
(1) Summer Session: More than fifty 1-week practical courses and master classes in music education, church music, piano, organ, voice, and choral

music; late June–August. Graduate credit available.

(2) High school programs: Vocal camp, 2 weeks; organ and piano programs, 1 week.

Accommodations
Dormitory, double occupancy; dining commons.

Cost
Write for information.

Cultural Opportunities
Recitals, concerts, oratoria, and nightly hymn sings.

Comment
Established in 1926, Westminster is a small school with a reputation for musical excellence. The Summer Session is one of the nation's largest and most diverse. Located in historic Princeton, Westminster attracts some of the world's leading musicians, including Robert Shaw, John and Helen Kemp, Sir David Willocks, and Margaret Harshaw. Participants include church musicians, music educators, college professors, performing artists, and amateur music lovers.

Further Information
(609) 924-7416

If we begin with certainties, we shall end in doubts, but if we begin with doubts (and are patient in them), we shall end in certainties.
            Francis Bacon

Art! Who comprehends her? With whom can one consult concerning this great goddess?
            Ludwig van Beethoven

NEW MEXICO

Santa Fe Chamber Music Festival
P.O. Box 853
Santa Fe, New Mexico 87501

Program
Chamber Music Festival season includes concerts, lecture-demonstrations, recitals, and open rehearsals; July–August. Schubert Series, American Composer Series, open discussion, and rehearsals.

Accommodations
Write for information.

Cost
Individual concert seats: $7.50–$20; season tickets available. Discussions, open rehearsals, youth concerts, and other events of the festival are free.

Cultural Opportunities
Santa Fe Opera, Taos Indian pueblos, museums, and art galleries.

Comment
The annual festival brings the best in chamber music to historic Santa Fe. World-class artists are featured.

Further Information
Daniel Koshabek
(505) 983-2075

NEW YORK

The Center for Music in Westchester
24 Hillside Avenue
Katonah, New York 10536

Program
Two 2-week chamber music workshops for students, young professionals, and adult amateurs; June–July. Instruction in strings, winds, piano, and voice.

Accommodations
Rooms on campus, homes, nearby hotels.

Cost
Write for information.

Recreation
Swimming, tennis, hiking.

Cultural Opportunities
Caramoor Festival.

Comment
The Center is located at the Harvey School in Katonah, forty miles north of New York City. Its program was first offered in 1980. It features coaching, master classes, student performances, and concerts by the faculty and visiting artists. Instructors are qualified musicians and university faculty members; private instruction is available. Average attendance is ten to fifteen per workshop.

Further Information
Alan Bramson, Director
(914) 232-4019

Dance, dance till you drop!
W. H. Auden

Country Dance and Song Society of America
505 Eighth Avenue
New York, New York 10018

Program
Weeklong programs of folk dance and music, July to early September. Included are sessions on early music, American dance and music, folk music, and English dance; also family week and a camper week.

Accommodations
Comfortable cabins in the woods at Pinewoods Camp, near Plymouth, Massachusetts.

Children
Minimum age for courses is 18. Children are welcome during the family and camper weeks but are the responsibility of their parents. Write for information.

Cost
Adults: $288–$315 per session; infants to teens: $13–$276, all inclusive. Membership in the society is $25.

Recreation
Swimming, boating, outdoor games.

Cultural Opportunities
Located near historic Plymouth, Massachusetts, and Cape Cod.

Comment
The Country Dance and Song Society of America was founded in 1915. It is a nonprofit organization devoted to the enjoyment, preservation, and study of English and American traditional dance, music, and song. The Pinewoods Camp is located between two large ponds and has large pavilions for dance and other activities. Instruction in dance, song, and a variety of instruments is provided by nationally known professionals from the United

States and England. Scholarships are available, with recipients asked to help in various camp activities. There is a dance and musical concert each night with group participation.

Further Information
Fall/Winter/Spring Programs:
Country Dance and Song Society of
    America
505 Eighth Avenue
New York, New York 10018

Summer Programs:
Pinewoods Camp
RFD #6, Box 451
Plymouth, Massachusetts 02360
(617) 224-3480

Madeira Bach Festival
437 Madison Avenue
New York, New York 10022

Program
Annual International Festival on Madeira Island, Portugal. Featured are renowned vocal and instrumental soloists, choral groups from both sides of the Atlantic, and the Madeira Festival Chamber Ensemble. The Festival is booked as part of a tour that includes the island and/or Portuguese mainland; 9 or 13 days.

Accommodations
Super-deluxe, deluxe, or first-class hotels, with corresponding concert seating and activities.

Cost
Write for information.

Recreation
Hiking, fishing, waterskiing, tennis, swimming available.

Cultural Opportunities
Tours of historic towns and buildings, scenic sites, museums; wine tastings.

Comment
The Madeira Bach Festival was first held in 1980. Concerts are held in different locations, such as the fifteenth-century Cathedral da Se. Works include Bach's major choral and instrumental works, as well as music of Vivaldi, Mozart, Brahms, and others.

Further Information
Extra Travel Value, Inc.
(212) 750-8800

Metropolitan Opera Guild
1865 Broadway
New York, New York 10023

Program
Opera lovers' tours to Europe held throughout the year. Itineraries feature numerous operatic performances, private tours and receptions, and recitals. Recent examples include a 17-day tour to southern Italy and Sicily as well as the Blue Danube and Adriatic Odyssey, a 16-day tour.

Accommodations
Deluxe.

Cost
For examples above: Italy, $4992 per person (double occupancy) plus $735 round-trip airfare from New York; Blue Danube, $4837 per person (double occupancy) plus $852 round-trip airfare from New York.

Comment
The Metropolitan Opera Guild sponsors more than ten trips throughout the year to important opera festivals, performances, and related events. Professional guides accompany all groups and side tours; related cultural and antiquarian sites

are always included. Guild membership is required.

Further Information
Shirley Bakal, Director
Members Travel Program
(212) 582-7500

> *Life calls the tune—we dance.*
> *John Galsworthy*

Mohonk Mountain House
October Fest of Chamber Music
Mohonk Lake
New Paltz, New York 12561

Program
Chamber Music Festival, 4 days, late October; concerts, master classes, workshops, readings, and discussions with professional musicians.

Accommodations
Double or single rooms, with or without bath. Mohonk Mountain House is a full-service resort and conference center, founded in 1869 on 2000 wooded acres near New Paltz, New York.

Cost
Single: $392–$512; double: $656–$804; complete with meals; partial packages also available. Small fees for players.

Comment
The October Fest, held annually since 1976, has events for musicians and nonmusicians. Those accepted as players are assigned to peer groups for morning sessions. An average of 300 people attend the fest annually, with 90 participating as musicians. Resident groups have included the Duncun Wind Quintet, the Mendelssohn String Quartet, and the Arden Trio.

Further Information
Music Director
(914) 255-1000
In New York City:
(212) 233-2244

Queens College/CUNY
Continuing Education Program
65-30 Kissena Boulevard
Flushing, New York 11367

Program
Backstage at the Berkshires, 1 week, August. Cultural seminar includes dance, music, and theater performances; field trips to museums and historic sites; lecture and discussion of play performed.

Accommodations
Double-occupancy dormitories, Simon's Rock of Bard College, Great Barrington, Massachusetts.

Cost
$490, includes tuition, room and board, local admissions, and transportation.

Recreation
Swimming pool, tennis, hiking, golf (nearby).

Cultural Opportunities
Trips to Jacob's Pillow (dance), Tanglewood (music), Berkshires Playhouse (theater), and other local sites.

Comment
The program, organized in 1983, is designed for people who have artistic cravings but no time or inclination to make decisions about where to go and what to see. It provides insights into the creative process through analysis of theater performances and observation of orchestra rehearsals.

Further Information
Elayne Bernstein, Assistant Director
(718) 520-7052

A talent is formed in stillness,
a character in the stream of
the world.
Johann Wolfgang von Goethe

Further Information
In the United States:
Rosemarie Fliegel
Austrian Music Festivals
Suite 2011 at the above address
(212) 944-6891
In Austria:
Tourist Office
Marketplatz 9
Salzburg, Austria

Salzburg Festival
Austrian National Tourist
   Office
500 Fifth Avenue
New York, New York 10110

Program
Annual 5-week festival, late summer.
Features more than one hundred
performances of opera, orchestral and
chamber music, lieder, instrumental
recitals, readings, and drama.
Performances by internationally
known artists. Works of all periods and
styles.

Accommodations
Write for information.

Cost
Advance sales of tickets in U.S.:
operas, $40–$115; orchestral concerts,
$17.50–$60; other events, $12.50–$60.

Comment
Founded in 1921, the Salzburg Festival
has become one of the largest in
Europe. Its mainstay continues to be
the works of Mozart; music, drama,
and dance from other composers and
periods are also performed. The
festival has attracted leading
conductors such as Arturo Toscanini,
Herbert von Karajan, and James
Levine.

Saratoga Performing Arts
   Center
Summer Festival
Saratoga Springs, New York
   12866

Program
Summer Festival offers ballet, drama,
classical and popular music, and the
Saratoga-Potsdam Chorus. A summer
school program offers courses in
orchestral studies, choral studies,
dance, and theater.

Accommodations
Responsibility of participants; lodging
nearby.

Cost
Write for details.

Recreation
Swimming, tennis, golf, mineral baths,
hiking, and biking. Saratoga Lake and
the Adirondack Mountains are nearby.

Cultural Opportunities
The Saratoga Performing Arts Center
is the summer home of the New York
City Ballet, the Philadelphia
Orchestra, and a Little Theatre.

Comment
The Performing Arts Center was
opened in 1966. Summer school courses
are taught by faculty of the State

University of New York system and by members of the leading performing arts companies. College credit for the Saratoga-Potsdam Chorus is available through SUNY College at Potsdam.

Further Information
(518) 584-9330

School for Singers
24 Hillside Avenue
Katonah, New York 10536

Programs
(1) Summer session with courses in all aspects of the singer's art, 4 weeks, July. Courses include opera workshops, performance classes, private and group lessons, and musical theater.
(2) Master classes for students, young professionals, and adult amateurs; late May–June. Include technique and interpretation, lieder, and opera.

Accommodations
Rooms on campus, homes, nearby motels.

Cost
Write for information.

Recreation
Swimming, tennis, hiking.

Cultural Opportunities
Caramoor Festival; chamber music concerts.

Comment
The School for Singers opened in 1980 and attracts a maximum of 150 students annually. It is located at the Harvey School in Katonah, about forty miles north of New York City, and offers a variety of courses for both adults and children. Instructors are highly qualified, conservatory-trained professionals. Concerts are given by faculty and visiting artists.

Further Information
Berenice Bramson, Director
(914) 232-4019

Tennanah Lakeshore Lodge
Chamber Music Holiday
Roscoe, New York 12776

Program
Annual holiday program for chamber musicians, three weekend sessions: Memorial Day, July 4th, and Labor Day.

Accommodations
Double or single rooms at the lodge, in the Catskills on the shores of Tennanah Lake.

Cost
$140 per person, Memorial Day; $155–$195, July 4th; $155, Labor Day. Rates include meals and use of lodge; single occupancy extra.

Recreation
Hiking, fishing, rowing, swimming, tennis, and more.

Comment
Held annually since 1977, the Chamber Music Holidays offer the opportunity to combine music and holiday celebrations. Musical direction is provided by competent instructors, and there is access to an extensive music library. Participants should bring their own music stands.

Further Information
(607) 498-4900

Dream what you dare to dream. Go where you want to go. Be what you want to be.
Calvin Coolidge

NORTH CAROLINA

Brevard Music Center
P.O. Box 592
Brevard, North Carolina 28712

Programs
(1) Educational program in music
theory and performance, 7 weeks,
June–August. Special sessions in
composition, chamber music, repertory
training, and orchestral performance.
(2) Brevard Music Festival, 6½ weeks,
July–August.

Accommodations
(1) Dormitories.
(2) Make own arrangements.

Cost
(1) $1095, tuition, room, board, private
lessons, music fee; special rates for
nonresident students.
(2) $5–$8.50 per performance.

Recreation
Tennis, swimming, hiking, canoeing,
basketball, dances.

Comment
(1) The Brevard Music Center opened
in 1937. Its educational program
admits students 12–28 years of age and
has three divisions. Teachers and guest
artists provide professional coaching.
Average class size is ten (largest is
twenty-five), and there is ample
opportunity for private lessons,
seminars, and master classes. College
credit obtainable through Converse
College in South Carolina.
(2) The Brevard Music Festival
features performances of symphony,
opera, and more by guest artists and
Brevard resident organizations. More
than 75,000 people attend each
summer.

Further Information
Mr. Louis Hrabovsky, Director of
Development
(704) 884-2011

> *Only the educated are free.*
> ***Epictetus***

Glickman-Popkin Bassoon Camp
Wildacres
Little Switzerland, North Carolina 28749

Program
Weeklong classes in all aspects of the
bassoon, late spring.

Accommodations
Lodges.

Cost
$260, tuition, accommodations, meals.

Comment
The Glickman-Popkin Bassoon Camp
was established in 1979. Its program
includes classes in orchestral
repertoire, auditions, solos and
chamber music, teaching methods, etc.
Also featured are reed classes, lectures
on bassoon design and repair, master
classes, and free bassoon repairs.
Schedule allows for daily performance
hours and solo and ensemble
performances. Instructors are all
experts in the bassoon. A beach camp
at Emerald Isle, North Carolina, is also
held.

Further Information
Mark Popkin, Director
Glickman-Popkin Bassoon Camp
740 Arbor Road
Winston-Salem, North Carolina 27104
(919) 725-5681

NORTH DAKOTA

International Music Camp
Bottineau, North Dakota 58318

Program
Summer school of fine arts; eight
weekly sessions, June–July.
Workshops and performance in music,
drama, dance, and visual arts;
computer camp recently added. Most
sessions for junior and senior high
school students, but some sessions
available for younger people and
adults.

Accommodations
Dormitories; cabins also available for
adults; camping for couples and
families only.

Cost
$150 per session, includes tuition,
room, and board; $15, private lessons.

Recreation
Swimming, volleyball, softball.

Comment
The camp was established in 1956 at
the International Peace Garden, on the
North Dakota–Manitoba border. Each
year 2000 students from all over the
world participate in the program. The
camp has a staff of 145, with additional
guest clinicians and conductors.
Facilities include large rehearsal halls,
studios, a music library, and
amphitheater. College credit available.

Further Information
Joseph T. Aline, Director
(701) 228-2277, ext. 46

> *What I could not learn was to*
> *think creatively on schedule.*
> *Agnes de Mille*

> *He who does not love art in*
> *all things does not love it at*
> *all, and he who does not need*
> *art in all things does not need*
> *it at all.*
> *Oscar Wilde*

OHIO

Oberlin College
Summer Organ Institute
Conservatory of Music
Oberlin, Ohio 44074

Program
One week, summer.

Accommodations
Dormitory rooms with shared baths.

Cost
Tuition: $225; housing: $125 weekly
(double occupancy). Private instruction
by arrangement additional.

Recreation
Swimming, tennis.

Cultural Opportunities
Art museum, concerts.

Comment
The Institute offers the opportunity to
study with some of the world's foremost
teachers and performers. The program
is designed for organists of
intermediate, advanced, or
professional standing and includes
master classes, lectures, and faculty
and student concerts. Enrollment is
limited.

Further Information
Professor Garth Peacock
(216) 775-8246

OREGON

***Portland State University
Haystack Summer Program in
the Arts
P.O. Box 1491
Portland, Oregon 97201***

Program
A summer arts program with 5- to 10-
day workshops in music, writing, and
art; June–August. Credit or noncredit
options. Specific subjects have included
songwriting, fiddle, steel drum, guitar,
watercolor, photography, storytelling,
fiction, and poetry.

Accommodations
A variety of housing in Cannon Beach
and nearby; campsites and trailer
spaces available. Write for details.

Children
Program for ages 4–13; music, art,
beachcombing, hiking, field trips,
other activities; throughout the season.

Cost
$160, 1 week; $210, 2 weeks; $45 per
week for first child; $35 per week for
other children; $10 per course, credit
fee.

Recreation
Fishing, charter craft, horseback
riding, hiking, bicycling, swimming,
tennis, golf; sand-castle-building
competition.

Cultural Opportunities
Art galleries, free concerts, summer
theater.

Comment
Established in 1969, the Haystack
Summer Program in the Arts (named
for Haystack Rock, a prominent coastal
feature) has no admissions
requirements, though some workshops

have prerequisites. Instructors are
university professors and other
experts. An average of 500–700 people
participate each summer at the
facilities of the elementary school in
Cannon Beach, Oregon, approximately
eighty miles northwest of Portland.

Further Information
(503) 229-4849
    or
In Oregon: (800) 452-4909
Outside Oregon: (800) 547-8887

PENNSYLVANIA

***Gettysburg College Chamber
    Music Workshop
Music Department
Gettysburg College
Gettysburg, Pennsylvania 17325***

Program
Two 1-week Chamber Music
Workshops, late June.

Accommodations
Housing on campus.

Cost
$185 tuition, room, and board; special
fee for commuting students.

Recreation
Tennis, swimming, bowling, games.

Cultural Opportunities
Gettysburg Battlefield National Park,
including museum.

Comment
The Gettysburg Chamber Music
Workshop was first held in 1972; in
1984 a second week was added. The
program features private lessons,
master classes, chamber music, and
ensembles. Its primary goal is to
provide an atmosphere conducive to

the study and performance of chamber music. Average number of participants is forty, ranging from 13 to 65 years of age. Eligible to participate are students, teachers, and others interested in playing chamber music and expanding their playing skills and teaching abilities on stringed instruments. The Mendelssohn String Quartet is in residence for the second week, providing coaching, master classes, and performances. Enrollment is limited; students accepted on the basis of musical ability and application date.

Further Information
Dr. Norman K. Nunamaker
Director, Summer Chamber Music
    Workshop
(717) 334-3131

The play's the thing . . .
                Shakespeare

International String Conference and Chamber Music Workshop
962 West Penn Drive
West Chester, Pennsylvania 19380

Program
Annual Conference, 10 days, August; programs for youth (junior-high and senior-high), a chamber music workshop with quartet in residence, and a special guitar orchestra. All programs include master classes, small and large ensembles, recitals, and social events.

Accommodations
Dormitory rooms, double or single occupancy. Motels and inns nearby.

Cost
Adults: $215; youth (12–18): $190; includes tuition, room, and board. Special fees for nonplaying family; single occupancy additional.

Recreation
Tennis, swimming, games.

Cultural Opportunities
Philadelphia, Valley Forge, Longwood Gardens, Brandywine Battlefield, art galleries, museums, zoo.

Comment
The conference began in 1962 and has been held at Immaculata College since 1972. It is presented in cooperation with the Pennsylvania and American String Teachers Associations and attracts over 400 participants annually. The faculty comes from educational institutions and symphony orchestras across the country. College credit is available through Catholic University of America, which is affiliated with Immaculata College.

Further Information
Dr. Constantine Jones, Executive
    Director
(215) 696-4092

Luzerne County Folk Festival
Luzerne County Tourist Promotion Agency
301 Market Street
Kingston, Pennsylvania 19704

Program
Held annually at the 190th Armory in Kingston, 4 days, late September to early October.

Accommodations
Available nearby; festival office will assist with arrangements.

Cost
Nominal ticket charges.

Cultural Opportunities
Wyoming County Historical Society
Museum and Library, three colleges,
two house museums, numerous
historical sites, Eckley Miners' Village
(a restored mid-nineteenth-century
community), Osterhout and Hoyt
libraries.

Comment
The Luzerne County Folk Festival was
first held in 1976. Its full-scale
multiethnic program features heritage
exhibitions, arts and crafts
demonstrations, music and dance
performances, and special food.

Further Information
Executive Director
(717) 288-6784

Music in the Mountains
214 Avon Road
Narbeth, Pennsylvania 19072

Program
Intensive coaching in chamber music
performance for violinists, violists,
cellists, and pianists, ages 13–20; 2
weeks; August. Culminates in final
concert; other performance
opportunities.

Accommodations
Local families and chaperoned
dormitory-style lodge in Eagles Mere,
Pennsylvania, in the Endless
Mountains, one hundred miles from
Philadelphia.

Cost
$200, tuition and lodging; meals
arranged with host family, cooked at
lodge, or bought at local restaurants.

Recreation
Hiking, canoeing, swimming, sailing,
cookouts, picnics, county fair.

Cultural Opportunities
Craft shows, concerts, plays, art
exhibits, and more.

Comment
Instruction by members of the
Philadelphia Trio; 3–6 hours of daily
coaching, rehearsal, theory class.
Ample time for recreation. Alumni
have gone on to such schools as
Eastman, New England Conservatory,
and Peabody. Ten to twelve persons are
selected by audition annually.

Further Information
Deborah Reeder or Barbara Sonies
(215) 664-0346

> *Music above all, and for this*
> *Prefer an uneven rhythm.*
> *Paul Verlaine*

RHODE ISLAND

Newport Music Festival
50 Washington Square
Newport, Rhode Island 02840

Program
Annual festival, 2 weeks, July;
performances of chamber and romantic
music from the nineteenth century.
The festival offers over thirty concerts,
usually combining solo and ensemble
performances, presented in historic
mansions, such as the Breakers, the
Elms, Belcourt Castle, Beechwood, and
Marble House.

Cost
$12–$21 admission per concert.

Cultural Opportunities
Tour of historic Newport homes, Touro Synagogue; many events held in connection with the festival.

Comment
The festival, established in 1969, includes morning, afternoon, and evening concerts. Repertory has varied from Tchaikovsky to American works, with an emphasis on pieces rarely or never before performed. Many performers of international acclaim have made their debuts here.

Further Information
Mark P. Malkovich III, General
    Director
(401) 846-1133

> *O body swayed to music,*
> *O brightening glance,*
> *How can we know the dancer*
>   *from the dance?*
>   *W. B. Yeats*

SOUTH CAROLINA

Spoleto Festival (U.S.A.)
P.O. Box 157
Charleston, South Carolina
*   29402*

Program
Annual festival of performing and visual arts in Charleston, South Carolina, 17 days, May–June. Featured are opera; ballet; modern dance; theater; jazz, symphonic, choral, and chamber music; and the visual arts.

Accommodations
Write to the Charleston Chamber of Commerce or call (803) 722-8338.

Cost
Tickets for individual events: $5–$34.

Comment
Held annually since 1977, the Charleston Festival is the American part of the Festival of Two Worlds, along with its counterpart in Spoleto, Italy. Artistic director is Gian Carlo Menotti; music director is Christian Badea. In recent years, attendance has averaged 100,000.

Further Information
Susan E. Kennedy, Marketing and
    Public Relations Manager
(803) 577-7863

TENNESSEE

Folk Life Center of the Smokies
P.O. Box 8
Cosby, Tennessee 37722

Programs
(1) Annual Cosby Dulcimer and Harp Convention, 3 days, June. Workshops on playing and building dulcimers and harp folk instruments, beginning to advanced level.
(2) Annual Folk Festival of the Smokies, 3 days, August; workshops on folk dancing, song collecting, others.

Accommodations
Camping on site, dormitory at local community center; other campgrounds and motels nearby. No firearms, firecrackers, or pets.

Children
(1) Special activities for children.
(2) Write for information.

Cost
$17 per weekend, including tent sites;
$8 per day, admission only.

Recreation
Great Smoky Mountains National
Park nearby, many trails and creeks.

Comment
Founded in 1971, the Folk Life Center
is dedicated to preserving the
traditions of American folk culture,
with emphasis on the southern
Appalachian region.

Further Information
Jean and Lee Schilling, Directors
(615) 487-5543

> *Music rots when it gets too
> far from the dance.*
>   *Ezra Pound*

TEXAS

*International Festival-Institute
   at Round Top
P.O. Box 89
Round Top, Texas 78954*

Programs
(1) Summer Season Classical Music
festival, 7 weeks, early June through
late July.
(2) Winter Series, 1 weekend per
month, August–April.

Accommodations
Arrangements should be made well in
advance; reservations required. Write
for information.

Cost
$7.50 per concert ticket. $50–$60 per
person, including ticket, room for 1
night, and continental breakfast.

Recreation
Lakes in the area.

Cultural Opportunities
William C. Wiederhold Library, with
largest private collection of materials
related to Toscanini known to exist.
Also historic restorations nearby; film
programs, weekends of August–April;
seminars on various topics.

Comment
Located an equal distance from Austin
and Houston, the Festival-Institute
was established in 1971. It has
acquired an international reputation
and is attended by distinguished
musicians, conductors, critics,
painters, and scholars.

Further Information
Lamar Lentz
(409) 249-3129

UTAH

*Snowbird Institute
Snowbird, Utah 84092*

Programs
(1) String Chamber Music Festival, 9
days; Youth Orchestra, 2 weeks,
August; workshops and performances.
(2) Modern Dance Workshops, two
sessions of 3 weeks each, June–August.
(3) Visual Arts Workshops: weaving,
lithography, photography.

Accommodations
First-class hotels, lodges, dormitories. No pets.

Children
Children and the Arts day camp, 1 week, July; $80 plus transportation. Daily day camp throughout the Institute session, age 5 and up.

Cost
(1) Chamber Music, $220; Youth Orchestra, $135.
(2) Dance Workshops, $300.
(3) $45–$165 per workshop.

Recreation
Hiking, tennis, tram rides, swimming, dancing, camping.

Cultural Opportunities
Utah Symphony, chamber music, dance, jazz, and rock concerts.

Comment
Snowbird was established in 1971 as both a summer and winter resort in Little Cottonwood Canyon in Wasatch National Forest, 45 minutes from Salt Lake International Airport. During the summer, several thousand people visit the complex. Workshops are taught in a beautiful alpine setting that is very conducive to learning.

Further Information
Linder Bonar
Director, Arts and Entertainment
(801) 742-2222, ext. 4080

> *The only way to be happy is to shut yourself up in art, and count everything else as nothing.*
> *Gustave Flaubert*

VERMONT

Brattleboro Music Center
Bach/Handel Performances Workshop
15 Walnut Street
Brattleboro, Vermont 05301

Program
Annual workshop includes coaching, rehearsals, and performances; 2 weeks; June.

Accommodations
Arranged in local homes.

Cost
$395, includes lessons, coaching, use of facilities and some meals; $75, room and breakfast. $75, auditor's fee for coaching only.

Comment
Artistic Director Blanche Honneger Mayse is assisted by guest coaches. Works from vocal and instrumental literature are assigned according to ability and combination of instruments. Music by Bach and Handel is highlighted. Workshop is limited to thirty; open to professional and advanced students and amateurs. College credit is available.

Further Information
(802) 257-4523

Vermont Music and Arts Center
Lyndon State College
Lyndonville, Vermont 05851

Program
Chamber music workshop, 3–4 weeks, July. Program covers chamber music of all periods, from Baroque to contemporary. Master classes,

informal and formal concerts, and varied ensembles are featured. Instruction in painting and ceramics is also available.

Accommodations
College dormitories and dining hall.

Children
Children may accompany parents but are solely their responsibility.

Cost
$325 per week, includes instruction, room, and board; $250 for accompanying nonparticipants. Minimum registration: 1 week.

Recreation
Tennis, swimming, golf, hiking.

Cultural Opportunities
College library, museums, theaters in nearby towns, chamber music concerts.

Comment
The Vermont Music and Arts Center was founded in 1953 and moved to Lyndon State College in 1971. Program atmosphere is informal, and participants can choose their own activities. Director is Samuel Flor, violinist and violist, a former Minneapolis Symphony member, professor, and author of books on string technique; other instructors are professional musicians and college faculty members. Participants come from all over the United States and from abroad. Average attendance each summer is 300.

Further Information
Summer:
Samuel Flor, Director
(802) 626-9371

Winter:
Vermont Music and Arts Center
c/o Samuel Flor, Director
1049 Holly Tree Road
Abingdon, Pennsylvania 19001

> *Architecture, sculpture, painting, music and poetry may truly be called the efflorescence of civilized life.*
> **Herbert Spencer**

VIRGINIA

Shenandoah Valley Music Festival
P.O. Box 12
Woodstock, Virginia 22664

Program
A festival of symphony, pops, and Big Band music; late July and Labor Day Weekend; held at the Orkney Springs Hotel in the Shenandoah Mountains, 120 miles northwest of Richmond.

Accommodations
Motels and hotels nearby.

Cost
Concert tickets: $6–$10 (adults), $1–$10 (children). Subscriptions available.

Recreation
Camping, fishing, hiking; golf, tennis, swimming nearby; ice cream social.

Cultural Opportunities
Arts and crafts show, Luray Caverns, New Market Battlefield Museum, Storybook Trail.

Comment
The Shenandoah Valley Music

Festival has been held annually since 1963. Music director and conductor of the Festival Orchestra is William Hudson, director of the Fairfax Symphony and professor at the University of Maryland. In 1984, total festival attendance was over 6500.

Further Information
Betsy Brockman
Administration
(703) 459-3396
    or
Shenandoah Valley Travel Association
(703) 740-3132

Wolf Trap Associates
1551 Trap Road
Vienna, Virginia 22180

Program
Annual trips to American cities, with specially arranged activities; varying durations. Example: 2-day trip to New York City for ballet and opera, as well as opportunities to meet the artists. Trips abroad offered periodically, including activities with performing artists.

Accommodations
In New York, participants stay at the Waldorf Astoria Hotel. Other trips generally use first-class accommodations.

Cost
Write for details; $35 membership fee prerequisite.

Comment
Wolf Trap Associates, a nonprofit organization for the advancement of

the performing arts, is located at Wolf Trap Farm Park in suburban Washington, D.C. More than 1000 people have participated in its trips since 1972.

Further Information
Nancy E. Brockman, Executive
    Director
(703) 255-1940

Music is love in search of a word.
                        Sidney Lanier

WASHINGTON

Centrum Foundation
Centrum Summer Session
Box 1158
Port Townsend, Washington
*   98368*

Program
Workshops and events in the performing arts throughout the summer. Festival of American Fiddle Tunes, International Folk Dance/ Music Festival, Jazz Workshop, theater, and more.

Accommodations
Dormitories, motels, hotels, other facilities nearby.

Cost
Varies with workshop; tuition: $100–$150; room and board: $140; room only: $58; 1 week.

Recreation
Tennis, picnic grounds, hiking, fishing, scuba diving.

Cultural Opportunities
Performances of music, theater, and dance throughout the summer; Port Townsend is a National Historic Landmark.

Comment
The Centrum Foundation was established in 1972 by the Washington State Arts Commission. Its purpose is to unite recreational, cultural, and educational opportunities. Workshops are conducted by professional artists and craftsmen.

Further Information
(206) 385-3102
(800) 742-4221

> *I get more help in my work from a good play than from any other kind of thoughtful rest.*
> **John Ruskin**

Seattle Opera Association
Pacific Northwest Wagner Festival
P.O. Box 9248
Seattle, Washington 98109

Program
Annual opera festival, 2 weeks, summer. Featured is the complete *Der Ring des Nibelungen,* Richard Wagner's Ring Cycle of four operas; performances in German with English translations. Festival previews and lectures by foremost musicologists and Wagner specialists.

Accommodations
Hotels, motels, and inns in Seattle and vicinity.

Cost
$72–$296 tickets for the four-opera cycle.

Recreation
Seattle Center, hiking and climbing in nearby mountains, fishing and boating.

Cultural Opportunities
Film festival, theaters; dance and music performances, both classical and popular.

Comment
The Seattle Opera Association first held the Wagner Festival in 1975. Seattle is one of the few places in the Western Hemisphere where the complete Ring Cycle is presented. The festival annually features an orchestra and great Wagnerian singers, making it a realization of the composer's vision of a festival devoted exclusively to his works. Attendance for each cycle averages 3000.

Further Information
Dorothy Dening Smith
Administrative Director
(206) 443-4700

> *It is not so important to be serious as it is to be serious about the important things.*
> **R. M. Hutchins**

> *And so we all of us in some*
>   *degree*
> *Are led to knowledge,*
>   *wheresoever led,*
> *And howsoever.*
>   *William Wordsworth*

AUSTRIA

International Vienna Festival
Austrian National Tourist
Office
Friedrichstrasse 7
Vienna, Austria

Program
Annual 5-week music festival, May–
June. Featured are operas performed
by Vienna State Opera and Volksoper
companies, concerts, symposia, and
theatrical performances;
internationally renowned and local
artists.

Accommodations
Write for information.

Cost
Many events are free. Write for
information.

Cultural Opportunities
Art and photography exhibitions,
films, readings, museums, gardens,
shops, and more.

Comment
The Wiener Festwochen (Vienna
Festival Weeks) were revived after
World War II. They are now among the
major European spring music festivals.
Occasionally the program features the
works of one composer.

Further Information
In Austria:
(0222) 579657
In the United States:
Austrian National Tourist Office
500 Fifth Avenue
New York, New York 10110
(212) 944-6880

CANADA

Banff Festival of the Arts
Box 1020
Banff, Alberta T0L 0C0
Canada

Program
An 8-week festival featuring opera,
ballet, drama, music, readings, and
more. Performers are students and
faculty members at Banff Centre
School of Fine Arts.

Accommodations
Hotels, motels, camping, trailer
facilities. Also bed-and-breakfast
arrangements.

Cost (Canadian dollars)
Musical performances: $10–$12.

Recreation
Hiking, mountain climbing nearby.
Lake Louis offers boating and
swimming.

Comment
The Banff Centre School of Fine Arts,
which produces the Festival, began in
1933 as an experimental theater
school, with music becoming an
integral part of its program soon after.

It has attracted an outstanding faculty that gives master classes and conducts workshops. Performances are held in principal theaters, churches, and schools, as well as out of doors, with concerts and recitals of varied types, including ballet, opera, and musical theater; also playwriting, readings, and art exhibitions.

Further Information
Banff Chamber of Commerce
Box 1298
Banff, Alberta T0L 0C0
Canada
(403) 762-3777

*Johannesen International
    School of the Arts
103-3737 Oak Street
Vancouver, British Columbia
    V6H 2M4
Canada*

Programs
(1) Summer school, 3- and 6-week courses in advanced music instruction, including contemporary music and chamber music, July–August.
(2) Victoria International Festival, July–August.

Accommodations
Provided on campus.

Cost (Canadian dollars)
(1) $1730, boarding student for 6 weeks, including admission to the festival; $945, for 3-week program.
(2) Write for details.

Recreation
Swimming, tennis; gym, playing field. Proximity to sea and beaches.

Cultural Opportunities
Local theaters where festival is presented, library.

Comment
Programs are held at St. Michaels University School on the outskirts of the city of Victoria on Vancouver Island.
(1) The school is named after J. J. Johannesen, an outstanding musician and music commentator, who established it in 1971 (when it was called the Shawnigan Summer School). Courses have limited enrollment; the chamber music course will be given credit at the University of Victoria. Students are exposed to great artists and attend daily master classes. Students desiring credit at other institutions should make arrangements with the colleges or universities concerned.
(2) The Victoria International Festival was also founded by J. J. Johannesen in 1971. It features renowned artists in solo, ensemble, symphonic, and operatic performances.

Further Information
Registrar
(604) 736-1611

*Dancing is the loftiest, the
most moving, the most
beautiful of the arts, because
it is no mere translation or
abstraction from life; it is life
itself.*
                        Havelock Ellis

Stratford Festival
P.O. Box 520
Stratford, Ontario N5A 6V2
Canada

Program
Plays by William Shakespeare; other
plays, both classical and modern;
musicals and pop/jazz concerts; May–
October.

Accommodations
Hotels and motels, bed-and-breakfast
homes, private homes. Write for
Stratford Festival Visitors Guide.

Cost
Write for information.

Recreation
Bicycling, canoeing, picnicking, and
more.

Cultural Opportunities
Gallery Stratford, Canadian
"Pennsylvania Dutch Country"
nearby.

Comment
Established in 1953 and now North
America's foremost classical repertory
theater, the Stratford Festival features
renowned actors, including Maggie
Smith and Peter Ustinov. Three
theaters perform Shakespeare's plays
and works of other playwrights,
including Chekhov, Molière,
Tennessee Williams, and Gilbert and
Sullivan. Concerts feature famous
artists like Judy Collins.

Further Information
Festival Theater Box Office (after
    mid-March)
(519) 273-1600

Administration (year-round)
(519) 271-4040

> ***If music be the food of love,***
> ***play on.***
> ***Shakespeare***

ITALY

Spoleto Festival (Italy)
Festival dei due Mondi
via Margutta 17
00187
Rome, Italy

Program
Annual music festival, 17 days, early
summer; featuring a variety of
international opera and ballet
companies, chamber music and choral
groups, and soloists.

Accomodations
In Spoleto, Italy, a provincial Umbrian
city, sixty miles north of Rome; write
for information.

Cost
$7–$50 per event.

Comment
Founded by Pulitzer-Prize-winning
composer Gian Carlo Menotti, the
Spoleto Festival was first held in 1958.
It is now considered one of Europe's
most stimulating musical events. Since
1977, it has combined with its twin in
Charleston, South Carolina, to fulfill
the founder's dream of a "Festival of
Two Worlds." In recent years,
attendance has averaged 100,000.

Further Information
(803) 722-2764

MEXICO

*Festival Internacional
   Cervantino
Emerson 304-90, Piso
Mexico City, Mexico 11570 D.F.*

Program
Annual 3-week festival each autumn,
featuring performances in music,
theater, dance, and opera and art
exhibits. One-act plays by Miguel de
Cervantes are highlighted.

Accommodations
Major hotels in Guanajuato (site of
festival), a colonial town 180 miles
northwest of Mexico City.

Cost
$15 per performance. Hotels: $65 per
night. Outdoor performances free.

Cultural Opportunities
Lectures, art exhibits, mimes, actors,
and street singers.

Comment
The Festival was first held in 1973 and
is considered a showcase for top
Mexican performers. Considered the
most important festival in Latin
America, the event offers five
performances daily beginning at 5 p.m.

Further Information
Public Relations
From the U.S.:
(01525) 250-0988/0345

*Without music life would be a
mistake.*
                Friedrich Nietzsche

PUERTO RICO

*Festival Casals
Apartado 41227
Minillas Station
Santurce, Puerto Rico 00940*

Program
Annual music festival, usually 2½
weeks in June. Features orchestral and
chamber music and individual recitals.

Accommodations
Responsibility of attendees.

Cost
Write for information.

Comment
The festival was established by Pablo
Casals in 1957, 1 year after he moved
to Puerto Rico. Performing artists have
included Isaac Stern, Andrés Segovia,
Rudolf Serkin, and others. Director is
Jorge Mester, also of the Aspen
Festival. Most events are held in San
Juan, but several may be scheduled in
other Puerto Rican cities.

Further Information
Maria E. Hidalgo, Administrative
   Officer

UNITED KINGDOM

*Aldeburgh Festival of Music
   and the Arts
The Britten-Pears School for
   Advanced Musical Studies
High Street
Aldeburgh, Suffolk 1P15 5AX
England*

Programs
The annual Aldeburgh Festival, 17
days, June; features a wide variety of

musical performances by symphony orchestras, string quartets, and individual musicians and singers, plus poetry readings.

Accommodations
Up to participant; hotels and private homes available.

Cost
£2–£27 (approximately $2.80 to $38 by exchange rate at time of publication).

Recreation
Riding, swimming, sailing, tennis, golf, and more.

Cultural Opportunities
The Britten-Pears Library in Aldeburgh, the Holst Library at the school, and more.

Comment
The Festival is managed by the Aldeburgh Festival–Snape Maltings Foundation Ltd. and was first held in 1948. Most of its events take place in Aldeburgh, about one hundred miles northeast of London, with others in Snape, Oxford, Blythburgh, Framlingham, and elsewhere.

Further Information
In England:
Festival: Aldeburgh 2935
School: Snape 671
In the United States:
Rhoda Altman
American Friends of the Aldeburgh
   Festival
P.O. Box 1857
New York, New York 10185
(212) 764-8520
In Canada:
Mrs. Marshall Sutton
The Canadian Aldeburgh Foundation
34 Glenallen Road
Toronto, Ontario M4N 1G8
Canada
(416) 481-1964

Edinburgh International Festival
21 Market Street
Edinburgh EH1 1BW
Scotland

Program
Three-week festival, mid-August through early September; features performances by accomplished artists and companies from around the world. The program includes opera, ballet, symphonies, chamber music, drama, poetry, and jazz.

Accommodations
Hotels, guest houses, private homes, or university halls.

Cost
Opera: £4–16; concerts: £6–18.50; theatrical events: £5.

Comment
The Edinburgh International Festival began in 1947. Participants have included the BBC Orchestra, the London and Boston symphony orchestras, and the Kent and Scottish operas. An international film and television festival, with other theatrical and musical events held concurrently.

Further Information
Regarding hotels, etc.:
Tourist Accommodation Service
9 Cockburn Street
Edinburgh EH1 1BR
Scotland
Regarding university halls:
Deputy Steward
Pollock Halls of Residence
18 Holyrood Park Road
Edinburgh EH6 5AV
Scotland

National Operatic and Dramatic Association
1 Crestfield Street
London WC1H 8AU
England

Program
Comprehensive theater courses in all aspects of voice, movements, prop-making, make-up, etc.; 1 week or longer; throughout the year.

Accommodations
University dormitories.

Cost
Write for information.

Comment
The course is divided into two sections, i.e., General and Directors. The 1-week course is appropriate for the very experienced or the amateur enthusiast.

Further Information
Joan Pickthall
c/o Joslin
6 Halsburg Road
Bristol BS6 7SR
England
(0272) 421501

7 MUSEUMS AND HISTORICAL SOCIETY EXHIBITS AND TRIPS

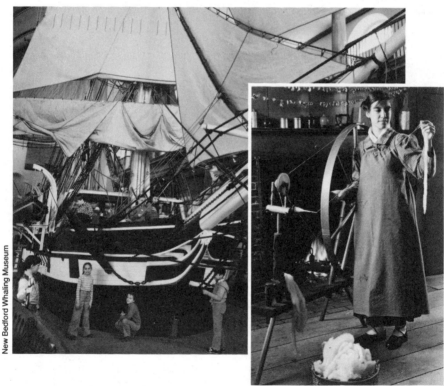

New Bedford Whaling Museum

Old Sturbridge Village

As repositories of artistic treasures and records of the past, museums and historical societies function for the benefit of current and future generations. Their exhibits and local programs provide enriching experiences, while their travel programs take participants to experience the world's great artistic and cultural treasures.

> *Art hath an enemy called ignorance.*
>
> Ben Jonson

ARKANSAS

Arkansas Arts Center Traveling Seminars
MacArthur Park
P.O. Box 2137
Little Rock, Arkansas 72203

Program
Traveling seminars of artistic and cultural interest are held several times during the year in the United States and abroad. Recent examples: Italy, Amsterdam, and Northern England/Scotland; all 2 weeks, except Amsterdam, 1 week.

Accommodations
Write for information.

Cost
Varies with tour. For Northern England/Scotland trip, $2546 including tour, accommodations, most meals, round-trip airfare, and tax-deductible contribution to the Arts Center.

Comment
All Arkansas Arts Center Traveling Seminars include four in-depth orientation seminars prior to departure, conducted by the Center staff or outside specialists. Trips in the United States are planned to take advantage of major art exhibits. Average number of participants per trip is twenty-five. Membership in the Arts Center is required.

Further Information
Martha Lancaster, Media Coordinator
(501) 372-4000

CALIFORNIA

San Diego Natural History Museum
P.O. Box 1390
San Diego, California 92112

Programs
(1) Whale-watching boat trips off the coast of California and Baja California, Mexico; 2 hours; October–January.
(2) Other area natural history trips, up to 1 week. Themes include geology, zoology, botany, and ecology.

Accommodations and Cost
Write for information.

Comment
The whale-watching trips have been a favorite since 1971. These and all the natural history trips are led by museum experts.

Further Information
Education Department
(619) 232-3821

COLORADO

Denver Museum of Natural History
Travel Series
City Park
Denver, Colorado 80205

Program
Foreign and domestic tours; various durations throughout the year. Themes include archaeology, whale watching, and outdoor activities. Recent destinations include East Africa, Central America, New Orleans, Turkey, Russia, and Arizona.

Accommodations
Vary with tour; write for information.

Cost
Range $525–$6700, all inclusive. Some examples: Arizona Birds, $525; Belize (Central America), $1200; Russia, $3000.

Comment
The museum's Travel Series, established in 1974, features tours with a wide range of subject matter and activities. Tour leaders are very familiar with the areas visited. Average group size is fifteen to twenty.

Further Information
Diana Lee Crew, Travel Coordinator
(303) 370-6307

CONNECTICUT

Jacqueline Moss Museum Tours
131 Davenport Ridge Lane
Stanford, Connecticut 06903

Program
Travel-study tours to Europe and the Orient; 15–25 days, two to four times annually. Emphasis is on art, architecture, and archaeology. Recent example: 25-day tour of China, visiting major cities and also the Mogao Caves at Dunhuang.

Accommodations
Deluxe or superior first-class.

Cost
Depends on tour. Example: China trip, $4000 complete (double occupancy), including round-trip airfare from New York and all meals.

Comment
Each tour is escorted by Jacqueline Moss, an art historian, lecturer, and

writer who has been planning and directing museum tours abroad since 1977. Itineraries include major museums and those off the beaten path, private art collections, art studios, and architectural sites. Average size of tour group is twenty-five.

Further Information
Jacqueline Moss
(203) 322-8709

DELAWARE

The Winterthur Museum
Winterthur, Delaware 19735

Programs
Annual trips with changing destinations, but generally to European countries. Examples:
(1) Northern Europe–Russia Cruise with land stopover in Leningrad, 16 days, summer.
(2) Winterthur Guild's anniversary tour of Switzerland and France, 2 weeks, September.

Accommodations
(1) Cruise portion is aboard *Royal Viking*. Land portion in first-class hotels.
(2) First-class hotels.

Cost
(1) $3446 per person, airfare plus tax-deductible contribution to Museum extra.
(2) $3495 per person, airfare plus tax-deductible contribution to Museum extra.
Trips require membership in Guild at $30 for individual or $40 for family.

Comments
(1) Trip has stopovers at Copenhagen, Amsterdam, Hamburg, Leningrad,

Helsinki, and Stockholm. Also features museum visits and lectures while at sea.
(2) Accompanied by Museum staff and highlights decorative arts with museum and special collection visits.

Further Information
Information: (302) 656-8591
Reservations: (302) 654-1548

> ***The adventurous student will always study classics... For what are the classics but the noblest recorded thoughts of man.***
> ***Henry David Thoreau***

DISTRICT OF COLUMBIA

Smithsonian Institution
Washington, D.C. 20560

Program
More than one hundred foreign and domestic study tours, 4 days to 3 weeks, year-round. Recent examples: China (several tours), Peru, Atlantic Crossing Aboard *Sea Cloud,* New England Seaports, Colorado Rockies, California Wine Country.

Accommodations
Vary with tour.

Cost
China: $3335 (17 days), $4395 (22 days), $5415 (18 days with Tibet); includes round-trip airfare, room and board, study leader, predeparture program. Peru: $2798 (16 days). Atlantic Crossing: $3240–$6140 (16 days). New England: $1495 (12 days). Colorado: $578 plus transportation (7

days). California: $960 plus transportation (7 days).

Comment
Travel programs are open to all associate members of the Smithsonian. The tours are culturally and scientifically oriented and under the guidance of museum curators or visiting scholars. They provide a combination of study, discovery, adventure, and vacation. In addition to the travel program, there are exhibits, workshop seminars, and lectures taking place year-round at the Smithsonian Museums in Washington. For details on these programs, see the membership publications.

Further Information
Barbara Tuceling
(202) 287-3362

FLORIDA

Museum of Arts and Sciences
1040 Museum Boulevard
Daytona Beach, Florida 32014

Programs
(1) Travel-study tours emphasizing art history, architecture, and/or natural regional history; numerous destinations, including Peru, Yucatán, the Galapagos Islands, Scandinavia, the U.S.S.R., and others. Also, shorter domestic trips to historic cities such as New Orleans and Charleston.
(2) Summer Institute for children ages 9–13, with classroom study and fieldwork in paleontology, archaeology, and marine biology. Directed by the science curator, the institute culminates in a 2-day field trip to Cumberland Island National Seashore.

Accommodations
First-class or best available.

Cost
(1) Varies with tour. Examples:
Yucatán, $387 (4 days, 3 nights),
complete, including three Mayan sites;
U.S.S.R., $2095 (2 weeks), complete.
(2) Summer Institute, $100 (2 weeks).

Comment
Tours are led by staff members with
extensive travel experience and
relevant expertise. Average group size
is fifteen to twenty.

Further Information
Sandra Lake Miller
Public Relations/Travel Coordination
(904) 255-0285

GEORGIA

Savannah Science Museum
Caretta Research Project
4405 Paulsen Street
Savannah, Georgia 31405

Program
Caretta Research Program, divided
into 1-week segments, mid-May to
September. Its objective is to learn
more about the habits of the Atlantic
loggerhead sea turtle (*Caretta caretta*).

Accommodations
Small house on Wassaw Island,
approximately ten miles southeast of
Savannah.

Cost
$275 per week, complete.

Comment
The project is conducted jointly by the
Savannah Science Museum and the
U.S. Fish and Wildlife Service. From
May to August, participants spend

evenings patrolling the island beaches,
tagging, measuring, and taking notes
on turtles found. In August and
September, participants monitor the
hatchery and beach nests and release
baby turtles. The program is led by an
experienced island coordinator;
participants must be in good physical
condition, due to the physical and
mental demands of the work.
Minimum age for participation is 15.
Maximum group size is six. College
credit available.

Further Information
Robert Graham, Coordinator of
    Caretta Project
(912) 355-6705

The Telfair Academy of Arts
*   and Sciences, Inc.*
121 Barnard Street
P.O. Box 10081
Savannah, Georgia 31405

Programs
(1) Tours of Telfair Mansion and Art
Museum, limited hours, year-round.
An 1818 English Regency House with
Federal Period furniture, paintings by
Samuel F. B. Morse, and several works
from various European and American
schools.
(2) Tours of Owens-Thomas House and
Museum, an 1817 Regency House
acquired by the Academy in 1957.
Contents include Philadelphia and
Duncan Phyfe tables, China Trade
porcelain, and Samuel Kirk silver.

Accommodations
Responsibility of tourist.

Cost
Tickets: $2 adult, $1 children.

Comment
The Telfair Academy is the oldest
public art museum in the South. Tours

and activities for children's groups can be arranged.

Further Information
Curator of Education
(912) 232-1177

ILLINOIS

Art Institute of Chicago
The Old Masters Society
Michigan Avenue at Adams
Street
Chicago, Illinois 60603

Program
Lecture series and tours of public and private collections in various cities led by professors of art history and/or curators of European art. Recent example: a trip to Toledo, Spain, to view the Spanish still-life exhibition.

Accommodations and Cost
Write for information.

Comment
The Art Institute of Chicago grew from an art school established in 1879 to a major museum (a drama school and theater were added some years ago). The Old Masters Society, established in 1977, supports the Department of European Painting and Sculpture of the Art Institute of Chicago. Society members have a close relationship with the department and are invited to lectures and tours sponsored by the society. Annual membership fee is $35. Members of the Old Masters Society must also be members of the Art Institute of Chicago.

Further Information
Elizabeth Silver-Schack, Coordinator
(312) 443-3615

> *Practical men (who believe themselves to be quite exempt from any intellectual influences) are usually the slaves of some defunct economics.*
>
> **J. M. Keynes**

INDIANA

Evansville Museum of Arts and
Science
411 Southeast Riverside Drive
Evansville, Indiana 47713

Program
Art and culture tours to East Coast cities several times a year; also European trips. Itineraries include historic tours, museum visits, theater, and social events. Some excursions open only to museum members.

Accommodations
Hotels.

Cost
Varies with tour. Example: $565 for 4-day New York trip, including accommodations, airfare, theater and museum tickets.

Comment
The Evansville Museum has been arranging trips since the late 1930s when it sponsored visits to Indian areas of the Southwest. Most of the art and culture trips are led by the museum director.

Further Information
John W. Streetman, Director
(812) 425-2406

KENTUCKY

J. B. Speed Art Museum
The Alliance
2035 South Third Street
Louisville, Kentucky 40208

Program
Art-oriented trips to sites in the United
States and abroad, throughout the
year. Recent destinations include
Mexico, British Isles, Minneapolis,
Baltimore, Annapolis, and Cincinnati.

Accommodations and Cost
Write for information. Membership is
required: $20 dues.

Comment
Orientation lectures prepare
participants for the exhibits they will
see; most trips include visits to private
collections. Average group size is
twenty-five.

Further Information
Travel Committee
(502) 637-6363

MARYLAND

The Baltimore Museum of Art
Art Museum Drive
Wyman Park
Baltimore, Maryland 21218

Programs
Art and culture tours to changing
destinations worldwide at various
seasons.
(1) China, 18 days, September;
highlights Shanghai, Beijing, Xi'an,
and Hong Kong.
(2) Northern Italy, 12 days, March;
stays in Florence and Venice with
visits to Padua, Ravenna, and Bologna.

(3) Paris, 9 days, March; includes visits
to special art collections and
excursions to Ecouen and Chantilly.
(4) Northern India and Nepal, 3 weeks,
October. Deluxe tour of Delhi, Jaipur,
Varanasi, Katmandu, and renowned
Tiger Tops game reserve. Optional
extension to Sikkim.

Accommodations
First-class.

Cost
(1) $3219, all inclusive.
(2) Approximately $2589, including
airfare.
(3) Approximately $2250, including
airfare.
(4) Approximately $4000, all inclusive.

Comment
Tours led by museum staff or others
knowledgeable in the topics to be
covered. Preliminary lectures are
given on focus of trip. Trips to northern
Italy and Paris may be combined.

Further Information
Terry Backmann
(301) 396-6314

Baltimore Museum of Industry
1415 Key Highway
Baltimore, Maryland 21230

Program
Recent example: Britain-Wales
Industrial Tour, 2 weeks, August.

Accommodations
Superior tourist-class hotels.

Cost
$1799 per person (double occupancy),
inclusive; $1899 per person (single
occupancy), inclusive.

Comment
Trip led by Dr. Dennis Zembala,
executive director of Museum and an

expert on British industrial history. Trip also features special lectures by curators or directors of sites visited.

Further Information
Ann Steele, Curator
(301) 727-4808

> *There is no knowledge that is not power.*
> *Ralph Waldo Emerson*

Maryland Historical Society
201 West Monument Street
Baltimore, Maryland 21201

Program
Cultural and historical tours to different locations in the United States and Europe, 2–3 weeks, annually. Recent examples:
(1) Eastern Europe (Prague, Budapest, Vienna, Dresden, Berlin), 16 days.
(2) Scandinavia (Finland, Copenhagen, Norway), 14 days.
(3) Ceramics Tour to England, including London, Bath, Broadway, Worcester, and Stoke-on-Trent, 10 days.

Accommodations
Deluxe and first-class.

Cost
Above examples:
(1) $2976 per person (double occupancy), complete.
(2) $2599 per person (double occupancy), complete.
(3) $2149 per person (double occupancy), plus $150 museum contribution.

Comment
The Historical Society has been offering tours since the mid-1970s. All trips focus on art, architecture, important sites, and history. Features relating to Maryland are especially emphasized. Average group size is twenty-five.

Further Information
Public Programs Office
(301) 685-3750, ext. 321 or 322

Walters Art Gallery
600 North Charles Street
Baltimore, Maryland 21201

Program
Three-week deluxe tour of India, including Bombay, Madras, the caves of Ajanta, Agra, and Delhi, visiting temples, private collections, with 1 night in a former maharajah's palace.

Accommodations
Deluxe or best available.

Cost
$2250 plus $1703 airfare, including $200 tax-deductible contribution to Museum.

Comment
The India excursion is led by John G. Ford, a distinguished collector and lecturer on Indo-Asian art. Group size on most trips is about thirty. Other trips are offered to varied destinations, highlighting the art and culture of each area visited.

Further Information
Patricia Barrett, Membership
   Secretary
(301) 547-9000, ext. 45 or 46

> *Education is an ornament in prosperity, a refuge in adversity.*
> *Aristotle*

MASSACHUSETTS

Harvard Museum of Comparative Zoology
Harvard University
Cambridge, Massachusetts 02138

Programs
Zoological trips worldwide, which vary from year to year, air and sea.
(1) Whale watching off the coast of Baja, California, Mexico, aboard *Qualifier 105,* 1 week, March.
(2) Antarctic Peninsula and southern Chili aboard *Society Explorer,* 15 days, January.
(3) Safari to Zambia, Zimbabwe, and Botswana, Africa, 3 weeks, August.

Accommodations
(1) 105-foot vessel.
(2) Cruise ship.
(3) Camps and Victoria Falls Hotel.

Cost
(1) $1050 plus $100 tax-deductible contribution to the Museum; airfare to and from San Diego extra.
(2) $3990–$14,500, based on accommodations; airfare from Miami, $1400 extra.
(3) $5380 (including airfare), plus $300 tax-deductible contribution to the Museum.

Comments
(1) Led by Leslie Copperthwaite, research biologist, and Bruce Wellman, naturalist and photographer.
(2) Led by James J. McCarthy, director of the Museum, and John E. McCoster, director of California Academy of Sciences, whose research has been used in *Jaws* and BBC "Nova" specials.
(3) Led by Mark Skinner, evolutionary ecology specialist, and limited to sixteen participants.

Further Information
Gabrielle Dundon
(617) 495-2463

> *Education is a treasure and culture never dies.*
> **Petronius**

Harvard University Art Museums
32 Quincy Street
Cambridge, Massachusetts 02138

Programs
(1) Weekend seminars on art-related subjects, such as Old Master Drawings: Origin, Function, Technique; year-round.
(2) Tours abroad emphasizing fine and performing arts, including Normandy, Egypt, Yorkshire, and Venice; year-round.

Accommodations
(1) Harvard Faculty Club or local hotel.
(2) Vary with tour, including inns, hotels, country houses, and shipboard cabins.

Cost
(1) $50; $25 for students.
(2) Varies with destination, duration, and tour content.

Comment
Seminars offer opportunities to learn from distinguished connoisseurs, using items from collections as examples. Tours abroad are led by museum curators and art history faculty members.

Further Information
Friends of Harvard Art Museum
(617) 495-4544

New Bedford Whaling Museum
18 Johnny Cake Hill
New Bedford, Massachusetts 02740

Program
Day trips, including whale watching, islands, and local historical sites; throughout the year. All trips are led by professional museum staff.

Accommodations and Cost
Vary with trip; write for details.

Comment
The New Bedford Whaling Museum is the largest museum in the United States devoted to the history and technology of whaling. Located in the historic waterfront district of New Bedford, the six-building complex also deals with local and maritime history. The Museum's educational program includes exhibits, lectures, films, and other related activities.

Further Information
Lalie Keeshan, Program Director
(617) 997-0046

Old Sturbridge Village
Sturbridge, Massachusetts 01566

Programs
(1) Crafts at Close Range, 1-day workshops on early nineteenth-century crafts.
(2) Summershops, weeklong programs for children ages 8–14.

Accommodations
Old Sturbridge Village Motor Lodge and Oliver Wight House, (617) 347-3327.

Cost
Call or write for specific costs.

Comment
Old Sturbridge Village is a living history museum that re-creates a New England town of the 1830s. In more than forty restored buildings on 200 acres, people in historical dress demonstrate the life, work, and community celebrations of the period. Programs are designed to provide insight into early New England life, including its crafts and skills.

Further Information
(617) 347-3362, ext. 303

MINNESOTA

St. Louis County Historical Society
506 West Michigan Street
Duluth, Minnesota 55802

Program
At least two historical and cultural tours annually, 1–3 days, spring and fall. Recent example: Southeastern Minnesota's Mississippi River Valley, 3 days.

Accommodations
Vary with location and duration of tour; write for more information.

Cost
Varies. For the example above: double occupancy, $165 (members), $185 (nonmembers); single occupancy, $185 (members), $200 (nonmembers).

Comment
Since its organization in 1922, the St. Louis County Historical Society has been actively engaged in preserving and interpreting the heritage of the county and northeastern Minnesota.

The society has sponsored tours since the mid-1960s, with society personnel as guides. Average group size is forty; travel is by air-conditioned motorcoach.

Further Information
Lawrence Sommer, Director
(218) 722-8011

NEW JERSEY

The Newark Museum
49 Washington Street
Box 540
Newark, New Jersey 07101

Programs
The museum conducts both domestic and foreign tours. Domestic trips visit museums, historic sites, restorations, and private collections. Some trips relate to Newark Museum exhibits. Examples:
(1) Visits to various collections in U.S. cities, 3–4 days.
(2) Spain, 2 weeks, with visits to private homes.
(3) Trip to Orient; 3–4 weeks.

Accommodations
First-class or deluxe.

Cost
(2) $275–$500.
(2) $2500, including airfare.
(3) $5000–$7500, including airfare.

Comment
Local tours travel by charter bus. They are accompanied by lectures from specialists, either prior to or during the trip. Membership in the museum (minimum of $15) is a prerequisite.

Further Information
(201) 733-6600, ext. 6585

Princeton University
The Art Museum
Princeton, New Jersey 08544

Programs
Tours in the United States and abroad, with emphasis on art and architecture. Recent tours:
(1) Ancient Landscapes, Turkey.
(2) Cruise through Australia and New Zealand.

Accommodations
Deluxe.

Cost
Varies with tour. Examples above:
(1) $3516 per person (double occupancy), complete with airfare and museum contribution.
(2) $3800, except airfare from Los Angeles to Auckland and museum contribution.

Comment
Guides from the Princeton faculty and other institutions accompany each group. Tours feature lectures on art, architecture, and archaeology and visits to museums and historic sites. Average group size is thirty; membership in the museum is a prerequisite.

Further Information
JoAnn Carchman
Director, Community Relations
(609) 452-3762

A morsel of genuine history is a thing so rare as to be always valuable.
                    Thomas Jefferson

NEW YORK

American Museum of Natural History
Discovery Tours
Central Park West at 79th Street
New York, New York 10024

Program
Various tours emphasizing natural history, throughout the year. Examples: Trinidad and Tobago Wildlife Tour, 10 days; Anthropology Tour to Morocco, 16 days; Art and Archaeology of Tibet and China, 29 days.

Accommodations
Write for information.

Cost
For examples above: Trinidad, $1950; Morocco, $1750; Tibet, $6500. Prices are based on double occupancy and do not include airfare.

Comment
Discovery Tours are led by distinguished scholars, many from the museum staff, who provide background information and discussion. Groups are limited in size to ensure personal attention. Predeparture information is provided.

Further Information
(212) 873-1440

Archives of American Art
41 East 65th Street
New York, New York 10021

Program
Generally annual, though destinations change. Recent example: The Art and Architecture of Ireland, visiting art and archaeological museums in Dublin and west coast of Ireland; 18 days; fall.

Accommodations
Travel by deluxe motorcoach; nights at hotels and castles.

Cost
$3500, including airfare from Kennedy airport. Membership extra and required for tour.

Comment
The Archives of American Art, which is affiliated with the Smithsonian Institution, launched its first Bon Voyage d'Art tour in 1960. Its tour program endeavors to arrange for special treatment that sophisticated travelers could not easily do on their own. Tours are led by experts in the field. Membership is a prerequisite for trip eligibility.

Further Information
Mrs. Otto Spaeth, Honorary Chairman
(212) 826-5722

Art Tours of Manhattan, Inc.
63 East 82nd Street
New York, New York 10028

Program
Guided tours behind the scenes to artists' studios, galleries, private collections, and museums. Trips in New York are 1 half-day or 1 full-day, throughout the year; trips to other cities in the region are 1 day to 1 week. Among the most popular destinations are Soho, 57th Street, and Madison Avenue; other destinations include Yale, Boston, Philadelphia, and Winterthur.

Accommodations
Hotel lodgings for longer trips.

Cost
Write for information.

Comment

The Art Tours program focuses on custom tours for groups of six or more, with individuals joining as space allows. Access is provided to collections not usually open to the public. Lectures cover topics such as Art as an Investment, Collecting Posters and Prints, Art Trends of the Eighties, and more. Out-of-town trips often include architecture and haute couture as well. Guides have degrees in art history, with some (including founder Barbara Guggenheim) holding doctorates.

Further Information

Ellen Sax, President
(212) 772-7888

Bronx County Historical Society
3309 Bainbridge Avenue
Bronx, New York 10467

Program

Walking tours and lectures, year-round. Tours in Bronx neighborhoods such as City Island, Hunt's Point, Riverdale, South Bronx, and West Farms, as well as along the Bronx Heritage Trail. Monthly lectures on Bronx history. Art shows and musical events at selected historic sites in the Bronx.

Cost

Write for information.

Comment

The Historical Society, founded in 1955, is dedicated to making known the heritage, growth, and development of one of the largest metropolitan areas in the United States.

Further Information

Education Coordinator
(212) 881-8900

> *The desire of knowledge, like the thirst of riches, increases ever with the acquisition of it.*
> Laurence Sterne

Metropolitan Museum of Art
Fifth Avenue at 82nd Street
New York, New York 10028

Programs

Art and culture tours worldwide, with changing annual destinations. Recent examples:
(1) Imperial Danube Passage, viewing Baroque marvels of Hapsburg, etc.; 2-week river cruise; August.
(2) China by Sea, cruise from Hong Kong aboard Royal Viking *Star;* 17 days; October.
(3) Northern India and Nepal, visiting Bombay, Katmandu, etc; 2 weeks by air; October.

Accommodations

(1) Best riverboat.
(2) Royal Viking.
(3) First-class hotels.

Cost

(1) $3270–$3470.
(2) $4180–$11,390.
(3) $5665.
Single accommodations on sea trips and hotels extra. Costs include tax-deductible contribution to Museum but do not include membership, which is prerequisite for any trip.

Comment

Tours are generally accompanied by curatorial or other staff member. The Museum has been conducting tours for 6 years. A portion of the fare represents a tax-deductible contribution to the Metropolitan Museum of Art.

Further Information
Raymond and Whitcomb Co.
400 Madison Avenue
New York, New York 10017
(212) 759-3960

New York State Historical
  Association
Seminars on American Culture
Cooperstown, New York 13326

Program
Annual weeklong seminars on
American culture, July. Subjects
include New York State history, art,
architecture, and general culture; arts
and crafts.

Accommodations
Participants make own arrangements;
facilities range from deluxe hotels to
moderately priced motels, rooms in
guest houses, and campgrounds. Write
for a complete list.

Cost
$150 per person per week, including
tuition and daily lunch (higher for out-
of-state residents).

Recreation
Cooperstown is located on Lake
Otsego, where swimming and water
sports can be enjoyed. Golf available
nearby.

Cultural Opportunities
Distinguished museums, including
Baseball Hall of Fame; professional
summer theater and Glimmerglass
Opera Theater. Home of James
Fenimore Cooper and his family, for
whom the town is named.

Comment
The Seminars on American Culture
were first offered in 1948. They
currently attract museum
professionals as well as interested

amateurs. Participants come from
throughout the United States and
Canada; instructors are nationally
renowned. Program includes evening
entertainment, lectures, and films.

Further Information
Education Department
(607) 547-2534

NORTH CAROLINA

Mint Museum
2730 Randolph Road
Charlotte, North Carolina 28207

Programs
Tours with changing foreign and
domestic destinations, with emphasis
on art, architecture, and ancient
civilization. Recent examples:
(1) Hudson River, 3-day trip by air,
fall.
(2) Flemish art, 2 weeks, late summer;
focusing on museums of Holland and
Belgium.

Accommodations
Vary; deluxe and first-class hotels
when available.

Cost
(1) $360, including airfare.
(2) $2600, including airfare.
Membership in the museum ($25) is a
prerequisite.

Comment
The Mint Museum was established in
1933. Trips feature visits to museums
and points of special interest, under
the direction of the professional staff of
the museum. Ample leisure time
provided.

Further Information
Colleen De Coursey
(704) 337-2010

> *History repeats itself. The fact is a testimony to human stupidity.*
>
> **Edith Hamilton**

OHIO

Toledo Museum of Art
P.O. Box 1013
Toledo, Ohio 43697

Programs
(1) One 2- or 3-week international trip annually, focusing on a specific style of art or period of art or history.
Examples: The Art, Architecture, and Wines of Medieval France; Holland and Belgium.
(2) Several domestic weekend trips to visit special exhibitions at other museums.

Accommodations
First-class luxury accommodations.

Cost
Depends on duration and destination of tour. Examples: Holland and Belgium, 3 weeks, $3000, including airfare from Detroit; Washington, D.C., 3 days, $532, from Detroit.

Comment
Groups are generally led by the director or a curator of the museum and include experts on the native art of the country visited. Trips are primarily art oriented and include lectures, museum tours, and visits to private collections. Group size averages thirty to forty.

Further Information
Cindy Rimmelin, Membership
    Coordinator
(419) 255-8000, ext. 313

PENNSYLVANIA

Pennsbury Manor
400 Pennsbury Memorial Road
Morrisville, Pennsylvania 19067

Program
Annual Fall Forum, 2 days, late September or October. Special celebrations and workshops, July–December. Tours of the manor and other restored buildings, year-round.

Accommodations
Nearby motels.

Children
Day camps, three sessions, July–August, ages 3–14; workshops, July–December.

Cost
Varying plans available: $50–$150 for tuition and most meals. Write for details.

Comment
The Fall Forum was first held in 1965. Topics have ranged from gardening to Colonial crafts and the Constitution. Forums feature expert speakers. Summer and fall events emphasize crafts, gardening, and living history. Pennsbury Manor is the only extant residence of William Penn in either England or America; twenty-one buildings re-create the milieu of a seventeenth-century country plantation.

Further Information
Nancy D. Kolb, Historic Site
    Administrator
(215) 946-0400

> *Venerate art as art.*
>
> **William Hazlitt**

> *So vast is art, so narrow human wit.*
> **Alexander Pope**

Pennsylvania Farm Museum
Institute of Pennsylvania Rural Life and Culture
2451 Kissel Hill Road
Lancaster, Pennsylvania 17601

Program
Three-day program, third week in June; seminars and workshops on antiques, rural culture, Pennsylvania German decorative arts, traditional crafts, and domestic skills.

Accommodations
Variety of motel and bed-and-breakfast accommodations nearby.

Cost
$100 institute registration, includes most meals and some entertainment; workshops additional.

Cultural Opportunities
Other museums nearby; President James Buchanan's home, "Wheatland"; walking tour of Lancaster.

Comment
The institute is held at the Pennsylvania Farm Museum, an outdoor museum that interprets Pennsylvania's rural life and culture from 1750 to 1900. Exhibits are housed in twenty buildings on one hundred acres of land. The museum displays an extensive collection of rural artifacts and presents living history through the demonstration of traditional crafts and domestic farm skills.

Further Information
John L. Kraft, Director
(717) 569-0401

Philadelphia Museum of Art
26th and Benjamin Franklin Parkway
Philadelphia, Pennsylvania 19101

Programs
Approximately sixteen different trips offered annually, domestic and foreign, all seasons. Recent examples:
Domestic:
(1) U.S. cities, 1 week to 10 days.
(2) Cruise, 5 days.
Foreign Trips
(1) Europe, 2 weeks, spring, summer, or fall.
(2) Egypt (land and air) 16 days, winter.
(3) China (land and air) 16 days, spring or fall.

Accommodations
First-class, deluxe.

Cost
Domestic:
(1) $500–$800.
(2) $1500–$2000, depending on accommodations.
Foreign:
(1) Write for information.
(2) $1599.
(3) $2859.
Membership fee: $30 (may be waived for out-of-state participant).

Comment
Trips include lectures prior to departure aimed at familiarizing participant with language, sociology, and cultural history of country to be visited. Museum staff participate in the lectures and usually accompany the trip. Trips are designed for educated travelers and are coordinated with the museum's own collection or exhibits. Participants must be a member of the Philadelphia Museum.

Further Information
Above address
   or
Mrs. William Wolgin
(215) 787-5496

*It is well to observe the force
and virtue and consequence
of discoveries.*
                    Francis Bacon

*University of Pennsylvania
University Museum Tours
33rd and Spruce Streets
Philadelphia, Pennsylvania
    19104*

Program
Tours to various locations, domestic
and foreign. Recent examples:
Indonesia, Central Mexico, Australia,
American Southwest.

Accommodations
Deluxe.

Cost
Write for information.

Comment
The University Museum has sponsored
trips for more than 20 years. Each is
led by a curator or university professor.
Personal and professional affiliations
of the tour leaders allow groups to visit
sites and meet people not normally
accessible to tourists. Lectures are
given before and during the trips.
Group size averages between fifteen
and thirty people.

Further Information
Women's Committee
(215) 898-4023

*Victorian Society in America
American Summer School
The Athenaeum
East Washington Square
Philadelphia, Pennsylvania
    19106*

Program
Seminar on American architectural
history and related subjects,
Philadelphia or other eastern city; 3
weeks; June–July.

Accommodations
International House of Philadelphia.

Cost
$780, tuition and room; meals extra.

Comment
The Victorian Society in America (a
sister to the Victorian Society in
England) is dedicated to the
appreciation and preservation of our
country's nineteenth-century cultural
heritage. In addition to the
concentration on architectural history,
lectures are given on the decorative
arts and the social and cultural history
of the period. Instruction is by
prominent scholars and professionals
and includes tours to relevant
buildings and sites.

Further Information
Johanna Levy
(215) 627-4252

VIRGINIA

*Colonial Williamsburg
   Foundation
P.O. Box C
Williamsburg, Virginia 23187*

Programs
(1) Antiques Forum, weeklong
program, includes lectures, tours, and

workshops; late January or early February.

(2) Learning Weekend, 3-day program of morning lectures and afternoon workshops on Colonial Williamsburg crafts; March.

(3) Garden Symposium, 3-day program includes lectures, trips, and tours; April.

(4) Senior Time, annual month-long observance with special activities for those 55 and older; September.

Accommodations
Williamsburg Inn, Williamsburg Lodge, The Motor House. Programs include some meals, receptions, coffees, and teas.

Cost
Write for information.

Comment
The Antiques Forum and Garden Symposium have been held since 1949.

Average attendance at these events is 500. Senior Time began in the mid-1970s.

Colonial Williamsburg is equally dedicated to research and scholarship in Colonial American subjects. All its programs are planned by experts in their fields. Williamsburg programs make use of their own and adjacent facilities, including Jamestown, Yorktown, and other historic sites.

Further Information
Trudy Moyles, Registrar
(804) 229-1000

To learn science easily . . . begin by learning your own language.
       Georges-Étienne Bonnet

8 WRITERS' CONFERENCES

Bread Loaf Writers' Conference

*U*seful information for novices and professionals. Work-shops and discussions covering all areas of writing and publishing, with numerous opportunities to make contact with knowledgeable and prominent people in literary fields.

> *Books are the treasured wealth of the world, a fit inheritance of generations and nations.*
> *Henry David Thoreau*

CALIFORNIA

California Study Tours
Writers in California
Mills College
P.O. Box 9813
Oakland, California 94613

Program
A summer course for men and women, consisting of four consecutive 1-week units, July–August. Many classes are held on location in northern California areas that inspired major writers associated with the state. Participants may enroll for entire course or individual units.

Accommodations
Campus facilities, conference centers, hotels, motels, all depending on location of class.

Cost
$300 per unit, includes tuition, field trips, and program expenses. Not included are accommodations, meals, and transportation to the unit site. Ride pools will be arranged. Write for information on accommodations.

Recreation
Facilities of Mills College and areas visited available to participants.

Cultural Opportunities
Guided tours to historic California sites; field trips are an integral part of every unit.

Comment
The Writers in California program, first offered in 1980, is equally suited for novices, published authors, or the merely curious. Participants study such writers as John Steinbeck, Jack London, Brett Harte, William Saroyan, and Mark Twain. Each weekly unit includes classes, on-site lectures, readings, and discussions. Program leaders are drawn from the Mills College community. Participants must be high school or college graduates; a maximum of thirty may enroll per unit. College credit obtainable (extra tuition charge).

Further Information
JoAnne Elias, Course Director
(415) 635-2499

California Writers' Club
Biennial Writers' Conference
2214 Derby Street
Berkeley, California 94705

Program
Three days, July, at different northern California locations.

Accommodations
College facilities, on site.

Cost
$210, including tuition, room, and board.

Comment
The California Writers' Club was founded in 1909 by Jack London, George Sterling, Herman Whittaker, and Austin Lewis. Every other year it sponsors a conference covering all aspects of writing in which knowledgeable professionals share their expertise with participants. Recent conferences have featured such speakers as Mary Higgins Clark, author of the best-selling novel *Stillwatch.*

Further Information
Dorothy V. Benson, Secretary
(415) 841-1217

> *The ideas of economists and political philosophers, both when they are right and when they are wrong, are more powerful than is commonly understood.*
> *J. M. Keynes*

Society of Children's Book Writers
P.O. Box 296, Mar Vista Station
Los Angeles, California 90066

Program
Annual Writers' Conference in Children's Literature, speakers, workshops, and manuscript consultation on writing books for children; 4 days; August.

Accommodations
Write for information.

Cost
Tuition: $140–$160; academic credit and individual consultation extra. Hotel reservations responsibility of participant.

Comment
The conference offers a chance for personal contact with prominent writers, illustrators, and publishers of children's books. Manuscript and artwork consultations are provided on an individual or group basis. It is cosponsored by the University of California, Los Angeles.

Further Information
Lin Oliver, Director
(818) 347-2849

DISTRICT OF COLUMBIA

American University
Washington Journalism Institute
Massachusetts and Nebraska Avenues, N.W.
Washington, D.C. 20016

Program
Washington Journalism Institute for college-bound high school students, a 2-week session for high school newspaper editors and writing students interested in journalism. Participants engage in writing laboratories and skill-oriented newspaper reporting and editing seminars, meet with members of the Washington Press Corps, and cover briefings with Executive Branch and Congressional personnel as part of their reporting assignments.

Accommodations
Dormitories on university campus.

Cost
$850 complete.

Recreation
Swimming, tennis, track and field.

Cultural Opportunities
Resources of Washington, D.C. Theater performance and field trips to museums and other sites are scheduled.

Comment
The Washington Journalism Institute was established in 1981 to help high school newspaper staff members take their first step toward a successful career in journalism. The Institute is administered by American University's Washington Semester

Program for college students, first held in 1947. Two faculty members from the School of Communication are assigned to a group of approximately thirty participants. In addition, students meet professional Washington journalists and public officials. College credit granted.

Further Information
Director, Washington Journalism
    Institute
(800) 424-2600

FLORIDA

Florida Suncoast Writers'
*   Conference*
University of South Florida
St. Petersburg Campus
830 First Street South
St. Petersburg, Florida 33701

Program
Annual writers' conference, 3 days, late January. Topics include short story, poetry, novel, science fiction, juvenile literature, inspirational writing, photojournalism, and more.

Accommodations
Participants arrange their own; headquarters is the Prince Martha Hotel, St. Petersburg.

Cost
$85, registration fee; $45 for teacher or student. Extra charge for work submitted for comment and criticism.

Comment
The Suncoast Writers' Conference was first held in 1973. It schedules more than forty workshops on writing topics. Manuscripts may be submitted before or during the conference for comment

and criticism by consultants. The conference is cosponsored by the University of South Florida Department of English and the Fine Arts Council of Florida. Annual attendance is 400–500.

Further Information
Edgar W. Hirshberg, Director
(813) 974-2421

GEORGIA

Epworth-by-the-Sea Creative
*   Writers' Workshop*
Saint Simons Island, Georgia
*   31522*

Program
Creative writing session held at Epworth-by-the-Sea Assembly Grounds, 1 week, mid-June.

Accommodations
Quality motel rooms available on grounds; meals available in dining room.

Children
Recreational facilities available; children not permitted in class.

Cost
Tuition: $75–$85, not including room and board. Write for information. Donations tax deductible.

Recreation
Golf, tennis, fishing, swimming pool, touring. In village: bicycles for rent, bowling, beach, volleyball, basketball, shuffleboard; also crabbing and shelling.

Cultural Opportunities
Fort Frederica National Monument/ Historic Preservations, Coastal

(Lighthouse) Museum, Methodist Museum, Island Art Center, Jekyll Island sites, and many other attractions.

Comment
These workshops, under the auspices of the United Methodist Church of South Florida, have been conducted annually since 1959 at historic Saint Simon's Island, Georgia. The beautiful surroundings are conducive to study, thought, prayer, and meditation. Everyone is welcome.

Further Information
Flora Buffington, Executive Secretary
3400 East Evans Mill Court
Lithonia, Georgia 30058
(404) 482-1340

> *. . . There is in writing the constant joy of sudden discovery, of happy accident.*
> *H. L. Mencken*

ILLINOIS

Mississippi Valley Writers'
Conference
Augustana College–College
Center
Rock Island, Illinois 61201

Program
Annually, 1 week, early June. Topics covered include fiction, nonfiction, short story, poetry, children's literature, writing romantic fiction, writing for religious markets, and the "beginning beginner."

Accommodations
Residence halls at Augustana College.

Cost
$25, registration; $35, one workshop; $60, two workshops; $125, room and board (fifteen meals and 6 nights' lodging).

Cultural Opportunities
College library, art gallery, theater, films, museum.

Comment
The Mississippi Valley Writers' Conference was first held in 1973 and is open to published and unpublished writers. Schedule includes eight workshops daily, evening writing events, seminars, and panel discussions. Program leaders include university professors and published authors. Average enrollment per session is seventy-five people; cash prizes are awarded.

Further Information
David R. Collins, Director
3403 Forty-fifth Street
Moline, Illinois 61265
(309) 762-8985

KENTUCKY

Eastern Kentucky University
Creative Writing Conference
Richmond, Kentucky 40475

Program
Annual Creative Writing Conference, 1 week, June. Evaluation and discussion of short-story and poetry manuscripts, lectures, and readings about creative writing.

Accommodations
Dormitory rooms, meals in cafeteria.

Cost
Tuition: $40–$140 per person; room:
$40–$50 per person per week.

Recreation
Tennis, swimming, Lexington horse
farms, Cumberland Mountains nearby.

Cultural Opportunities
Library and Kentucky History
Museum.

Comment
The conference was established in 1963
and averages twenty-two participants.
Individual attention is given to
participants' writing. The university is
located in the heart of the Bluegrass
country near many areas of historic
and scenic interest. College credit is
available.

Further Information
William F. Sutton
Department of English
(606) 622-5661

> *It is a funny thing about life;
> if you refuse to accept
> anything but the best, you
> very often get it.*
> *Somerset Maugham*

MAINE

Maine Writers' Conference at
*   Ocean Park*
P.O. Box 296
Ocean Park, Maine 04063

Program
Annual conference, 4 days, late
August. Program covers a wide variety
of topics, especially those related to
Maine and New England.

Accommodations
Hotels and motels nearby.

Cost
$30, registration; $15 if under age 21.

Recreation
Tennis, swimming, fishing, golf
nearby.

Cultural Opportunities
Local library; museums in Saco,
Kennebunk, and Portland; 10-week
Ocean Park Assembly session of
religious, cultural, and educational
programs.

Comment
The conference was first held in 1941.
It is the highlight of the Ocean Park
Assembly, which was first held in
1881. Conference leaders include
writers, publishers, and editors.
Approximately seventy-five persons
attend the conference each year.

Further Information
Richard F. Burns, Director
(207) 934-5034 (summer only)

Maine Writers' Workshops
Box 905
Stonington, Maine 04681

Program
One-week seminars in fiction, basic
writing, and poetry; August; located in
1820s home of director in Stonington,
Maine.

Cost
$400 per week includes tuition, room
and board, bay cruise, and manuscript
evaluation.

Recreation
Tennis, fresh and saltwater fishing.

Comment
Quality staff includes lecturers
Buckminster Fuller, Pulitzer Prize

winner Richard Eberhart, Carlos Baker, Kay Boyle, and publisher George Garrett.

Further Information
G. F. Bush, Director
(207) 367-2484

MARYLAND

The Johns Hopkins University Summer Writers' Conference
102 Macaulay Hall
Baltimore, Maryland 21218

Program
Annual writers' conference, 2 weeks in June. Workshops in fiction, nonfiction, and poetry.

Accommodations
Modern air-conditioned dormitory.

Cost
Tuition: $550; room and board: $295.

Recreation
University tennis courts, track, gym; Memorial Stadium within walking distance.

Cultural Opportunities
University library and other campus facilities; close to museums, art galleries, and theaters; other sightseeing attractions include Baltimore's Inner Harbor.

Comment
The conference was first held in 1985. Designed for both experienced and aspiring writers, it includes workshops, individual consultations, and discussions on the writer at work. Evening sessions feature readings by faculty and distinguished visiting

writers, such as John Barth. Enrollment limited to sixty.

Further Information
Michael C. Alin
Director, Division of Continuing
    Education
(301) 338-8500

> *The good ended happily and the bad unhappily. That is what fiction means.*
> *Oscar Wilde*

MINNESOTA

Upper Midwest Writers'
    Conference
Bemidji State University
Bemidji, Minnesota 56601

Program
A conference for teachers and authors, second and third weeks of July.

Accommodations
University residence halls.

Cost
$60.

Recreation
Swimming, sailing, tennis, canoeing, fishing, hiking, golf.

Cultural Opportunities
Library, art gallery, summer theater; repertory theater off campus.

Comment
The Upper Midwest Writers' Conference was first held in 1969 and is open to teachers and writers. Its

professional writing staff, which changes from year to year, has included Carol Bly (fiction), John F. Nims (poetry), Emilie Buchwald (children's literature), Robert Treuer (nonfiction), and Paul Burtness (screenwriting). The average number attending is forty-five. College credit is available.

Further Information
William D. Elliott
Director, Humanities Division
(218) 755-2813

NEW YORK

International Women's Writing Guild
Box 810, Gracie Station
New York, New York 10028

Program
Annual writing conference at Skidmore College, Saratoga Springs, New York; 1 week; late July. More than forty workshops open to all women writers.

Accommodations
Air-conditioned dormitory rooms, single or double occupancy.

Cost
$440, 7-day conference; $475, including 2-day excursion; $200, weekend only.

Recreation
Tennis, swimming, hiking, kite flying, jogging, bathing in mineral spa.

Cultural Opportunities
Ballet, music, and theater at the nearby Saratoga Arts Festival.

Comment
Founded in 1976, the Guild and its workshop help women express their concepts through writing. Open to all women regardless of professional portfolio, the workshop and nightly readings stress the use of writing for personal growth and professional advancement. The workshop is attended annually by 250 women from the United States and abroad. Adult education credit is available from Skidmore College, and a tax deduction is allowed for improvement of professional skills.

Further Information
Hannelore Hahn, Executive Director
(212) 737-7536

> *Genius is one percent inspiration and ninety-nine percent perspiration.*
> *Thomas Alva Edison*

Long Island University
Southampton Campus
Writer's Conference and Workshops
Southampton, New York 11968

Program
Annual conference, 12 days, July. Program includes classes with visiting writers, readings, and lectures; workshops on fiction, playwriting, and poetry.

Accommodations
Dormitories.

Cost
Tuition: $171–$182 per credit; campus fee additional. Housing: $60–$75 for non-LIU students, lower for students. Meal plans: $45–$60 per week.

Recreation
Swimming, tennis, fitness trail,
University facilities.

Cultural Opportunities
Campus library, art galleries, summer
theater, museums, botanical gardens.

Comment
The Writer's Conference has been held
since 1976. Visiting writers have
included George Plimpton, Russell
Banks, and poet André Lorde and a
host of renowned artists. Enrollment is
limited.

Further Information
William Robertson
Conference Coordinator, Library
(516) 283-4000, ext. 151

*New York University
   Publishing Institute
School of Continuing Education
126 Shimkin Hall
New York, New York 10003*

Program
Annual 6-week institute, summer.
Features a comprehensive look at the
book and magazine publishing
industries and takes students through
every phase of the publishing process.

Accommodations
Responsibility of participants; they are
encouraged to live on campus due to
the demands of the program.

Cost
Tuition only: $2200.

Recreation
Parks, athletic fields, tennis courts
nearby.

Cultural Opportunities
New York City has a wealth of cultural
institutions and events.

Comment
The Publishing Institute combines
classroom lectures and discussions
with workshop sessions and field trips.
Under the tutelage of industry
professionals, participants explore the
business and editorial aspects of
publishing and acquire marketable
skills in editing, writing, design, and
sales.

Further Information
Dorothy Durkin
Director, Public Relations
(212) 598-2026

*New York University Summer
   Writers Conference
School of Continuing Education
Division of Arts, Sciences and
   Humanities
332 Shimkin Hall
New York, New York 10003*

Program
Annual New York University Summer
Writers Conference, 2 weeks, July; 70
hours of courses and seminars in
fiction, nonfiction, poetry, and drama.

Accommodations
NYU dormitories in the Washington
Square area available; Housing Office
will assist those wanting off-campus
accommodations.

Cost
$1032, undergraduate; $744, graduate;
$670, noncredit.

Comment
Instructors include established
novelists, playwrights, poets, and
editors. Participants may discuss their
work in private conferences with
faculty members. Undergraduate and
graduate credit available.

Further Information
(212) 598-3091

Niagara Frontier Christian Writers' Workshop
6853 Webster Road
Orchard Park, New York 14127

Program
Christian Writers' Workshop held at
Houghton College, Buffalo; 1 day; late
June. Past topics include Writing for
Children, Using Personal Anecdotes,
Skeleton of a Feature Article, and
Writing the Short Poem.

Accommodations
Rooms for overnight stay can be
arranged.

Cost
Tuition: $15; room: $5. Write for
information.

Comment
The Niagara Workshop was first held
in 1971 and attracts both professionals
and amateurs. Average attendance is
fifty. Instructors live in the Buffalo
area and are involved in writing for
religious markets. A workshop will
critique participants' manuscripts
(length limit: 2000 words) if included
with preregistration fee.

Further Information
Don Booth, Director
(716) 622-5259

Pauline Bloom Workshop
Writer's Holiday Workshop
20 Plaza Street
Brooklyn, New York 11238

Program
Writer's workshop, eight 1-week
sessions throughout the year.

Accommodations
Responsibility of participants;
recommendations available.

Cost
$60 per session.

Comment
Classes are conducted by Pauline
Bloom with emphasis on writing
techniques, help with manuscripts,
and the marketing of stories and
articles. Participants may submit
manuscripts (no longer than 3000
words) 1 month prior to workshop for
detailed evaluation. Novices and
published writers are equally welcome.

Further Information
Pauline Bloom
(718) 789-8054

Spa Writers' and Educators' Conference
47 Hyde Boulevard
Ballston Spa
Saratoga, New York 12020

Program
Workshops in fiction, poetry,
nonfiction, and promotions and
advertising; educators' lab; July.

Accommodations
Nearby motels and restaurants.

Cost
Tuition: $200 per week, $600 per
month.

Recreation
Swimming, boating, golf, polo, parks.

Cultural Opportunities
Houseman Theatre, Lake George
Opera Company, Hyde Art Museum,
Albany Historical Museum, Saratoga
Performing Arts Center.

Comment
The Spa Conference was first held in 1967. Workshops are under the direction of Harry Barba, writer, editor, teacher, publisher, and director of several writers' conferences. Average group size is fifteen to twenty. Manuscripts produced at the conference will be considered for publication by Harian Creative Books.

Further Information
Dr. Harry Barba, Publisher and
    Director
(518) 885-7397

University of Rochester
Writers' Workshop
Rochester, New York 14627

Program
Intensive sessions of writing, study, and discussion, working with a faculty of distinguished writers, plus a day of consultation with publishers; 1 week; early July. Faculty of talented professional writers, all of whom have published widely; past faculty include Nora Sayre, William Stafford, Linda Gregg, Jarold Ramsey, Penelope Gilliatt, and Hayden Carruth.

Accommodations
Dormitory.

Cost
Tuition: $195.

Recreation
Swimming pool, tennis courts, golf course.

Cultural Opportunities
Summer theater and weekly concerts on campus, oratorio reading group, night readings by workshop staff, art gallery, museum of science, George Eastman House.

Comment
People with a serious interest in writing are encouraged to attend. An average of sixty people per year participate.

Further Information
Annual Writers' Workshop
127 Lattimore Hall
University of Rochester
Rochester, New York 14627
(716) 275-2347

A good discussion can draw out wisdom which is attached in no other way.
                Lord Lindsay of Birker

NORTH CAROLINA

Blue Ridge Assembly
P.O. Box 188
Black Mountain, North
*   Carolina 28711*

Programs
(1) Blue Ridge Christian Writers' Conference, program of workshops and seminars by editors, publishers, and established authors; instruction in all genres of writing; discussion on the writing profession; 1 week; July–August.
(2) Inspirational Romance Writers' Conference, instruction, discussion, and other activities focusing on the inspirational romance; 5 days; August.

Accommodations
Blue Ridge Center (double occupancy, double beds, air-conditioned) or Abbott Hall (double occupancy, single beds).

Cost
(1) Tuition: $150; room and board: $161–$174.
(2) Tuition: $130; room and board: $121–$130.

Recreation
Swimming, tennis, basketball, hiking, sightseeing. Blue Ridge Parkway, Mt. Mitchell, and Grandfather Mountain nearby.

Comment
The Blue Ridge Conference was first held in 1976; the Inspirational Romance Conference in 1984. Both are designed for the Christian writer, published or unpublished. Participants benefit from the experience of established authors and learn the needs of editors and publishers. Enrollment averages seventy to eighty.

Further Information
Yvonne Lehman, Writing Conferences Director
(704) 669-8421

OHIO

Akron Manuscript Club
Akron, Ohio 44325

Program
Annual writers' workshop, second Saturday in May at University of Akron.

Accommodations
Participants make own arrangements.

Cost
$30.

Comment
Workshop features lectures and roundtable discussions. The workshop is the oldest writers' club in Ohio and provides written critiques on all manuscript material submitted.

Further Information
Bea McLaughlin or Helen Backus
P.O. Box 510
Barberton, Ohio 44203
(216) 867-3691

VERMONT

Bread Loaf Writers' Conference
Middlebury College
Middlebury, Vermont 05753

Program
Annual program, 2 weeks, August. Lectures, workshops, and discussion groups covering all fields of writing.

Accommodations
Dormitories and guest houses.

Cost
$850, inclusive, for contributors with manuscript.

Comment
The Bread Loaf Writers' Conference was first held in 1926 and is the oldest meeting of its kind in the United States. Over the years it has attracted notables such as Robert Frost, Bernard De Voto, Louis Untermeyer, and John Ciardi. Average attendance is 300 or more.

Further Information
Carol Knauss
(802) 388-3711

WASHINGTON

Centrum Foundation
Port Townsend Writers'
  Conference
Fort Worden State Park
P.O. Box 1158
Port Townsend, Washington
  98368

Program
Port Townsend Writers' Conference, usually 10 days, annually in July. Limited-enrollment workshops with well-known writers of fiction, poetry, nonfiction, and children's literature. Discussions, lectures, panels, special workshops on reading, manuscript preparation, and related areas.

Accommodations
Dormitories, restored Victorian houses, motels, bed-and-breakfast houses, campgrounds, hostels.

Cost
$200, tuition; $198, dormitory room and three meals a day. Other accommodations from $12 per night.

Recreation
Beaches, hiking, tennis, fishing, scuba diving, sailing.

Cultural Opportunities
Port Townsend National Historic site, consisting of several square blocks of restored Victorian buildings and houses, in "the best-preserved Victorian seaport north of San Francisco." Performance by resident theater company; also chamber music and jazz performance.

Comment
The Port Townsend Writers' Conference was first held in 1974. The conference attracts serious writers of various levels of experience; the primary focus is on the writing process rather than the business aspects of writing and publishing, though many participants are widely published. Faculty meets daily with students in limited-enrollment workshops and is joined by other well-known visiting writers. Participants come from across the United States and Canada. Many combine attendance with vacations in the Olympic National Park, the San Juan Islands, or Vancouver Island. Attendance averages 130–180 participants annually.

Further Information
Carol Jane Bangs, Director
(206) 385-3102

Chance favors the prepared mind.
                    Louis Pasteur

9 *THE WORLD OF GASTRONOMY*

The Great Chefs at the Robert Mondavi Winery, photo by Faith Echtermeyer

*T*hese programs can benefit both light-snack and full-course menu preparers, whether amateur or experienced in the art of cooking. Program samples for all tastes.

> *"Bread," says he, "dear brothers is the staff of life."*
>   *Jonathan Swift*

CALIFORNIA

The Great Chefs at the Robert Mondavi Winery
P.O. Box 106
Oakville, California 91562

Program
Cooking sessions with famous name authors, 2–5 days, spring and fall.

Accommodations
Lodging in Napa Valley.

Cost
$1040 (2 days), $3100 (5 days); 5-day program includes round-trip limousine service from San Francisco.

Comment
Courses have been given by Julia Child and Simone Beck and include visits to wineries and receptions. Limited to twenty-four participants.

Further Information
(707) 944-2866

Judith Ets-Hokin Culinary Company
Traveler's Package
3525 California Street
San Francisco, California 94118

Program
Cooking classes for out-of-towners interested in learning more about San Francisco's many gastronomic delights. Minimum of three classes per week (up to nine offered); year-round.

Accommodations
Responsibility of participant.

Cost
$55 for three classes; $18, each additional class.

Comment
The Company's Cooking School, established in 1973, offers courses covering all the basics of cooking meat, fish, pasta, pastry, and more. Judith Ets-Hokin holds certificates from cooking academies in France, Italy, and England. She is author of the prize-winning *San Francisco Dinner Party Cookbook*. The school has a staff of five; each class is 2 hours. Lessons are also offered by mail.

Further Information
Judith Ets-Hokin, Director
(415) 668-3191

NEW YORK

Cigahotels
Landia International Services, Inc.
745 Fifth Avenue, Suite 404
New York, New York 10151

Programs
(1) Annual summer cooking courses at the Hotel Gritti Palace, Venice, Italy; six courses of 3–5 days; June–August. (2) Other programs at Cigahotels throughout Italy, year-round; subjects include the arts, history, and tennis. Write for details.

Accommodations
Deluxe hotels.

Cost
$196, 5-day programs.

Recreation
(1) Swimming, sailing, more.

Cultural Opportunities
Sightseeing excursions.

Comment
Held annually since 1975, the summer cooking courses are designed for the serious amateur cooking student. They include lectures, demonstrations, and service with appropriate wines. Instructors are famous chefs from the Gritti Palace in Venice and elsewhere and noted authors of cookbooks. Enrollment is fifteen to twenty students per course.

Further Information
In the United States:
(800) 221-2340 or (212) 935-9540

In Italy:
Compagnia Italiana Grandi Alberghi—Ciga S.P.A.
Executive Office
Largo Donegani No. 2
20121 Milan, Italy
Hotel Gritti Palace, Venice
(041) 26044 or Telex 410125

E & M Associates
Rome Gourmet Adventure
45 West 45th Street
New York, New York 10036

Program
Italian cooking classes in Rome, 9 days, several sessions during the year; tour combines classes at La Scaldavivande Cooking School with related sightseeing, for those who want to experience Rome and its food intimately.

Accommodations
Superior first-class hotel.

Cost
$1150 per person (double occupancy); includes course fees, room, and breakfast, but not airfare.

Recreation
Ample time for sightseeing and shopping.

Comment
E & M Associates has offered the Rome Gourmet Adventure since 1976. It features three 4-hour class sessions in English. Enrollment is limited to twelve; tours can be arranged for those not taking classes. Other gourmet and cultural tours are available.

Further Information
Wendy Louise Boor or Martha Morano
(800) 223-9832 or (212) 302-2508

German Wine Academy
79 Madison Avenue
New York, New York 10016

Program
Wine Academy courses in West Germany, several 1-week sessions between May and October. Basic courses and a postgraduate course; instruction in English.

Accommodations
Hotel Schwan in Oestrich-Winkel, the heart of Germany's Rheingan winegrowing region.

Children
Children are not permitted at the Academy.

Cost
$500, basic course, $560, postgraduate course; includes accommodations,

meals, and local travel. Airfare and transportation to and from Frankfurt Airport not included. (Costs based on exchange rates at time of publication.)

Cultural Opportunities
Castles, wine museums, cathedrals, Rhine River tour, and more.

Comment
Wine Academy courses have graduated more than 1200 wine lovers since 1973. Each course attracts thirty to forty participants for lectures and discussions. Schedule includes tasting over 200 wines, visits to vineyards and to the wine research center at Geisenheim, and more. Passage of test at program's conclusion entitles participant to certificate.

Further Information
German Wine Academy
c/o Reisebüro A. Bartholomae GmbH
Wilhelmstrasse 8
D-6200 Weisbaden
Federal Republic of Germany
In the United States:
Carol Sullivan
    or
Lamar Elmore
(212) 213-7036/7035
In Canada:
Michael Wilson
German Wine Information Service
2200 Yonge Street, Suite 1002
Toronto, Ontario M4S 2C6
(416) 489-3131

> *We have chosen to fill our hives with honey and wax; thus furnishing mankind with the two noblest of things, which are sweetness and light.*
> *Jonathan Swift*

The World of Oz
3 East 54th Street
New York, New York 10022

Programs
(1) L'École du Moulin-Roger Verge, cooking adventure in the South of France, 1 week, February–December; five 4-hour cooking lessons.
(2) Ruffino's Tuscan Experience, cuisine, wine, and culture tour of Italy's Tuscany region; 9 days; spring and fall; five cooking demonstrations and two wine-tasting sessions.
(3) Numerous special interest tours focusing on food, cooking, wine, art, culture, astronomy, archaeology, etc., in Europe, East Asia, and the South Pacific, throughout the year.

Accommodations
(1) Deluxe Hotel Gray d'Albion, Cannes.
(2) Superior first-class hotels.

Cost
(1) $2089, low season; $2265, high season; land only.
(2) $1980, land only.

Comment
The World of Oz has been offering these cooking and other special interest tours since 1976. Gourmet programs are conducted by established, well-qualified experts and feature meetings with respected restaurateurs.

Further Information
C. Wynne Oz
(800) 223-6626 or (212) 940-8463

OREGON

Richard Nelson's Cooking School
P.O. Box 2795
Gearhart, Oregon 97138

Program
Two 1-week sessions stressing fish and shellfish cooking, held in Astoria, Oregon; early July.

Accommodations
Gearhart by the Sea Condominiums available on weekly basis.

Cost
Tuition: $600 per week (accommodations additional).

Comment
Richard Nelson, who was associated with the late James Beard for many years, is assisted by a staff of six instructors. Classes are limited to about twenty-four to ensure maximum attention to individual needs. Although courses are advanced, enrollees of different levels of experience are accepted.

Further Information
(503) 738-3755

PENNSYLVANIA

Giuliano Bugialli's Cooking in Florence
2380 Gordon Street
Allentown, Pennsylvania 18104

Program
Series of cooking classes in Italy, 1 week, June–October; most classes held in Florence, with additional tours to other sites in Italy. Past themes include The Italian Tradition, Four Regions of Italy, and Florence in the Fall. There is also a special 1-week July program for professionals.

Accommodations
First-class hotels, usually air conditioned with private bath.

Cost
$1250–$2450, includes room, most meals, and classes. Price depends on amount of travel involved; airfare not included.

Cultural Opportunities
Concerts, ballet, sightseeing, visits to vineyards and unique restaurants, many special events. Emphasis of all programs is on blending knowledge of cooking with that of Italy's culture and people.

Comment
Founded in 1973, Cooking in Florence is the first Italian cooking school to cater to English-speaking students. Instructor Giuliano Bugialli, who personally teaches every class, is well known as a cookbook author. Participants include professionals and nonprofessionals from all continents. Average enrollment is twenty; a diploma is granted upon completion of the course.

Further Information
Audrey Berman, Registrar
(215) 435-2451

> *Weeds spring up along the wholesome plants . . . It's hard to tell at first which is the weed!*
> *Romeyn Berry*

> *Great chefs are not born . . . they are educated!*
> M. Taillevent

RHODE ISLAND

**Johnson and Wales College
Culinary Arts Division
8 Abbot Park Place
Providence, Rhode Island 02903**

Program
Cook 'n Tour, cooking classes, good food, New England sightseeing; weekends; July and August.

Accommodations
Rhode Island Inn, Warwick, Rhode Island; owned and operated by the college.

Cost
Approximately $350 per person (double occupancy), all inclusive.

Recreation
Swimming pool on premises, beaches, golf, fishing, tennis nearby.

Cultural Opportunities
Theater, museums.

Comment
Organized in 1980, the Cook 'n Tour programs are sponsored by the Culinary Arts Division of Johnson and Wales College. Classes are conducted by an international faculty of award-winning chefs. Escorted tours of nearby attractions, including a Newport mansion and Mystic Seaport in Connecticut. Average group size is thirty.

Further Information
Dr. Allan Freedman, Director of Admissions
(401) 456-1120

WEST VIRGINIA

**The Greenbrier
White Sulphur Springs, West Virginia 24986**

Program
Five-day cooking courses offered during the winter months; morning and afternoon sessions cover preparation of U.S. regional and European dishes. New trends in cooking are also discussed.

Accommodations
The Greenbrier is a five-star resort hotel.

Cost
$295, course tuition; hotel rooms additional.

Comment
The Greenbrier cooking school was first offered in 1977. The morning session instructor has been head of a cooking school for the past 20 years, and the afternoon sessions are led by the Greenbrier's executive chef. Class size ranges from twenty-five to thirty.

Further Information
Ann Walker, Marketing
(800) 624-6070

UNITED KINGDOM

**L'École de Cuisine Française
Saline de Mirbeck
Clapham House
Litlington BN26 5RQ
England**

Programs
(1) Diploma course in traditional French cooking, 5 months, beginning

in February and September.
(2) Intensive summer course, 1 month,
July.

Accommodations
Private home, guest house, castle.

Cost
Write for information.

Comment
Courses are conducted by chefs trained
at the Cordon Bleu de Paris. The
diploma course includes restaurant
management (silver service, wine,
accounting, marketing, etc.) and is
followed by an optional 5-month
training session in a first-class
restaurant.

Further Information
(0323) 870047

*Knowledge is the food of the
soul.*
                              Plato

10 SENIOR CITIZENS' PROGRAMS

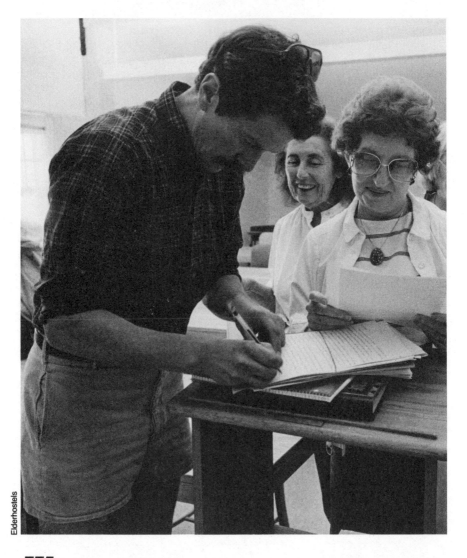

Elderhostels

With emphasis on the slogan "You are never too old to learn," go back to the campus of your choice without the worry of exams and credits. Just relax and enjoy as you learn.

ELDERHOSTELS

Programs for senior citizens age 60 and over (and their spouses or companions) have been growing in popularity, particularly since the formation and development of the Elderhostel Network in 1975. Beginning in New England, it spread rapidly throughout the United States and Canada and is now worldwide.

Institutions belonging to this organization generally offer programs of a week's duration (although participants may elect to stay on longer) that usually comprise three subjects. Although most take place in summer, many are available throughout the year. Class size averages from thirty to forty, and many participants move from one institution to another if program dates make it convenient.

Costs of domestic programs of the Elderhostel Network are modest, averaging $205 per week, which is all-inclusive. Participants live in the dormitory of the sponsoring institution and enjoy its recreational and cultural facilities.

A few examples of recent subject matter follow:

Institution	Courses
University of North Carolina Chapel Hill, North Carolina	A. Russians and Missiles B. Books and Ideas C. Supply Side Economics
University of South Florida Tampa Campus Tampa, Florida	A. Logic of Animals B. History of Books and Manuscripts C. The Victorian Era
Cornell University Ithaca, New York	A. Utilizing the Media B. How to Get Political Clout C. The Victorian Era

The names and addresses of institutions, listed elsewhere in this book, that *also* have Elderhostel programs follow. For a complete list of those belonging to the Elderhostel Network and for registration purposes, write its headquarters:

Elderhostel
80 Boylston Street
Suite 400
Boston, Massachusetts 02116
(617) 426-8056

ALABAMA
University of South Alabama
Elderhostel Director
2002 Old Bayfront Drive
Mobile, AL 36615

CALIFORNIA
San Jose State University
Elderhostel Director
Washington Square
San Jose, CA 95192-0135

FLORIDA
Florida State University
Elderhostel Director
Tallahassee, FL 32306

University of West Florida
Elderhostel Director
Pensacola, FL 32504

ILLINOIS
Northern Illinois University
Elderhostel Director
De Kalb, IL 60115

INDIANA
Indiana University Bloomington
Elderhostel Director
Union Memorial Building
Bloomington, IN 47405

KENTUCKY
Eastern Kentucky University
Elderhostel Director
Richmond, KY 40475

Western Kentucky University
Elderhostel Director
Bowling Green, KY 42101

MAINE
Chewonki Foundation
Elderhostel Director
RFD #3
Wiscasset, ME 04578

MARYLAND
Anne Arundel Community College
Elderhostel Director
101 College Parkway
Arnold, MD 21012

Towson State University
Elderhostel Director
Towson, MD 21204

University of Maryland College Park
Office of Experiential Programs
Hornbake Library, Room 0119
College Park, MD 20742

MASSACHUSETTS
Hampshire College
Director of Summer Programs
Amherst, MA 01002

MICHIGAN
Michigan State University
Elderhostel Director
Kellogg Center of Continuing
   Education
East Lansing, MI 48829

MINNESOTA
University of Minnesota, Duluth
Elderhostel Director
Continuing Education and Extension
403 Darland Administration Building
10 University Drive
Duluth, MN 55812

MONTANA
Montana State University
Elderhostel Director
Bozeman, MT 59717

NEBRASKA
Chadron State College
Elderhostel Director
Chadron, NE 69337

NEW YORK

Chautauqua Schools Office
P.O. Box 1098
Chautauqua, NY 14722

Cornell University
Elderhostel Director
626B Thurston Avenue
Ithaca, NY 14850

NORTH CAROLINA

University of North Carolina
  at Chapel Hill
Elderhostel Director
Chapel Hill, NC 27514

OHIO

College of Wooster
Elderhostel Director
Wooster, OH 44691

OKLAHOMA

University of Oklahoma
Elderhostel Director
1700 Asp Avenue
Norman, OK 73037

OREGON

Northwest Christian College
Elderhostel Director
828 East 11th Avenue
Eugene, OR 97401

PENNSYLVANIA

Kutztown University of Pennsylvania
Elderhostel Director
Kutztown, PA 19530

Pennsylvania State University
University Park
Elderhostel Director
University Park, PA 16802

TEXAS

Texas Tech University
Elderhostel Director
Lubbock, TX 79406

UTAH

Brigham Young University
Elderhostel Director
Continuing Education Building
Provo, UT 84602

VERMONT

Goddard College
Elderhostel Director
Plainfield, VT 05667

VIRGINIA

Eastern Mennonite College
Elderhostel Director
Harrisonburg, VA 22801

Washington and Lee University
Elderhostel Director
Lexington, VA 24450

CANADA

Mount Allison University
c/o Elderhostel Canada
P.O. Box 4400
Fredericktown, NB E3B 5A3
Canada

*Old minds are like old horses;
you must exercise them if you
wish to keep them in working
order.*
        John Quincy Adams

INTERHOSTELS

Another interesting experiment in programs for adults age 50 or older is that of Interhostels. This concept of providing mature adults with international educational experiences began in 1980 at the University of New Hampshire. It is a cooperative exchange arrangement between American and foreign—primarily European—institutions allowing study of the history, social structure, art and music, and other aspects of various foreign cultures. The following description of the University of New Hampshire's program is illustrative:

University of New Hampshire Division of Continuing Education
6 Garrison Avenue
Durham, New Hampshire 03824

Programs
Interhostel, a series of 2-week international educational programs for adults age 50 and over. Programs are jointly sponsored by a European institution and include sightseeing, field trips, social activities, and instruction in English. Examples of recent destinations are Greece, Sweden, Great Britain, Germany, and Spain. Programs take place from early spring through fall.

Accommodations
University residence halls or hotels; single or double rooms, depending on program.

Cost
Ground program: $950, includes tuition, room and board, local travel. Air-fare: $550–$730, depending on departure and destination.

Comment
The programs, developed in 1980, are designed for active older adults. They are fully scheduled and may be extended by those with additional interests. Groups range from twenty to forty people and are accompanied by a UNH representative. Topics include history, politics, economy, literature, arts, and daily life of the host country.

Further Information
Joanne Piper, Interhostel Coordinator
(603) 862-1088

> *My interest is in the future, because I'm going to spend the rest of my life there.*
> *Charles F. Kettering*

DIRECTORY OF PROGRAMS FOR CHILDREN AND FAMILIES

DIRECTORY OF PROGRAMS FOR HIGH SCHOOL AND TEENAGE YOUTH

SPONSOR INDEX

GEOGRAPHIC INDEX

This index lists sponsoring institutions according to where their representative programs take place.

Travel programs have been classified in several ways and can be found as follows:

(a) Those going to a specific location are indexed at that location.

(b) Tours embracing a number of countries of a particular continent are indexed by the name of that continent.

(c) Others going to a specific region (for example, South Pacific or Latin America) are listed regionally.

(d) When the sponsoring institution's travel programs are too numerous and far-ranging to be specific, look under the Worldwide heading.